Politics
and the
Support
of
Libraries

Edited by
E. J. Josey and Kenneth D. Shearer

Neal-Schuman Publishers
New York   London

Published by Neal-Schuman Publishers, Inc.
23 Leonard Street
New York, NY 10013

Copyright © 1990 by Neal-Schuman Publishers, Inc.

Printed and bound in the United States of America

Library of Congress Cataloging-in-Publication Data

Politics and the support of libraries / edited by E.J. Josey and
    Kenneth D. Shearer.
        p.   cm.
    Includes index.
    ISBN 1-55570-073-X
    1. Library finance—Political aspects—United States.   2. Library
fund raising—Political aspects—United States.   3. Federal aid to
libraries—Political aspects—United States.   4. Libraries and
community—Political aspects—United States.   5. Libraries and
state—Political aspects—United States.   I. Josey, E. J., 1924-
II. Shearer, Kenneth D.
Z683.2.U6P64   1990
021.8'3'0973—dc20   90-49654
                                                       CIP

Contents

Preface

The parson who said that "the Lord helps those who help themselves" was correct. Sweet reason alone will not pay the library's mounting bills. To get support for libraries, librarians—with help from other parishioners who value libraries—must explain why the bills are mounting. They also must determine how much money they will need to pay those bills. To carry out this mission, librarians must participate in the political process. Adequate support depends upon this activity. *Politics and the Support of Libraries* is dedicated to assisting librarians to help themselves to support libraries: not only their own but others in the community and across the United States.

The scope of this book is broader than that of its related volume, *Libraries in the Political Process*, a Neal-Schuman Professional Book, published in 1980 by The Oryx Press, Phoenix. The earlier book emphasized politics at the federal and state levels. In addition, it concentrated on public library issues. Building on that foundation, this book more explicitly addresses local politics. It also goes beyond public library issues to discuss the political environments of university, college, community college, and special libraries by drawing on authors with experience in all these diverse settings.

Because most libraries are publicly supported institutions, politics in the public sector receives more attention than politics in the private sector. Nonetheless, the private academic library is represented by its own chapter, and the privately supported special library is not neglected. Of course, since privately supported libraries seek some funding from public sources just as publicly supported libraries seek some funding from private sources, the reader must not conclude too quickly that any part of the book is of no practical use. For example, fund-raising campaigns, usually conducted in the private sector, will be of practical value to most readers no matter what kind of library they serve. Therefore, both general guidelines for a fund-raising campaign and a case study of the recent $307 million campaign at the New York Public Library are included. The editors believe the expanded, explicit, up-to-date coverage in *Politics and the Support of Libraries* will prove to be of practical benefit.

Some of the familiar players on the political stage reappear in this work. For example, the American Library Association's Washington Office continues to play a coordinating role at the federal level. The importance of state libraries and state library associations is highlighted repeatedly. For instance, some state library associations present well-conceived agendas to gubernatorial candidates while they are actively campaigning and are, therefore, most open to requests for library funding. At the local level, one author after another stresses the role of management as the art of politics and the art of politics as good management.

Unless libraries are resoundingly and unambiguously praised, libraries will not earn the support they merit. In his chapter of this book, the first, and at the time of this writing, the only librarian ever to serve in the United States Congress, Representative Major Owen (Democrat, New York) makes the point that much is irretrievably lost when conflicting and half-hearted testimony is given by library leaders at congressional legislative hearings. In her chapter, New York State legislator and librarian, Cynthia Jenkins stresses the need for every librarian to bear witness to the fact that libraries are essential to American society.

Politician-librarians and other politicians who are committed to library support may help to define political campaigns, but it is the community that must bring these campaigns to life. Library advocates must become a powerful political force, mustering the strength to stay the often arduous course. They must commit to whatever effort is needed for each and every library campaign. And then, when the plate is passed and they see that plate overflowing, they will all rejoice together.

E.J. Josey
Kenneth D. Shearer

Politics
and the
Support
of
Libraries

Introduction

Politics and the Support of Libraries contains 24 essays most of which were written explicitly for this book in response to the editors' requests. Three of the essays appeared while the book was in progress. They fit the concept exactly and were actively sought.

The volume is divided into four parts. Part One focuses on national politics. Even though in most library budgets the fraction of funds coming from the federal level is minor, it does provide important seed money for projects. These funds tend to multiply as they pass through the state capitols on the way to the local level. Perhaps most important, they often set goals and agendas that serve as models for librarians at other levels.

Thomas Wall provides an overview of library policy-making at the federal level. After inventorying agencies involved with library policy-making nationally, Wall concludes:

> None of the agencies, however, have proposed or articulated a single, unified policy for the country. . . . Yet surely it is possible to bring information professionals together to become familiar with the issues, to express their views, to understand how they can be active participants in the policy-making process, and to affirm their place in the process.

Congressman Major R. Owens argues persuasively for a unified policy representing the library community. Further, he sees a chance for renewed library support at the federal level in the early 1990s:

> If indeed, we are entering a new era and a probable federal breakthrough on education is only a few years away, then the development of a new approach within the library community is very much in order.

Owens provides a welcome pep talk to the field and surveys recent legislative initiatives, along with practical ideas on how to proceed.

Michael H. Harris and Dennis P. Carrigan provide a sweeping

1

history of presidential intervention in library affairs. They conclude that, " . . . the president . . . must be ideologically inclined towards library support if any significant funding is to be forthcoming." They think it is unlikely that the current administration is so inclined. Yet even with Mr. Bush's expressed concern with the improvement in education and Mrs. Bush's expressed concern for literacy—both of which evidence widespread bipartisan support—it remains to be seen at this writing whether the administration will propose significant funding for libraries. Still bipartisan support for literacy training, in particular, seems to be growing at the federal level.

Part Two is devoted to the treatment of state politics and the support of libraries. It opens with Assemblywoman Cynthia Jenkins' "The Political Process and Library Policy." She urges the profession to become ever more astute politically. She views such a pursuit as the top priority for the field:

> From my vantage point as a legislator and as a trained librarian, I would say that this lack of knowledge of the legislative process on the part of librarians is the major reason for the low priority which libraries hold with legislative bodies.

Following Jenkins' remarks, three state librarians relate their accounts of both state politics and also state library policies in the making: California's Gary Strong; Florida's Barratt Wilkins and New York's Joseph Shubert.

Strong's story is interesting in that California has been coping with the blow that was delivered by the passage in 1978 of Proposition 13 causing severe declines in the support of public library services ever since. But, at the same time, " . . . there have been a number of major initiatives which have strengthened library services . . . [requiring] . . . the attention and collaboration efforts of the State Library, the state library association, and trustees and friends of libraries."

The most recent decade has brought to Florida and New York a better fiscal environment than was experienced in California. Wilkins takes us on a roller coaster ride through Florida's politics. After all the ups and downs, he still can conclude:

> I cannot think of any more exciting times than these for librarians to get involved in the legislative process. But, they should be prepared—nobody in the process always wins. However, I have found that unless you are willing . . . to accept a less than perfect outcome—little progress will ever occur, and we will be reduced to holding out our "tin cups."

In New York, ranked first in total state funds for public library support, we witness a model of what is possible when librarians speak carefully and with one voice:

> The $28.7 million 1989 comprehensive bill includes . . . aid to public library systems, reference and research library systems, school library systems, public library construction, outreach and literacy services, parent and child services, conservation/preservation, automation and databases, hospital library programs, coordinated collection development and aid to the Research Libraries of the New York Public Library.

This section on state-level politics concludes with two essays which may be unique in the literature. First, David Shavit discusses "The Politics of the State Budgetary Process and Library Funding." Contrasting state politics today with those of a mere decade ago, Shavit observes that:

> State legislatures today are more political and more partisan, they are more fragmented, with power dispensed among leadership, standing committees and individual members each with their own agenda; and more aggressive, particularly with the executive branch.

Closing up this section of the book, Benjamin F. Speller, Jr., deals with the political environment of the state university library, noting that:

> By the very nature of their establishment and governance structure, state universities are part of . . . and in some instances . . . at center stage of the political environments of the state.

Part Three moves to the local political level of library support. Most libraries, of course, receive most of their monies and political support at the local level. We begin with three essays on the public library before turning our attention to multitype networks, community college libraries and the private academic library. Arthur Curley deals with the curiosity that:

> The public library is something of an anomaly in American society: revered as fundamental to the nation's values, yet without mandate or secure fiscal niche at any level of government in most areas of the country.

Marilyn Gell Mason ties politics to the role of public library manager in an amusing manner in order to underscore her point that:

> The elements that are most useful in acquiring political support for the library budget are an understanding of political pressure points, and the willingness and ability to lean on them.

Paul Fasana follows with an account of a campaign to raise nearly a third of a billion dollars for the operation of New York Public Library from public and private sources, lamenting that,

> Donors want to give money for something that they know and understand, and for efforts that they can be proud of and for which they receive recognition. These desires do not necessarily coincide with the library's objectives.

Janet Welch's essay depicts a balancing act in which,

> . . . external political forces and realities must be balanced and integrated, in the multitype library organization, with . . . internal issues of coordination, representation, equality, governance and administrative power.

Ngozi Agbim asserts that learning resource center professionals ". . . must wake up to the fact that their Library is no longer a passive, service-oriented social institution, but is now a political animal . . . " John Lubans, Jr., and Sheryl Anspaugh present the private academic library's political situation where:

> Some large private schools subscribe to the funding notion of "every tub its own bottom." This refers to the Harvard model wherein each unit is responsible, more or less, for raising its own revenues and spending it.

Part Four of the book opens with the key players in library politics at the various levels of government. David R. Bender identifies members of the national library team, the " . . . numerous players who work to support the funding of libraries in Washington . . . as elected officials in Congress, as members of the federal bureaucracy, in professional associations, and in private institutions." Howard F. McGinn, uses a marketing model, in which "like Proctor and Gamble, General Foods, and General Motors, libraries have to become adept at dividing the community into manageable parts such as children's services, business services, adult's services and so forth." Virginia G. Young draws on a large cast of players at the local level all of whom may be tapped, according to their appropriateness for " 'one-shot' funding, i.e., of construction or renovation of a library building . . . or for support of a special programming activity . . . [or] to the basic funding of the on-going library operations."

The book then turns to its final theme, the major strategies used in engaging in library politics. Richard B. Hall dissects strategies for "Winning a Bond Issue." In one part of his essay, Hall analyzes the reasons for success in the Chesapeake, Virginia, referendum where "the steering committee listened to the community, obtained political savvy, and responded effectively even in a political atmosphere which was unfriendly." Keith Curry Lance follows with his essay on the important role of presenting attractive statistical evidence in building a case for library support, identifying five winning techniques:

> ... 1. presenting figures from the users' point of view, 2. presenting trends for a library, 3. comparing one library with another (or group of others), 4. relating the library to its community institutions or environs, and 5. using graphics to present statistics.

Eileen Cooke demonstrates with charm and lucidity that "In the legislative arena, there is no secret to success; it calls for eternal vigilance. There are no shortcuts or easy victories. . . . Persistence and flexibility are essential." Robert B. Ford, Jr., takes up the important strategy of public relations, using a marketing approach and writing that:

> ... effective public relations tells the library story in such a powerful manner that it will positively influence public opinion to the extent that city and county commissions and state legislatures are forced to deal with the financial ramifications. . .

Pamela Bonnell gets to the point at once in her advice on private funding and the role of the Board, subtitling her chapter, "Give, Get, or Get Out" and she notes that:

> Any fund-raising campaign will fall into one or a combination of the following categories: 1. annual appeal, 2. capital campaign, 3. deferred giving, 4. memorial gift program, or 5. a special event.

E. J. Josey's "Building Coalitions to Support Library and Information Services" concludes the volume with a call to battle:

> We have been fairly successful in developing an army of librarians, library advocates, library trustees, citizen groups, and library friends to battle for legislative support for libraries. What is still needed in the 1990s and beyond is to develop a cadre of people at the grass-roots level or the neighborhood-action levels in our communities.

Well, that gives you some highlights and a sense of the book's scope. It presents the history, offers the vision, describes the tools, warns of the dangers, identifies the people, and calls for continuing vigorous support for libraries. We hope you find it as helpful as we believe it to be.

E.J. Josey
Kenneth D. Shearer

I
National Politics and the Support of Libraries

Federal Library Policy- making: An Overview

Thomas B. Wall
SLIS Library
University of Pittsburgh

INTRODUCTION

When the federal government enacts a law, it establishes policy with respect to a particular issue. As a result, many people are affected. In some instances, those affected accept the policy, and the policy-decision stands. At other times, people challenge the policy through legal action, and the law may be overturned in a court of law. In both cases, people on both sides of the fence are involved: those whose interests lead to enactment and those whose interests lead to a challenge of the law. If the challenge reaches the Supreme Court, the outcome of the case generally depends on a reading of precedential cases that interpret the Constitution, and not on public opinion. In contrast, through the enactment process, the legislative and executive branches create laws that implement public policy. Thus, the process is more directly subject to the lobbying efforts of various interest groups. With universal suffrage, lobbying is one of the two basic practices of democracy in America.

However, policy-making is not merely a matter of law-making, lobbying, and voting. The policy-making process is a highly complex operation with potentially far-reaching consequences.[1] The process has many facets. These, in turn, raise a variety of underlying questions. The first of these questions addresses clarity, i.e., what is the issue and *why* does a policy need to be established?

The next question is sometimes more difficult: it addresses *who* is involved. The question of involvement is complicated. The people affected fall into either "passive" or "active" groups. In-between exists a large gray area. The "passive" people are those who are not necessarily affected immediately, or directly. In some cases, it is appropriate to consider the passive group as latent participants. Only after the "trickle down" do they begin to feel the effects of a policy. The active group includes people who have participated in forming or implementing the policy: the lobbyists, the legislators, and the members of organizations or agencies whose current policies will be altered. This active involvement is especially likely on the part of the agency charged with enforcing the policy.

Establishing (or appointing) a governing body is yet a third issue in the policy-making process. The governing body is charged with implementing policies and procedures to ensure that the enacted policy achieves its desired end. Planning and developing such a body involves providing personnel, financing, and information resources.

In addressing the policy-making process vis-à-vis libraries, an examination of some key lobbying groups and their roles is helpful. The difficulties in providing such an overview, however, are manifold. For example, it is problematic to identify all the legitimate library-related lobbyists. The question of which library-related issues to focus on is rather subjective. The dilemma is compounded further (1) because the issues and groups are interdependent and (2) both components are constantly changing: new players continually enter the game and issues come and go. Moreover, the conflicts that arise in one arena may serve as a backdrop to another.

One can conjecture that the intertwining of issues and lobbying groups is becoming more pronounced as communication channels reach wider audiences, and many issues will reach global proportions in the not-too-distant future. Although some of the issues—such as literacy—have warranted attention for years, they have only recently come to the forefront. Other issues, driven by social and technological forces, have arisen since the computer has become commonplace. All, however, have complexities and subtleties that extend well beyond the discussion presented here. Rather than attempting to explore in-depth the intricacies of these many important areas, this essay provides an overview. However, the hope is that by highlighting key concerns, the essay gives readers the opportunity to focus on those areas which interest them most.

NATIONAL COMMISSION ON LIBRARIES AND INFORMATION SCIENCE

The official advocate of library and information issues for the United States government is the National Commission on Libraries and Information Science (NCLIS). Established in 1970, NCLIS is "a permanent, independent agency of the Federal government charged with advising the Executive and Legislative Branches on national library and information services, policies, plans and needs."[2] By virtue of being recognized as the official commission which the executive and legislative branches consult on matters of library and information science, NCLIS enjoys the benefit of a formal channel for communicating the needs and concerns of the profession to these branches.

NCLIS has a vocal and influential role in the lobbying efforts on policy decisions related to library and information science. Recent activities of the group illustrate this influence. Often consulting with the American Library Association (ALA), NCLIS has been instrumental in calling attention to a number of key issues, which have subsequently been enacted as federal law. As one might expect, the types of issues in which NCLIS is involved have national implications. Recent projects include: the Federal-State Cooperative System for Public Library Data; the National Library Card Campaign, services to older Americans; literacy; and issues concerning the dissemination of government information.[3]

Despite its successful cooperative ventures with the ALA and other professional organizations, NCLIS does not always agree with the profession. Library and information science is a diverse field that is replete with professional associations. As a result, reaching a consensus is not an easy matter. In fact, controversial issues with wide-ranging ramifications constitute the politics. Decisions have to be made on tough issues and rarely, if ever, are all those affected satisfied with the outcomes.

As the official agency for the government, NCLIS holds a politically sensitive position. NCLIS has to consider and balance the interests of the library community and the political infrastructure. What a particular presidential administration believes is a wise policy decision may not meet with approval of library and information science professionals, and certain decisions may make NCLIS unpopular with the library community, which views NCLIS as its representative to the United States government. In fact, it is sometimes unclear whether NCLIS is an advocate for the government or the library and information profession. Understandably, but perhaps not always justifiably, NCLIS has not enjoyed universal approval or support from the professional community, which has recently expressed its ire in reaction to two particular issues : (1) the United States withdrawal from the United Nations Educational, Scientific, and Cultural Organization (UNESCO), and (2) the Federal Bureau of Investigation "Library Awareness Program."

The United States Withdrawal from UNESCO

It is clear to the library and information science profession that innovations in information and telecommunications have brought the peoples of the world closer together. The idea of a global information network is not as quixotic as it may have appeared only a decade ago. Yet despite this understanding, the United States government believed it was sound policy to withdraw its support of UNESCO, a key source for gathering and disseminating information relevant to the library and information sciences on an international level.

The library community has questioned this decision. At the 1989 ALA Annual Conference, for instance, the ALA issued a strong statement in support of renewed aid for UNESCO. The library and information science community almost unanimously agreed.[4] Although the aspects of the issue are extremely complex,[5] the policy underlying the decision raised some questions about NCLIS. In the final analysis, how much power does NCLIS really wield? Moreover, does NCLIS accurately reflect the position of the field or the administration?

Prior to United States withdrawal from UNESCO in 1987, NCLIS served as the secretariat to the organization for the United States. Now, because UNESCO had provided much of the information on the international situation and possible ramifications of library and information policies, the responsibility for information gathering has partially fallen on ALA, NCLIS, and other similar groups. Although UNESCO still produces many relevant documents, without United States funding, the future availability and scope of UNESCO's information gathering publications and activities remains uncertain. Subsequent to the UNESCO withdrawal, NCLIS has assumed responsibilities for advising the government on which international conventions, organizations, and related matters it should support.[6]

UNESCO is ostensibly an organization dedicated to goals congruent with those of democratic nations, including the United States. One of UNESCO's specific goals is to achieve worldwide literacy. Other goals include sharing culture, the exchange of information, and information access. Access, however, involves such basic issues as confidentiality and getting one's hands on the information itself, which in turn, involves various related concerns—the economics of information, for example.

The FBI Library Awareness Program

To the astonishment of library and information science professionals, it was disclosed recently that the Federal Bureau of Investigation (FBI) launched a "Library Awareness Program." The FBI designed the program to use librarians to identify library patrons, primarily of foreign backgrounds, who may be using United States library resources for subversive activities.[7] Needless to say, the profession has serious ethical problems with the program, which flies in the face of the values in which most librarians believe—such as freedom to disseminate and give access to information—moreover, the program is antithetical to a basic tenet of the field, namely the right to privacy and confidentiality on the part of the library user.[8]

The fact that the FBI succeeded in implementing the program, though probably conceived with good intentions, illustrates that many people still do not understand the humanistic values and educational roles that libraries promote. Thankfully, however, the ALA was clear in calling the program a curtailment of intellectual freedom and of the free speech civil liberties protected by the First Amendment. Virtually every news article on the subject contained a strong statement of disapproval from a librarian. Moreover, Judith Krug of the ALA's Office of Intellectual Freedom appeared on the popular television news program, "Nightline," to explain the view taken by the ALA on the issue. In addition, as soon as ALA's Intellectual Freedom Committee found out about the program, the Committee issued and distributed an advisory notice describing the program as "an unwarranted government intrusion upon personal privacy . . . that threatens the First Amendment right to receive information."[9]

NCLIS, however, was not as forthright in its reaction to the FBI program. Its disapproval was perceived as mild compared to that of ALA. At the 1988 Mid-winter meeting of the ALA, NCLIS met behind closed doors for a briefing on the awareness program. Only after the transcripts of the meeting were released under the Freedom of Information Act (with some parts excised) did NCLIS acknowledge the existence of the program. Later, after knowledge of the controversy was widespread, and pressure from the library community mounted, NCLIS issued its own statement reaffirming its commitment to the right to privacy of library users, open access to information, and unequivocal support of First Amendment rights.[10]

A major lesson to be learned from the awareness program is that censorship and more insidious forms of oppression may occur any time. Library and information science professionals have traditionally been advocates of civil liberties and humanistic values. This does not, however, guarantee that they will maintain such a stand in the future. It remains important for professionals to unite, to reaffirm the ethics of the profession, and to work to ensure that professionals continue to embrace these democratic principles.

WHITE HOUSE CONFERENCE ON LIBRARY AND INFORMATION SERVICES

Perhaps the most important role of NCLIS is that of a consultant for government policy-makers. In this capacity, the Commission is responsible for "planning and conducting" the White House Conference on Library and Information Services (WHCLIS). The first WHCLIS was held in 1979 and explored "Information for the 1980's."[11] The second conference is scheduled to occur July 9–13, 1991.

The purpose of the conference is to focus attention on issues and concerns related to library and information services in the United States. The 1979 conference, for example, issued a number of resolutions related to literacy, government information policy, preservation, funding, and intellectual freedom. Moreover, the conference provides an educational opportunity for policy-makers to discuss and debate a variety of complex issues with practitioners and theorists alike.

Unfortunately, the relationships among the various library and information science interest groups are not as strong as they could be. Each group has particular concerns. When these overlap, cooperation does occur. But it would be useful if legislators and representatives of the major organizations of the field would discuss and debate some of the overriding issues, especially those which concern the future of the profession in an "information age." Provided personalities do not detract from the debates and discussions, the 1991 WHCLIS offers great promise for better understanding, if not agreement.[12]

Other key interest groups in the library and information science arena include, but are not limited to: the Urban Libraries Council, the Research Libraries Group, the Association of Research Libraries, the Council on Library Resources, the Society of American Archivists, and the American Society for Information Science, and governmental agencies including the Educational Resources Information Clearinghouse (ERIC) and the National Endowment for the Humanities (NEH). Significant policy decisions would affect each of these groups, often in a similar manner. The importance of the conference is crucial: it alone may provide the opportunity for policy-makers and library and information professionals to engage in debate on an entire forum of issues. It would be an educational experience for everyone involved.

The 1991 WHCLIS is an excellent opportunity for professionals to discuss the role of the federal government vis-à-vis library-related issues. The opportunity is double-edged, however, in terms of structure and agenda. If too many issues are covered, the discussion will risk being superficial. Although there is much to be discussed, it may be wiser to focus on a few pressing concerns. Worthwhile issues number too many to list; even a single topic could not be given exhaustive treatment. Thus, what might work best is to use the WHCLIS as a means of heightening awareness of the relevance and interdependence of a wide range of concerns.

LITERACY

Literacy has emerged as a key theme for the 1991 WHCLIS. Certainly, illiteracy is a problem that will not simply disappear. As noted earlier, though, no issue stands alone; literacy is no exception. The literacy question not only raises issues of democracy, but also raises a plethora of related issues, such as access, the general role of libraries in the educational process, and the specific role of the public library. In line with the examination of the "purpose" questions, the library community may want to explore further how libraries can continue to be a public good into the next century. Promoting literacy may be a powerful way for libraries to maintain relevance. After all, an educated populace is the basis for a democracy's success. Yet the problems of the profession will not be resolved by simply equating education to democracy and then expecting support to follow.

PUBLIC/PRIVATE TENSION

The issue of whether access to information should be free of charge in public libraries has created tension between public and private interests. The public-private tension has existed a long time and promises to remain a basic consideration in all policy matters. The increasing commercial value of information exacerbates the tension since the private sector relies more heavily on the dissemination, production, and sale of timely information. Yet, while the private sector has been assuming a central role in the information economy, access to information resources for many members of society—especially the economically disadvantaged—is becoming less and less available.[13] This issue is particularly thorny, especially since the public/private aspect dovetails into a variety of other related economic concerns. For example, where does a public library set the limit in providing information when the source is online and costs $130 an hour.

The more general question is: does every citizen, by virtue of simply being a citizen, have the right to information? Or, does this right apply only to government-produced information? These questions lead to the funding issues, followed closely by questions of access: how is the information to be provided? By which agency? The public library? And if there is no right governing information, should the government establish policy on the issue? Clearly, access to—and provision of—information resources are important concerns. The policies the government establishes are likely to help to shape the information economy in the future.

A balance of priorities and responsibilities between the public and private sectors of the economy would be ideal. Some public libraries have developed strong ties with their local business communities, and these relationships work quite well. But can such ties be legislated? Moreover, are such relationships even viable in lower-income communities where both businesses and libraries may be impoverished?

FEDERAL INFORMATION POLICY

The idea of a federal information policy can have many interpretations. Perhaps the narrowest interpretation would view the policy as governing only government-sponsored information. In this case, questions would tend to address the access to and provision of government-produced documents and information, not those produced in the private sector. For example, it is clear that the Reagan Administration had a consistent record of restricting access to government information. In *Less Access to Less Information*, the ALA explicates an alarming pattern of increasingly restricted access to government publications.[14] The legislative steps documented by ALA raise doubts concerning the Reagan Administrations' commitment to, and understanding of, information access issues specifically, and its commitment to libraries generally. One important aspect of the problem was the policy decision to allow the National Technical Information Service (NTIS) to contract out certain parts of its operation to private firms. Although the information was compiled at government expense, the private sector became free to sell it as a commodity.

The decision to permit partial privatization of NTIS may be a harbinger of how the Bush administration will deal with the public/private issue. The NTIS is the "central source for public sale of government-sponsored research, development, and engineering reports, foreign technical reports, and other analyses prepared by U.S. and foreign governments and their contractors worldwide."[15] The goal of this research is to keep the United States competitive internationally. Prior to the privatization of NTIS in 1989, these documents were readily available at relatively inexpensive cost in many public and academic libraries. Whether access to these documents is limited in the future remains to be seen. Hopefully, NTIS will be run more efficiently, and hence the price of the information will lessen. Since technical information is usually more costly, however, prices may increase. But it would appear that NTIS documents will remain available as a vital source of technical information.

A broader interpretation of federal information policy takes the stand that information is information irrespective of its origin. This view is radical because, in essence, it attempts to centralize both public and private sources of information. This point of view could become a controversial issue in the medical profession with respect to AIDS. The possibility of any comprehensive policy based on a muted public/private distinction seems very far from reality in the foreseeable future.

Yet another interpretation of federal information policy may be more encompassing. This policy in principle supports libraries as a public good, and then provides them with the financial means to pursue their ends. In fact, this policy has been exercised to a certain degree since the enactment of the Library Services Act of 1956.

LIBRARY SERVICES AND CONSTRUCTION ACT

Due in large part to effective lobbying efforts by the ALA, the Library Services Act (LSA) was adopted in 1956. The act was designed to provide public library services to rural areas. By 1964, the scope of LSA was expanded. Title II was introduced to include library construction and services to urban areas. Thus, LSA became LSCA, the Library Services and Construction Act. During the past 25 years, LSCA has grown significantly in terms of scope and funding.[16] The overriding purpose of LSCA is to provide library services to all groups, with particular attention devoted to the disadvantaged. The credit for the initial success of LSA and LSCA goes to the ALA, which has consistently lobbied for more funding and more enhancements to the scope of LSA (now LSCA) since enactment.

LSCA funding originates in the United States Department of Education, which channels the funds to state library agencies. Then, state library agencies distribute the funds[17] in the form of grants to individual libraries. The grants may take a variety of forms and address any number of issues. In this regard, the state library agencies have the responsibility to exercise sound judgment in managing the funds, to identify the library needs of the state, and then to show results. Finally, as is the case with other instances of funding or support, much of the onus falls on the grant recipient. Librarians in the field have to make it work.

AMERICAN LIBRARY ASSOCIATION

The ALA remains active on a range of policy matters—from copyright to intellectual freedom—that have a bearing on the profession. Indeed, the ALA Washington Office is the primary lobbying agent for the association and for the profession at large. The ALA Washington Office was established in 1945. In fact, many association members believed the ALA Headquarters should be moved to Washington.

Washington had particular appeal at that time because of ALA's successful involvement with legislators in trying to procure government funding for library development. This involvement later evolved into LSA and LSCA.

The ALA monitors—and informs members of—legislative and regulatory developments, issues, and actions through the *ALA Washington Newsletter*. As the national official professional association for librarians, the ALA also communicates current issues and news to its members across the United States. Publications from its various divisions report on specific concerns, and these, in turn, provide a fairly solid communications system. The ALA is active in virtually all areas of the profession, for which it is arguably the true advocate, if not the "official" one, in matters of federal policy. The steps taken by ALA in response to the FBI Awareness Program are merely one recent and highly visible example of how ALA can influence matters of policy.

CONCLUSION

This chapter has presented a number of ideas and related issues, along with a short discussion of some of the key programs and agencies involved in the federal policy decision process. None of the agencies, however, have proposed or articulated a single, unified information policy for the country. They are satisfied in working in their own area, often in isolation, on information programs. Perhaps the fact that myriad issues confront the profession makes concerted efforts to establish a unified policy so difficult. Yet surely information professionals can get together to become familiar with the issues, to express their views, to understand how they can be active participants in the policy-making process, and to affirm their place in the process.[18] These goals are too important to neglect.

References

1. See, for example, Bill Crowley, et.al., "Information Policies and the State Library Agencies," *Interface* 11(4):2-4. Also, for a more detailed analysis, see Ines Welsey-Tanaskovic, *Guidelines on National Information Policy: Scope, Formulation, and Implementation* (Paris: UNESCO, (1985).
2. Dorothy P. Gray, "National Commission on Libraries and Information Science," *The Bowker Annual, 1987–1988*, 32nd ed. (New York: R.R. Bowker, 1988), p. 266.
3. United States National Commission on Libraries and Information Sciences.

Annual Report 1986–87 (Washington, D.C.: Government Printing Office, 1988).

4. *"Resolution on the Return of the United States of America to UNESCO."* Resolution voted by the American Library Association on the occasion of the Director General of UNESCO, Mr. Frederico Mayor, at the 108th Annual Conference, Dallas, 24–29 June 1989.

5. See, for example, C. James Schmidt, "Rights for Users of Information: Conflicts and Balances Among Privacy, Professional Ethics, Law, National Security." *The Bowker Annual, 1988–89*, 33rd ed. (New York: R.R. Bowker, 1989), pp. 83–90.

6. Gray, *op. cit.*, p. 266.

7. Schmidt, *op. cit.*, pp. 85–87.

8. See the "ALA Policy Manual," in virtually all editions of the *ALA Handbook of Organization* for ALA policies on professional ethics, intellectual freedom, and other policy-relevant issues.

9. Schmidt, *op. cit.*, p. 86.

10. Susan K. Martin, "National Commission on Libraries and Information Science." *The Bowker Annual 1989–1990*, 34th ed. (New York: R.R. Bowker, 1990), p. 102.

11. White House Conference on Library and Information Services. *Information for the 1980's: Final Report of the White House Conference on Library and Information Services 1979* (Washington, D.C.: U.S. Government Printing Office).

12. See, for example, John N. Berry, "NCLIS and the White House Conference: A Plea for Bipartisan Participation and Nonpartisan Results," *Library Journal* 113 (November 1, 1988): 4.

13. See, for example, the essays presented in *Unequal Access to Information Resources: Problems and Needs of The World's Information Poor*. Proceedings of the Congress for Librarians, February 17, 1986, St. John's University, Jamaica, N.Y. Jovian P. Lang, ed., OFM. (Ann Arbor, MI: Pierian Press, 1988).

14. See American Library Association. *Less Access to Less Information By and About the U.S. Government*. Two chronologies dating from 1981–1986. Reprinted in *Unequal Access, op. cit.*, pp. 172–214, and Anne Heanue, "Less Access to Less Information by and about the United States Government," in *Unequal Access*, pp. 127–131.

15. Wernberg, Alan R. "National Technical Information Service." *The Bowker Annual, 1989–1990*, 34th ed. (New York: R.R. Bowker, 1990), p. 104.

16. For a historical analysis of LSA and LSCA, their evolution, and the pivotal role played by ALA in the evolution, see Edward G. Holley and Robert F. Schremser, *The Library Services and Construction Act: An Historical Overview From the Viewpoint of Major Participants*. (Greenwich, CT: JAI Press, 1983).

17. For a view of the role of the State Library see Gary E. Strong, "Impact of the Federal Government on State Library Services." *State Library Services and Issues*. Charles R. McClure, ed. (Norwood, NJ: Albex Publishing Corporation, 1986), pp. 50–61.

18. These final recommendations are more clearly articulated by Toni Carbo

Bearman in "National Information Policy: An Insider's View." *Library Trends* 35 (1) (Summer, 1986): 105–118. See especially pp. 117–118.

Bibliography

American Library Association. *Libraries and the Learning Society*. Chicago: American Library Association, 1984.

American Library Association. *Policy Statement on "Confidentiality of Library Records."* Chicago: American Library Association, 1970.

American Library Association. *Statement on Professional Ethics*. Chicago: American Library Association, 1981.

American Library Association, Washington Office. *Less Access to Less Information By and About the U.S. Government: A 1981–1984 Chronology*. In *Unequal Access to Information Resources:Problems and Needs of the World's Information Poor*. Proceedings of the Congress for Librarians, February 17, 1986, St. John's University, Jamaica, N.Y. Edited by Jovian P. Lang, OFM. Ann Arbor, MI: Pierian Press, 1988, pp 172–187.

American Library Association, Washington Office. *Less Access to Less Information By and About the U.S.Government 2: A 1985-1986 Chronology*. In *Unequal Access to Information Resources: op. cit.*, pp. 187-214.

Bearman, Toni Carbo. "National Information Policy: An Insider's View." *Library Trends* 35(1) (Summer 1986):105–118.

Berry, John N. "NCLIS and the White House Conference: A Plea for Bipartisan Participation and Nonpartisan Results." *Library Journal* 113 (November 1, 1988).

Bowker Annual Library and Book Trade Almanac. 34th Edition, 1989–1990. New York: R.R. Bowker, 1990.

Cooke, Eileen D. and Henderson, Carol C. "Legislation Affecting Libraries in 1987." In *The Bowker Annual of Library and Book Trade Information*. 33rd Edition. New York: R.R. Bowker Co., 1989, pp. 201–211.

Crowley, Bill; Johnson, Veronica; and Walters, Clarence. "Information Policies and the State Library Agency." *Interface* 11(4) (Summer 1989):2–4.

Day, Melvin S. "National Information Policy: The Broader Context." *Government Information Quarterly* 6(2) (May, 1989):159–164.

Federal-State Cooperative System for Public Library Data Task Force. *An Action Plan for a Federal-State Cooperative System for Public Library Data*. Washington, D.C.: U.S. Department of Education, April 1989.

Fineberg, Gail and Price, Douglas. "200 Years of Issues in Federal Information Policy." *Library of Congress Information Bulletin* 48(22) (May 29, 1989):195–197.

Garceau, Oliver. *The Public Library in the Political Process*. New York: Columbia University Press, 1950.

Gray, Dorothy P. "National Commission on Libraries and Information Science." In *The Bowker Annual of Library and Book Trade Information*. 33rd Edition, 1988, pp. 266–268.

Hanson, Bob. "Can Congress Take the Necessary Steps to Ensure an 'Informed Nation'?" *Government Information Quarterly* 6(2) (May1989):153–158.

Heanue, Anne. "Less Access to Less Information By and About the United States Government." In *Unequal Access to Information Resources, op. cit.*, pp. 127–131.

Heim, Kathleen. "Articulating a Compelling Reason to Take Action." *Government Information Quarterly* 6(2) (May 1989):149–153.

Holley, Edward G. and Schremser, Robert F. *The Library Services and Construction Act: An Historical Overview From the Viewpoint of Major Participants.* Greenwich, CT: JAI Press, 1983.

"LC MARC Licensing—A Furor Waiting to Happen." *Library Hotline* 18(34), August 28, 1989.

Martin, Susan K. "National Commission on Libraries and Information Science." In *Bowker Annual 1989–1990, op. cit.*, pp. 101–105.

Mason, Marilyn Gell. *The Federal Role in Library and Information Services.* White Plains, NY: Knowledge Industry Publications, 1983.

Milevski, Sandra N. "National Commission on Libraries and Information Science." *ALA Yearbook of Library and Information Services*, Volume 14, 1989.

Molz, Redmond Kathleen. *Federal Policy and Library Support.* Cambridge, MA: MIT Press, 1976.

Molz, Redmond Kathleen. *National Planning for Library Service 1935–1975.* Chicago: American Library Association, 1984.

Morrow, Carolyn Clark. "Preservation Comes of Age." In *Bowker Annual 1989–1990, op. cit.*, pp.71–76.

Resolution on the Return of the United States of America to UNESCO. Resolution voted by the American Library Association on the occasion of the Director General of UNESCO, Mr. Federico Mayor, at the 108th Annual Conference, Dallas, 24–29 June 1989.

Riley, James P. "Federal Libraries and Information Access." In *Less Access to Information Resources, op. cit.*, pp. 119–126.

Schmidt, C. James. "Rights for Users of Information: Conflicts and Balances Among Privacy, Professional Ethics, Law, National Security." In *Bowker Annual 1989–1990, op. cit.*,pp. 83–90.

Shavit, David. *Federal Aid and State Library Agencies.* Westport, CT: Greenwood Press, 1985.

Shavit, David. *The Politics of Public Librarianship.* Westport, CT: Greenwood Press, 1986.

Shields, Gerald R. "Federal Legislation and Libraries." In *Libraries in the Political Process*, edited by E.J. Josey. Phoenix: Oryx Press, 1980, pp. 3–14.

Strong, Gary E. "Impact of the Federal Government on State Library Services." In *State Library Services and Issues*, edited by Charles R. McClure. Norwood, N.J.: Ablex Publishing Corporation, 1986, pp. 50–61.

Unequal Access to Information Resources: Problems and Needs of the World's Information Poor. Proceedings of the Congress for Librarians, February 17, 1986, St. John's University, Jamaica, N.Y. Edited by Jovian P. Lang, OFM. Ann Arbor, MI: Pierian Press, 1988.

United States Department of Education. *Alliance For Excellence: Librarians*

Respond to "A Nation At Risk". Washington, D.C.: U.S. Government Printing Office, July 1984.

United States National Commission on Libraries and Information Science. *Annual Report 1986–1987.*

United States Scientific and Technical Information (STI) Policies: Views and Perspectives. Edited by Charles R. McClure and Peter Hernon. Norwood, NJ: Ablex Publishing Corporation, 1989.

Wernberg, Alan R. "National Technical information Service." In *Bowker Annual 1989–1990, op.cit.,* pp. 104–107.

White House Conference on Library and Information Services. *Information for the 1980's: Final Report of the White House Conference on Library and Information Services, 1979.* Washington, D.C.: U.S. Government Printing Office.

Wood, Fred B. "Directions in Federal Information Dissemination Policy in 1989." In *Bowker Annual 1989–1990, op. cit.,* pp. 90–100.

Young, Virginia G. *The Library Trustee: A Practical Guidebook.* 4th Edition. Chicago: American Library Association, 1988.

The Congressional Legislative Process and Library Policy

Congressman Major R. Owens

Ideas and concepts are at the heart of the legislative process at every level of government. At the federal level, the ideas and concepts must have a long gestation period. Decades sometimes pass between the time a legislative concept is launched and the date of final passage. Social Security, a program now universally taken for granted, was proposed at least thirty years before it was enacted. Federal aid to elementary and secondary education followed a similar pattern. And, we are all familiar with the long obstacle course which had to be traversed before the first federal dollars flowed to libraries.

We can predict the legislation of the twenty-first century by reviewing the ideas and concepts under discussion now. Certainly not every proposal will survive the long marathon from first initiative to law. However, the ideas that are not today in evidence at the starting line will probably be out of the race altogether. During seven years of service in Congress, I have developed a great respect for the thoroughness of the Capitol Hill legislative process. I have been particularly impressed by the fact that the initiatives with the least powerful sponsors are forced to run the longest marathons. In the 101st Congress the perfect contrasting examples are the savings and loan association bailout bill versus the bills for child-care programs. The former which obligates the American taxpayers for one hundred and sixty-six billion dollars was rammed through both houses in less than three months. On the other hand, child-care legislation which is requesting less than two billion dollars was abandoned in 1989 and held over until the second year of the 101st Congress. The drive for federal child-care legislation originated during the Nixon administration in the late sixties.

Of course, the one certain way to abbreviate the lengthy legislative process is to obtain the sponsorship of the President. The nation's chief executive was the driving force behind the controversial bailout of the collapsing savings and loan associations, a law which numerous leaders are beginning to question rigorously. The important point here, however, is the power of the presidency in the legislative process. As we seek to make projections for library legislation for the nineties and for the twenty-first century, it is important to note the fact that the office of the presidency may be solidly placed behind a drive to greatly improve education at every level in America.

The Virginia education summit was more than the beginning of a propaganda show. That highly publicized meeting of the nation's governors to discuss education is generating a momentum which can not be stopped. Too many sincere and serious players are now involved in the effort to improve education for it to halt before meaningful changes are made. Eight years of rhetoric without commitment has made a large segment of the political and business leadership of the nation ashamed and eager to make up for lost time and opportunities. In the next five years there will be a major breakthrough with respect to the federal role in educational improvement. Is the library community ready to take advantage of such a historic breakthrough? What concepts, ideas, policies, program proposals and mission statements exist now which may be transformed into federal legislation? Not all of the library family's dreams, hopes and brilliant innovative proposals can be realized. But if the vital embryos are not already implanted we may be assured that the prospects that libraries will benefit from the coming positive changes related to education are indeed grim.

At the end of the first year of the 101st Congress the federal calendar of legislative items related to libraries may be summarized as follows:

S.J. Res. 57 (Pell)/H.J. Res. 226 (Williams): Declares it to be the policy of the United States that federal records, books, and publications of enduring value be produced on acid-free permanent papers. Directs the Librarian of Congress, the Archivist of the United States, the Director of the National Library of Medicine, and the Administrator of the National Agricultural Library to monitor progress in implementing such policy.

S. 339 (Glenn)/H.R. 957 (Snowe): Intergenerational Library Literacy Act—Amends the Library Services and Construction Act to authorize the Secretary of Education to make grants to local public libraries to establish demonstration projects using older adult volunteers to provide intergenerational library and literacy programs for school children during after-school hours.

H.R. 1255 (Owens (NY)): Requires that the Librarian of Congress be appointed from among individuals who have specialized training or significant experience in the field of library and information science.

H.R. 2054 (Owens (NY)): Library and Information Technology Enhancement Act of 1989—Amends the Library Services and Construction Act to direct the Secretary of Education to make grants to States which have had approved long-range and annual State plans and programs required by such Act for library and information technology enhancement programs.

H.R. 2357 (Frenzel): Amends the Library Services and Construction Act to direct the Secretary of Education to make competitive grants to State and local public libraries to purchase and deliver children's books, videos, tapes, and toys to licensed or certified family-based or group child-care providers.

H.R. 2742 (Williams): Library Services and Construction Act Amendments of 1989—Amends the Act to revise its programs and extend the authorization of appropriations through FY 1994. Among other things it directs the Secretary of Education to: 1) coordinate specified programs; 2) give the head of the State library administrative agency opportunity for comment on applications for foreign language and for library literacy grants before the award, to assure that the purposes of such grants are consistent with the long-range state program; 3) limits the authority of the Department of Education to contract out or otherwise transfer activities or functions of the Department of Education Research Library; and 4) provides grants for the establishment of experimental Family Learning Centers or Literacy Centers.

H.R. 3123 (Sawyer): Adult Literacy and Employability Act of 1989—Amends the Library Services and Construction Act to establish a library literacy program.

S. 1257 (Dole)/H.R. 3170 (Goodling): Library Services Improvement Act of 1989—Provides assistance for: 1) library services for economically disadvantaged or disabled individuals; 2) library resource sharing; and 3) library research and assessment of services. Offered as an alternative to the Library Service and Construction Act Amendments.

S. 1310 (Simon): Comprehensive Illiteracy Elimination Act of 1989—Amends the Library Services and Construction Act to extend through FY 1995 the authorization of appropriations for making specified grants under Title VI (Library Literacy Programs) of LSCA.

Before continuing with possible projections for the future it would be appropriate and useful to examine the ALA and SLA legislative program statements:

The ALA

1. Supported the reauthorization of the Library Services and Construction Act.
2. Urged the House and Senate Appropriation Committees to appropriate during 1989 the authorized and required $6 million for the White House Conference on Library and Information Services II so that State and local activities may proceed.
3. Urged federal agencies to follow the clear intent of Congress in waiving fees for Freedom of Information Act requests from information disseminators, including libraries, reversing an "egregious" misinterpretation by which some agencies exclude libraries. Also, ALA recommended Congressional action should the agencies continue to charge fees for library requests.
4. Urged Congress to designate federal libraries and information centers as "inherently government functions," not subject to contracting out.
5. Urged appropriate members of government to control expenditures in ways other than cutting back on federal library acquisitions which adversely affects the nation's well-being and security. (In 1988, the Defense Department placed a moratorium on purchase of materials for its libraries).
6. To ensure the dissemination of government publications to depository libraries and access to publications through the GPO *Monthly Catalog*, urged Congress to carefully weigh agency exemptions from GPO printing and distribution requirements, and to allow no exemptions from *Monthly Catalog* listing requirements under the law.
7. Urged Congress to immediately hold hearings on the possible restrictive OMB Circulars A-3 and A-130, "Management of Federal Information Resources," and to assure a government-wide electronic information policy guaranteeing dissemination through the Depository Library Program for equal and ready access to federal government electronic information products.
8. Requested Congress to increase LSCA appropriations to allow for the critical enhancements in H.R. 2742, proposed LSCA amendments.
9. Urged Congress to restore and increase funding for Higher Education Act II-B, which, in part, provided fellowship assistance to minority library school students.
10. Urged Congress to address the need for guaranteed family and medical leaves from the workplace, and offered ALA participation in partnerships working toward this end.

11. Strongly supported passage of H.R. 50, regulating FBI conduct in certain matters (such as the Library Awareness program).

The SLA

1. Encouraged enactment of legislation which advances library and information services in the public and private sectors.
2. Encouraged the enactment of legislation which will foster the uses of new information technologies.
3. Encouraged the enactment of postal legislation which will allow for the mailing of information in an efficient and cost-effective manner.
4. Encouraged the enactment of legislation which will foster international exchange of information, regardless of its format.
5. Encouraged the enactment of legislation which would serve to protect an individual's intellectual freedom by guaranteeing the confidentiality of library records maintained in public institutions.
6. Monitored various government activities/regulations to ensure that the library and information services mission of each governmental agency is not adversely affected.
7. Monitored legislative and executive branch activities to ensure that government documents and information are easily accessible and readily available to the special library community.
8. Monitored library and information personnel practices, including standards and wage comparability, which will impact on the development and delivery of library and information services.
9. Monitored developments in telecommunications that affect the transmission of data used in education, research, and the provision of library/information services.
10. Monitored copyright legislation ensuring that libraries in the public and private sectors receive equitable treatment.
11. Monitored funding for library and library-related programs.

After the policy statements and legislative programs are clearly set forth, the next important step is the achievement of a consensus within the library community. The recent tendency of the Special Libraries Association to act more aggressively, independent of the larger and more broadly based American Library Association, may be a healthy development. Or it may be a constant source of division which weakens the political effectiveness of all advocates for library legislation. Certainly this legislator has experienced the devastating impact of this internal division. After lecturing for several years about the need for libraries and librarians to have greater visibility and more recognition at the federal level, I introduced legislation requiring that the qualifications for the position of Librarian of Congress must include training and/or experience as a professional librarian. The objective was to take a giant step toward the achievement of maximum recognition for the library profession.

The introduction of a bill is an easy matter. It was not easy, however, to obtain a hearing for the bill since I do not serve on the committee which has jurisdiction. We were quite pleased when, after several requests and some begging, Congresswoman May Rose Oakar, Chair of the Subcommittee on Libraries and Memorials of the House Committee on Administration, agreed to hold hearings on the bill. We were further delighted by the fact that the witnesses were chosen in consultation with my staff. On October 29, 1987, the hearing was held with representatives of the American Library Association, the Special Libraries Association, and the Association of Research Libraries. During the question period we were shocked by the following responses:

Dr. F. William Summers, then President-elect of the American Library Association, when asked if only librarians would be qualified for the Librarian of Congress position under the criteria of the bill, replied, "As I read the bill, it would provide for persons who have either specialized training or appropriate kinds of experience in the directing and organizing of large-scale library operations." Asked if library trustees, friends of libraries and others dedicated to the improvement of library and information services could be candidates for the Librarian of Congress position, Dr.Summers said, "I think many of them would. The definition of library has been drawn very, very broad in the last 20 or 25 years and it includes a great many things other than the kinds of buildings we might traditionally think of as libraries." He said *the ALA supported the bill*. Herbert F. Johnson, President of the Association of Research Libraries said his organization had taken no position on the measure, and added that other than knowing of the two librarians— Quincy Mumford and Herbert Putnam—who served as Librarians of Congress, he had not done any personal research of the Librarians of Congress as a whole, other than knowing their names and when they served.

Asked if Putnam and Mumford who would have been qualified for the position under the bill were better librarians or were more likely to be better librarians than others who have served in that capacity, Johnson said, "I am not anxious to get into the business of comparing one with another." Emily Mobley, President of the Special Libraries Association, told the Subcommittee, "While we (SLA) support the bill, I think it can be a bit too narrow and I believe you must watch to make sure it is not so narrow, because some good people would be missed."

Needless to say, following this exchange, the bill was doomed for the foreseeable future. While the division on this critical point does not represent an earthshaking tragedy, it does represent a serious setback in the long-term political process. First, the library profession is on record with a two-to-one vote indicating that it doesn't really care whether it receives high level recognition in Washington. Second, three major organizations have publicly indicated that they do not consult with each other to attempt to resolve their differences on important matters of strategy and tactics. And, finally, the credibility of a major Congressional library advocate was damaged by the official display of disunity among those he sought to represent.

Advocates, sponsors and cosponsors are of critical importance. After agreement is reached on a set of legislative initiatives, nothing of significance will happen unless a group of inside supporters is recruited. Sponsors and cosponsors for each bill are needed in both the House and the Senate. There is also a need for all interested parties to work together. The Washington lobbyists sometimes play an invaluable role in achieving this kind of coordination. Unfortunately, in the seven years that I have served in the House, I have never seen the Washington ALA Office or any other library serving entity test its advocacy strength or identify and introduce its chief supporters to each other. There is a residue of goodwill among Congressmen and a reservoir of support among constituents which has still never been appropriately exploited.

The eight years of Ronald Reagan were fearful years. So much time and energy had to be consumed in preventing the eradication of key programs that already existed or the strangling of such programs through budget cuts; in this environment not only were new initiatives neglected but new strategies and methods of operation were also overlooked. If, indeed, we are entering a new era and a probable federal breakthrough on education is only a few years away, then the development of a new approach within the library community is very much in order.

A more creative agenda is needed immediately and a greater amount of staff power is needed to carry out such a long-term master plan while at the same time holding the line for existing programs. Failure to achieve greater unity on a legislative program for the nineties would expose a critical weakness; it would foreshadow a deadly final fragmentation within the library profession. Such splintering will cause a reduction in the size of a critical mass which is already too small. Not only will lawmakers stop listening to library representatives, they will begin to listen to pseudo information specialists who have learned a few tricks with computers and databases. And, of course, they will listen more and more to the well organized representatives of the information industries.

How many and which lawmakers do you have access to and what influence can you exert with them or through them? These are the bottom line questions which must be addressed when one is considering the Congressional legislative process. When you gain access what amount of time and attention will you receive? How will the all important staff of the decision-makers be directed to interact with library representatives? Where will the Congress members place library matters on their list of priority concerns? What degree and quality of participation will the library activists and lobbyists be able to get from the members as they mobilize around specific and timely legislative concerns?

In recent years there has been an escalation of the criticisms of influence peddling and misuse of powers in Washington as a result of ties to powerful lobbying interests. Indeed, Ronald Reagan succeeded in thoroughly confusing the situation when he accused welfare recipients, community action agencies, and senior citizens of being dangerous special interests. Deliberately obscured is the fact that only when money is being used to promote a special interest is the political process corrupted and distorted. True democracy requires that all special interests be heard in order to reach some conclusion about where the interests lie. But the case for each interest group should be made on its own merits. Big contributions and unregulated honorariums mutilate the desirable democratic process of considering all arguments equally. The power of money must be greatly reduced or removed from the Congressional legislative process.

On the other hand, more aggressive citizen lobbying is badly needed in Washington. It is strongly recommended that as much as one-fourth of the budget and staff of national library organizations be dedicated to the efforts to achieve positive and productive decisions and programs from the Congress. What would the Washington operation do with all of those resources and staff people? There are some handbooks and readings which can readily provide a practical answer to this question.

For the purposes of immediate illumination of this argument, however, a few examples will be provided. Consider the well financed South African lobbying effort: These merchants of propaganda to perpetuate the evil system of apartheid have a profile on every member of Congress with a rating system indicating the members' position on their concerns. Accompanying such profiles are recommendations indicating ways to minimize the influence of certain opposition members; ways to maximize the influence of supportive members; and ways to change the minds of certain hardline members. Probably the cigarette lobby, the dairy lobby, each major defense contractor, the automobile lobbyists against effective measures to curb acid rain; all of these have similar profiles. And even a poorly funded nonprofit lobbying group like the environmentalists have such well organized files.

There are lobbying groups who regularly interact with members' offices in the following positive ways:

Organizations such as the National Education Association, the

National Council on Independent Living, the Child Welfare League and others, act as a bridge between Congress members and communities in the field. They may arrange activities in the members' districts that will bring the members closer to their issues (as we, for instance, can arrange for tours of depository libraries). They form networks providing members with the latest information on the most recent innovative practices or research in a given field. They issue voting record ratings every year, documenting the voting patterns of those members who have been supportive of their issues. Some organizations, such as the Wilderness Society, the Sierra Club, and others concerned with environmental and conservation matters, write thank you letters to those members who have been supportive of environmental and wildlife protection legislation. Many organizations, particularly labor groups, place members' names on mailing lists to receive books, pamphlets, newsletters and periodicals to keep the lawmakers informed and up-to-date. Several members of lobby groups make it a point to regularly visit or meet with Congressional staff, just to stay in touch with them, even when there is no specific legislation pending which has to do with the lobby group's issue area. And they generally act as conduits, letting members' staffs know what is going on within the constituencies they represent, whether it is educators, disabled Americans, libraries, or economically disadvantaged children and youth.

In closing I will not offer a set of basic recommendations. Such a set of practical do's and don'ts can be found in a number of other places. My closing exhortation would instead call for the launching of the kind of legislative program which America needs in the twenty-first century. We must dust off some of the old dreams, ideas and concepts and place them on the front burner again. We must listen to the most creative among us and allow some new proposed solutions to old problems to surface. And most of all we must commit the time, energy and resources to achieve passage of the majority of our legislative initiatives. While others might find it hard to believe, librarians must continue to assume that the contributions of libraries to the overall American cultural enrichment and educational improvement effort is a vital one.

We must identify, assemble and empower the leaders of the library profession who are "great communicators." Whatever strategy for legislative success is developed, such "great communicators" must be a central and vital component of the overall mobilization. To energize the rank and file as well as some cynical commanding officers we must have "great communicators" forcefully repeating the message that the key to the "learning society" of the future is the library of the future. The Congressional legislative process must begin with vision and inspiration.

The President and Library Policy

Michael H. Harris
Dennis P. Carrigan
College of Library and Information Science
University of Kentucky

INTRODUCTION

Even though librarians become involved in the political process, at times they appear naive about the effects of presidential intervention in national library affairs. The literature gives the impression that many librarians think they only need to make a strong moral and intellectual case for federal support, and they will get it. With rare exception, this optimism has proven unjustified.

Librarians who seek to understand the nature of presidential intervention in national library affairs must do so not within a moral and/or intellectual context but rather within the context of the political economy of national communications policy. Political economy is a concept which enjoyed widespread use in the eighteenth and nineteenth centuries, after which it fell from popularity. Recently, the concept has been revived as a useful construct for understanding aspects of decision-making by the president and others. Applied to presidential decision-making, political economy generally connotes the detailed study of the relationship between the state, society, and the economy. The concept suggests the dynamic interdependence among all three elements. If librarians are to understand the process of presidential intervention in library affairs, they must abandon the ingenuous idea that libraries operate in a vacuum, free from the influence of political, economic, and social considerations. Instead, librarians must understand and fully appreciate the vital political economy which powerfully influences their work.

This essay proposes a model for understanding presidential intervention in library affairs. Framed within current thinking about political economy, the discussion will provide library policy-makers with a tool for understanding how various forces enter into presidential decision-making. Due to space constraints, the discussion of the historical development of presidential involvement in national library affairs will be limited to the last thirty years.

It is essential to recognize that presidential intervention in national library affairs represents conscious political choices about the nature and value of library services in American society. Decisions are made within the context of politics, the economy, and various ideologies. In turn, these frameworks are directly influenced by the availability of information pertinent to the outcomes expected from the various policy options proposed to the president.

It may be assumed that when a particular group gives information to the president, the information will reflect the interest of that group. Thus, the group will design the information to provide support for a particular policy option. Further, a number of interest groups usually have a stake in the outcome of a policy decision; therefore, they will do everything in their power to influence the decision-making process. Within economic and political parameters, they will subsidize the production of information, which the president and his advisors will consume. This subsidized information, framed in a self-interested argument, will be more likely to influence policy decisions favorably if the president sees it as falling comfortably within his ideological framework.

THE INTERESTS

Four interest groups are vitally concerned with influencing presidential intervention in national library affairs.[1] First are the *consumers*. They comprise the users of libraries throughout the nation, and to a lesser extent the general public, even though they may never use libraries. Second are the *librarians*. Their jobs and professional performance are significantly influenced by any national policy relating to library affairs. Third are the *producers* of goods and services consumed by libraries. This group includes authors, publishers, book vendors, building contractors, and those who produce supplies and equipment designed for libraries. Finally there is *the executive* himself. All four of these groups have interests—often conflicting—that are briefly explored below.

Library Users

Generally, library users have one goal in supporting libraries: to maximize the benefits they derive as library patrons. Clearly this goal means different things to different users, but to most it means an interest in library buildings and library materials (i.e., books, periodicals, and, increasingly, materials in other formats). Generally, the user group can be counted on to provide support for enhanced funding for libraries. Frequently they are especially eager to have federal support for local library service. In addition, support from the nonuser portion of the public may be forthcoming, especially if increased taxes do not result.

The Librarians

As a group, librarians have a considerable stake in persuading the government to invest substantial sums of money in library programs. Thus, librarians generally support appeals for presidential intervention in library affairs, provided the intervention takes the form of increased financial support and does not carry with it direct federal involvement in local decision-making. Federal support often provides substantial funding for the training and employment of librarians, the modernization and construction of library buildings, and the acquisition of library materials. Because the government supports these crucial areas, the librarians' lobby, as represented most visibly in the American Library Association's Washington Office, actively gathers and provides information that might contribute to greater federal investment in the national library system.

The Producers

Historically, the strongest advocates of federal involvement in library services have been the nation's book publishers, who have a major and, in some cases, vital stake in the size of library materials budgets. Libraries acquire vast numbers of books and periodicals with, it often appears, little or no attention paid to whether these materials will be used. Moreover, the publishers of high-culture books and the publishers of scholarly periodicals have become dependent upon the library marketplace for survival. As a result, they have proven to be particularly potent supporters of libraries (witness National Library Week) and have lobbied intensely for presidential, or national, intervention in library support.

The motivation for publishers to support library funding is obvious. A decline in library support would have a direct and serious impact on the survival of the high-culture publishing industry in this country. In contrast, an increase in library support would directly contribute to the success of the same sector. The support of the high-culture industry comes heavily freighted with liabilities; the industry's interests are (as was reflected in the Library Services and Construction Act) limited to securing support for programs that would allow libraries to consume more books. These publishers appear generally uninterested in programs that might enhance cooperation among libraries, especially cost-saving attempts to share books and periodicals.

For years, publishers were the dominant component of the producer lobby in library affairs. Recently, however, producers of technology for libraries—especially computer manufacturers and database vendors—have taken an increased interest in the library marketplace. These latecomers complicate the work of the producer lobby since they frequently advocate a "paperless library," an idea book publishers and vendors find both distasteful and dangerous to the industry.

The President

It is reasonable to expect that the president's interest in libraries will be primarily political, use of the term "political" is not meant to be pejorative. Understandably, the president considers each policy choice in light of his need to maximize votes in elections or other forms of political support. The president first considers the voting power of the constituencies on both sides of the battle for and against federal support for libraries. He also carefully scrutinizes the extent to which the voters are indifferent to any issue.

In the light of these considerations, the president predictably will propose legislation that a majority of voters would favor. *At the same time,* the legislation would be consistent with his ideological views on the role of the library in the larger context of evolving national communications policy.

PRESIDENTIAL INTERVENTION IN NATIONAL LIBRARY AFFAIRS

The preceding pages set forth a model that explains the process of presidential decision-making relative to federal support for library services. Four distinct groups have considerable, and in certain cases intense, interest in national support for libraries. Three of the interest groups—users, producers, and librarians—have clearly defined reasons for supporting one or another of the policy options that might be proposed for library support. While the president is clearly interested in policy options that promise continued voter support, his ideological frame will influence policy decisions. As a result, it may be more difficult to predict how he will act relative to the proposals being considered.

An examination of the presidential decision-making process in operation follows. To test the explanatory power of the model, examination will focus on two quite different cases of presidential intervention in library affairs. The first case is the massive government support for library services initiated under the broad rubric of the "Library Services and Construction Act." The second case was the equally dramatic attempt on the part of the Reagan Administration to redirect the federal role relative to libraries while at the same time explicitly attempting to redefine the very purpose of libraries in the context of national communications policy.

The Library Services and Construction Act and Other Federal Legislation: 1956 to 1974

In 1944, Fremont Rider, then Librarian at Wesleyan University, declared that academic libraries in the United States were "actually doubling in size every sixteen years."[2] Rider concluded that if such growth rates were projected into the future, the results would be "astronomical," and clearly could not be supported by the nation's library system. As a solution, he proposed a paperless library based on the new technology of the micro-card. Although the idea seemed rational enough, it fell on deaf ears among the members of the library and book communities. Yet how could the library community members ignore the facts and comfortably assume that they could continue to raise the resources necessary to sustain such growth and house these dramatically increased holdings? From a current vantage point, the answer is obvious: librarians fully expected massive intervention from outside sources to supply the necessary funds. They mainly anticipated support from the federal government. And their expectation has indeed been met.

As early as the late forties, forces were set in motion that were designed to encourage federal intervention in the support of libraries.[3] Certain observers began to sense the symbiotic relationship that had developed between American libraries and the high-culture publishing industry. Libraries had become essential markets for the consumption of serious literature, scholarly books and periodicals, and quality children's books. Indeed, libraries represented the only market for much of this material.

Over time, publishers of this material came to see the American library system as essential to scholarly and high-culture publishing—and concomitantly to the research and literary output of the country. Both the widespread demand for cooperation and the introduction of non-book formats threatened the destruction of the close relationship between libraries and the high-culture industry. At the same time these developments threatened a dramatic restructuring of both institutions. In the face these threats, the nation's libraries marshalled powerful forces to find the resources necessary to alleviate their imminent problems.

The book producers' agenda was quite clear. In order to deal with the space problem that Rider had predicted they first had to convince the national government to supply resources for the construction of a substantial number of libraries across the land. They also had to block all discussion of cutting back on library acquisitions or eliminating the book altogether. Second, they had to gain support for federal funding for the acquisition of library materials. And third, they had to encourage support for the training of professional librarians and provide funds for the employment of these same librarians.

Library users and professionals all liked this agenda. Of course, patrons would support any proposal that would enhance access to library materials. Librarians saw the agenda as a means of addressing the central problems facing libraries at the time—crowding, inadequate acquisitions budgets, and a shortage of staff—without giving in to the jarring implications of Rider's suggested paperless library. In short, despite Rider's dire predictions, libraries could survive. All that remained was to convince the federal government of the need for massive support.

The government provided that support in the Library Services Act of 1956, which extended library service to rural Americans through state and public libraries. When the government amended the law in 1965 as the Library Services and Construction Act, it included a provision to assist in the financing of library buildings. The two acts together resulted in federal expenditure of some $425 million for books and staff salaries and some $168 million for library construction by 1974. In addition, Title II of the Elementary and Secondary Education Act provided some $750 million for the acquisition of library materials by 1974. This Bill was quickly followed by Title II-A of the Higher Education Act, which provided some $150 million in federal money for academic library acquisitions through 1975. Another $40 million was made available for the training of professional librarians, principally under the provisions of the National Defense Education Act and the Higher Education Act. While estimates vary as to the exact extent of federal investment in libraries, a conservative figure would be $2 billion from 1956 to 1980. This enormous infusion of money resolved the space, acquisitions, and staffing problems of libraries at that time, and constituted the most significant increase in library support ever experienced in this country.[4]

How could such enormous federal intervention in library affairs have come about? As previously discussed, forces in the book community naturally came together to lobby for the passage of legislation to support the status quo in libraries. But the general support for libraries by Presidents Kennedy and Johnson appears to be the key to the success.

As Kathleen Molz has rightly suggested, the proposals for national support of library programs were couched in a liberal ideology that conceived of education as the key to civic virtue, and placed considerable emphasis on the library's role in the equalization of educational opportunity in the United States.[5] Both Kennedy and Johnson agreed that the federal government had a moral responsibility to further the development of an educated citizenry. They were persuaded that libraries could contribute in a significant way to this vital national goal. In addition, however, two other forces were at play—the good health of the economy (which turned out to be short-lived) and the aggressive pressure the high-culture lobby brought to bear on the two presidents and congress.

But the success of the high-culture lobby brought with it substantial liabilities for the library profession. The massive support for the acquisition of books and periodicals, the construction of buildings, and the training of staff firmly embedded the American library system in the high-culture industry. As a consequence, the library profession's power to direct its own destiny has clearly been affected. Starting in the mid-sixties, the library's structural and functional characteristics have been determined by its role as an institution contrived to consume, preserve, transmit, and reproduce high-culture in printed form. This allegiance proved to be a serious problem at the dawn of the "post-industrial era," during which a series of presidents took office whose ideologies encompassed diminished federal support for the cultural life of the nation.

Beyond The Reagan Administration

The election of Ronald Reagan as president heralded a dramatic shift in federal policy towards libraries. In many ways he was the most ideologically committed president ever to occupy the White House. Dedicated to a conservative ideology, he believed that the government's role in the life of the nation should be strictly limited. Thus, he immediately set about to reduce federal involvement in the lives of ordinary Americans. He insisted that the federal government had no right to interfere in local affairs, and that local governments had the right and responsibility to direct their destinies in a whole range of social and cultural concerns.

Further, he was intensely committed to laissez-faire economics, and insisted that the government relinquish its alleged "stranglehold" on the American economy in order to let the free market work. Along with much of the society at large, President Reagan and his advisors were also quite taken with Daniel Bell's vision of the emergence of a new "Post-Industrial Society." In it, information would be a commodity capable of fueling a dramatic economic recovery in America.[6] In the context of his firm ideological commitments and his belief in Bell's vision of society, the president proposed a number of policy initiatives that were to have widespread ramifications for the society at large, and more specific ramifications for the nation's libraries.

As Dickson and Noble concisely point out, these policy initiatives fell into four broad ideological campaigns:

1. The rediscovery of the self-regulating market, the wonders of free enterprise, and the classical liberal attack on government regulation of the economy, all in the name of liberty.
2. The reinvention of the idea of progress, now cast in terms of "innovation" and "reindustrialization," and the limitation of expectations and social welfare in the quest for productivity.
3. The attack on democracy, in the name of "efficiency," "manageability," "governability," "rationality," and "competence."
4. The remystification of science.

The president and his advisors soon sent a message that they were not committed to supporting local library services with federal money, but instead would leave such support to local resources. President Reagan not only proved indifferent to appeals for federal support for libraries; he actually took a hostile stand. He insisted that information as a commodity was the key to future economic development in the country. Thus, he quickly made it clear that he intended to nurture the private sector information industry, and cast an indifferent eye on the high-culture aspirations of the public sector library programs in the United States.

The consequences of Reagan's stand have been apparent for some time, and the election in 1988 of the conservative George Bush, suggests more of the same. There are several implications for libraries. First, despite increasing cries of cultural decline from the high-culture industry, there is little reason to expect the federal government to provide the resources necessary to remedy the problems faced by libraries. The conservative ideology simply does not promise a return to generous federal support for libraries. At the same time, the Bush Administration will most likely continue to support private sector initiatives in the information industry, further exacerbating the problems for the nation's public sector library system. It is unlikely that the high-culture lobby will be able to reverse these trends, and the alliance of the library profession with the high-culture interest now appears to be a liability.

This situation promises to divide the library profession further. Advocates of the library as a "public good" will encounter stronger resistance from the information-industry wing of the profession. Until now, the library has successfully deferred the awkward self-examination that Fremont Rider called for in the mid-forties. Once again, the profession faces the prospect of having to abandon the cherished high-culture goals of the American library system as a result of economic exigency and the conservative ideology now dominant in the White House. As a result, librarians find themselves absorbed in intense debate about the very role of the library in American society.

CONCLUSION

The foregoing outlines a model that provides a useful framework for analyzing and predicting the nature of presidential intervention in national library affairs. A number of fairly distinct interest groups, led by the producer lobby, have sought increased federal support for the nation's library system. While these groups may have clear objectives in mind, they must nevertheless confront the matter of presidential ideology, which constrains presidential policy options. The library profession may have suffered as a result of its intense and very close relationship with the high-culture print industry in the United States. Furthermore, the library profession's historic commitment to the library's role as a publicly subsidized element in the process of civic enlightenment is most likely out of step with the Bush administration's conception of libraries and librarians as players in the private sector information market. How the library profession deals with the current administration's ideology of information policy remains to be seen. It is clear, however, that the president must be ideologically inclined towards library support if any significant funding is to be forthcoming.

References

1. The so-called "realist" analysis of political power in the United States has been extensively documented. The portrayal of the interest groups active in library affairs heavily depends upon Randall Bartlett, *Economic Foundations of Political Power* (New York: The Free Press, 1973).
2. Fremont Rider, *The Scholar and the Future of the Research Library: A*

Problem and its Solutions (New York: Hadham Press, 1944), p. 3. This startling fact has remained true to this day, and has also proven to be the case for school and public libraries.

3. Due to the brevity mandated by the editors of this volume, developments are outlined in the following pages without benefit of extensive documentation. However, both authors of this essay have written extensively on aspects of the material covered here, and readers are encouraged to consider that work, and the documentation therein, as an extended footnote to the current paper. Dennis P. Carrigan has written a number of essays on the political economy of current library services; see especially his "The Director's Dilemma," *The Journal of Academic Librarianship* 13 (1988): 349–52; "Librarians and the Dismal Science," *Library Journal* 113 (1988): 22–25; "The Political Economy of the Academic Library," and *College and Research Libraries* 49 (1988): 325–331. For the historical case for the linkage of libraries with the high culture industry in America, and a detailed argument about the future of libraries in America, see Michael H. Harris, "State, Class, and Cultural Reproduction: Toward a Theory of Library Service in the United States," *Advances in Librarianship* 14 (1986): 211–52; and for an analysis of the use of libraries see Michael H. Harris and James Sodt, "Libraries, Users and Librarians: Continuing Efforts to Define the Nature and Extent of Public Library Use," *Advances in Librarianship* 11 (1981): 109–33.

4. Federal funding for libraries continued after 1974, but at steadily diminishing levels. The article argues later that this decline was due primarily to the election of two presidents who did not share the liberal ideological commitments that influenced Kennedy and Johnson. There is a substantial literature on the federal support for libraries from 1956–1974, but perhaps the most useful volume on the whole process is Genevieve M. Casey, ed., "Federal Aid to Libraries: Its History, Impact, Future," *Library Trends* 24 (July, 1975), whole issue.

5. Redmond Kathleen Molz, *Federal Policy and Library Support* (Cambridge: MIT Press, 1976). Professor Molz's book clearly represents the most perceptive assessment of the federal role in library affairs. However, it should be noted that the authors disagree with her conclusion that the dramatic flowering of federal support for libraries in the sixties "stemmed directly from the activities of the national professional association", p. 16. The evidence would suggest that it was the producer lobby that carried the day, and that their motives were clearly tied to their need to enlarge the library market for their products.

6. Daniel Bell's views have, in a popularized version, become the common sense of contemporary American society; the "information society" has become a commonplace in national discourse. For Bell's most thorough deployment of his spectacularly influential metaphor see Daniel Bell, *The Coming of Post-Industrial Society: A Venture in Social Forecasting* (New York: Basic Books, 1973). Perhaps the most successful of the many popularizations of Bell's ideas will be found in the widely read book by John Naisbitt, *Megatrends: Ten New Directions Transforming Our Lives* (New York: Warner Books, 1982). Despite the many powerful critiques of Bell's idea, it remains the dominant metaphor in contemporary American society.

7. David Dickson and David Noble, "By Force of Reason: The Politics of Science and Technology Policy," in Thomas Ferguson and Joel Rogers, eds., *The Hidden Election: Politics and Economics in the 1980 Presidential Campaign* (New York: Pantheon Books, 1981) p. 267.

II
State Politics and the Support of Libraries

The Political Process and Library Policy

Cynthia Jenkins
Member, The Assembly, State of New York

For a profession that specializes in the business of information, the library profession suffers from a great paucity of research on its role in an area on which its very existence depends. Research on the legislative process and how libraries—whether school, university, prison, or special ones—can use it effectively in library policy-making and implementation is practically nil. In my search for background information to draw from in the preparation of this chapter, I was hard put to find one substantive paragraph of research from which to draw.

From my vantage point both as a legislator and as a trained librarian, I would say that this lack of knowledge of the legislative process on the part of librarians is the major reason for the low priority which libraries hold with legislative bodies. I would suggest that a definitive study on libraries and the legislative process be done in the very near future.

Following is a brief description of the legislative process and how to use it to effect library policies.

THE LEGISLATIVE PROCESS AS IT APPLIES TO THE LEGISLATIVE BODY

What is known as the legislative process can be simply described in two parts. The basic process of legislation is essentially the same for city, state and federal governments. Although there may be variations

45

in government procedure from state to state and city to city, there are two major parts to all legislative bodies on all levels of government.

Part one deals with how the legislators divide the monies. These are the monies that have been collected through various taxes from the people and are to be returned to the people in services. The time table for this return varies at state, city and federal levels. In New York where I serve, the process must be finalized by April 1st.

In part two, the legislators must deal with laws affecting the people. On the federal level these laws involve international, national, state and local affairs. On the state level these laws involve state and local affairs. And on the city and county levels the affairs are, of course, local. As you can see, the legislative process is very concise and clear. It is working through the process that is complicated, involved and time-consuming. Nevertheless, until the library profession learns how to use the process effectively, it will always remain the stepchild of legislative concerns and special favors.

USING THE LEGISLATIVE PROCESS TO EFFECT POLICY GOALS

Giving credit where due, I must concede that librarians have been improving in their understanding of the legislative process and in their lobbying techniques. This progress is reflected in the increased funding levels of the general needs of libraries as well as of special programs such as Literacy Volunteer Program and special funding for foreign language books to serve the increasing population of non-English speaking people. For instance, recently through the legislative process, the New York State Legislature encouraged the New York State Board of Regents to approve a three part strategy to update the 1950 regulations affecting public libraries which would assure quality library service to every man, woman and child in the State. The New York State Board of Regents is the top state education governing board. Although we applaud these efforts, much more must be done to ensure quality service for every citizen.

There are several ideas I wish to explore which I know will help to advance the position of librarians in the concerns of legislators.

To begin, the library profession must realize that it has to compete with all other groups for a part of ever-decreasing funds from the taxpayers' dollars. The operative phrase is "the taxpayers' dollars." Librarians must convince the taxpayers that libraries are as essential in their everyday existence as any other service needs. When the library profession achieves this consideration for libraries, the profession will come to its fullest potential and reach an undreamed of height and respect.

How can the profession best get its policies through the legislative process? The profession must learn how to be more precise and clear in its stated aims and goals.

There must be a clear statement of how the library's policy will benefit the people to be served.

The library profession must have a stronger, more demanding feeling about its importance. The profession must exude more confidence in itself and its uniqueness. Librarians should learn how to capitalize on the fact that theirs is the only information base that all people may use to meet information needs.

To augment the point of their profession's uniqueness, librarians can demonstrate to legislators that lawmakers depend on information that is supplied to them through libraries in order for them to function. Without the information stored in the legislative libraries and the state research libraries, the legislators would have to operate at less than a snail's pace. Above all professionals, legislators cannot make a single move without first doing research on what they purport to do to accomplish the legislative and/or funding needs of their constituents.

Librarians must flex their muscles for the legislators at every level of government. They must play their uniqueness to the hilt. There is no discipline in the world that can function without the information supplied by libraries. Thus, librarians must develop the presence that will lead them into the forefront of the information and service society of the twenty-first century.

The second big step in getting policies through the legislative process is to have the people—the tax-paying people—on your side. This is an absolute must for all service institutions and organizations that require government help, whether private or public. The people must be active participants in whatever librarians wish to accomplish. Without input and participation from the people, the best intended policies get nowhere.

Again, it must be emphasized that policies must be clearly stated if the people are to work with librarians in trying to effect policies through the legislative process; they must have a clear and full understanding of what it is the library wants to accomplish. The goals and objectives must, unquestionably, be beneficial to those to be served. Everyone on a lobbying team should be thoroughly knowledgeable of what he or she is asking for whether it affects them directly or indirectly. For instance, few people including other librarians, fully understand library networking and how it can add to the effectiveness of their local services.

Development of Political Awareness

Staying close to home, the profession has often looked at itself as a group; however, every library should strive to develop a program of orientation in the political process. Every institution—be it college, school, prison, or public library—should have as part of its employee orientation program a segment on the political process in the life of the organization.

Every librarian should be taught that the political process does not begin and end in the legislative assemblies of Washington, D.C. or the state capitals or city halls of the nation. The political process begins in the neighborhood institutions of each individual—the churches, community meetings, block associations, parents' associations, etc. Thus, librarians should lobby for libraries every opportunity they get.

In the orientation classes each individual should receive the names and both local and official addresses and telephone numbers of their elected officials. They should also receive a capsule explanation of the function of each office and the committees on which the person serves.

All employees should be encouraged to communicate with any elected official who resides in their neighborhood or election district, to articulate the library's needs, and to promote its services and programs whenever the opportunity presents itself. Community relations, if done well, can be highly beneficial.

Librarians in whatever type of library (regional, public, school, university) should strive to develop an on-going, meaningful relationship with their resident elected officials on every level of government. They should try to keep in touch generally as well as through written communications in a meaningful way. Librarians in managerial positions on the local levels should encourage their constituents to do the same on an individual and organized basis. School librarians should encourage parents' associations and volunteers to make at least one group visit to local officials for the purpose of promoting library policies and articulating the services of the library and the part it plays in the lives of their children.

The key for librarians in the legislative process is the establishment of a good relationship with legislators on committees concerned with funding and legislation. Librarians should also establish relationships with whatever other committees in the individual states would impact on libraries. They should seek ways to be in touch with those legislators on an ongoing basis.

The legislative process should not be a one-day affair. ("state capitol," "Washington, D.C.," or "City Hall" Lobby Day.)

It is most important in the establishment of a meaningful relationship with legislators to impress on them how library policies will impact on local community needs. By developing creative lobbying, librarians can present the goals of the library in exciting and readily understandable ways. They should be sure that goals are included which have been proven to contribute to the educational and social needs of the community. They should not try to push programs that have not proven successful.

Central to the success of any library's policies are the people on the Board of Trustees. Trustees should not be getting political payoffs. First and foremost, they should be people interested in libraries as a vital institution in the lives of people. Trustees should be very capable, articulate and influential citizens who are truly committed to the preservation and growth of libraries and dedicated to the promotion of their policies.

PUBLIC RELATIONS AND THE PROMOTION OF LIBRARY POLICIES

Library policies and programs, in general, suffer from a lack of creative packaging and from low visibility. A survey of 37 American libraries concluded that if libraries engaged in more pubic relations, they would definitely get much more in their budgets. Increased library awareness and public image help to create confidence in the library, and people are more apt to support something in which they have confidence.

Political public relations is the most significant part of the whole public relations package. The need is growing for library management to develop political awareness and better skills in the political process. Management might learn how to accomplish its goals in conjunction with other government agencies, as a part of a public relations package, rather than in isolation. Management should contact other agencies to see what services they offer or to determine which needs might be met centrally through the library. Management should work closely with local government agencies in fulfilling reference and research needs. Also, management should keep agencies posted on special programs which relate to agency needs and proffer the use of meeting rooms if needed. By striving to learn about the special interests of some of the heads of the agencies and by contacting them personally, management can tap a politically invaluable source.

The library should encourage staff to attend meetings of other government agencies and encourage them to be active in various professional associations. It is important to develop a lobbying network composed of the people from a wide range of backgrounds who would serve as spokespersons for library policies and related matters. Sources for contacts include trade unions, Departments of Election, Federated Community Groups, churches, and community service groups. For instance, the organization which I founded, Social Concern Committee of Springfield Gardens, Inc. in Queens, New York has 2,000 employees. No one from the local library, which is three blocks away from this agency, has ever approached the management to see if they could work out a library program that would benefit the employees and the library.

Librarians need more mass media exposure. Their public relations departments should learn to use the approaches of any viable, highly respected big business. Note the distinction: *highly respected*, big business. I do not propose that libraries become hucksters in their public relations.

The main library of every major city or town should make better use of the public service spots that are available to communities on radio, and television and in newspapers. And, more celebrities, other famous people and local elected officials are willing to donate their time to public service announcements promoting positive social and educational programs.

THE LIBRARIES' UNIQUE POSITION

I would like to summarize by reiterating that the library profession should make better use of its unique position: Libraries are centers of lifelong learning and information retrieval for everyone at all age levels. In the rapidly changing world of knowledge, children must be taught how to learn on their own so that they can keep up with what is happening in the world. Researchers in every field must know the latest findings. The legal profession must know the latest changes in law. Doctors must know the latest findings in drugs and medical procedure. Only through a variety of sources found in libraries—whether school, public, college or special—can information needs be met.

To illustrate further the unique role of libraries in the education process, I would like to quote the *National Commission On Excellence In Education* in their report *A Nation at Risk*. "We have been losing ground at a time when we need to expand and redefine the kinds of services we provide to meet the new and expanding learning needs in an information society."

Lifelong learning is not simply a catch phrase; it is a concept referring to a constantly evolving set of skills necessary for effective participation in society and achievement of a full life. "Only library institutions are equipped to serve in this unique capacity."

The idea of the educated man being one who has "learned how to learn, the man who has learned to adapt and change; the man who has realized that no knowledge is secure, that only the process of seeking knowledge gives basis for security" is not new. It was expounded by Carl Rogers, noted psychologist of the early 1900 s. According to his views, through the cooperation of professional teachers and librarians, students would have a better chance to become truly educated and learn what they need to know all of their lives. Moreover, he believed that when the learning needs of students become the first priority of the educational system and are reflected in budgets, class size, and support systems, all education will be gifted.

Without question, the library in its unique role as the center of learning and information is the only institution equipped to fulfill the need of lifelong learning and independent learning. Libraries are the only centers of learning with access to a broad world of information. This is especially true today with the practice of library cooperation, networks, and interloan systems. No other institution or agency can offer this broad range of material and services in education and general information. It is imperative that the libraries begin to act as centers of learning and information and become more involved with people rather than materials. They are the only institutions that can quickly furnish in one place a variety of rapidly changing knowledge. This is the library's uniqueness and the profession should learn how to use this fact in affecting the policy needs which require legislative action.

When the library field has a ready answer to the question "How do library policies serve the everyday needs of people?" and when libraries are considered a basic community need, over half of the battle with legislators will be over. And libraries will step into the forefront of education and information.

State Policy in California

Gary E. Strong
State Librarian of California

In the decade following the passage of the Gann Initiative and Proposition 13, library politics in California has experienced tremendous changes. These initiatives have changed the basic structure of funding and the ways in which libraries can control their own destinies. These public policy phenomena have created stress on libraries, including the California State Library, and have slowed expansion and growth in public library service for a rapidly changing and growing population. As legislative consultant Fred Silva states:

> California has experienced three revolutions: the Bear Flag Rebellion of 1846; the Populist Movement during the early part of this century that brought the initiative, referendum, and recall provisions to the California Constitution; and the "Great Tax Revolt"of 1978. The Great Tax Revolt has affected California's system of government as profoundly as the populist revolt. The initiative provision worked exactly as it was intended. It has become a release valve for pressure built up by a political stalemate in Sacramento. A combination of factors in the mid-1970s, including rapidly increasing property taxes and a growing mistrust in government's ability to deal with the problem, brought Proposition 13 to the ballot in June 1978. It proved that the reformers 70 years ago were right. You can fundamentally change the system if the government apparatus was unresponsive.[1]

Those who voted for Proposition 13 continually claimed that they had not intended to hurt their libraries. People would state again and again, "We were just voting against more taxes." The results were to the contrary. For the past ten years, the California State Library has monitored the status of public library service in California. That investigation found a 22 percent reduction in library service hours, a 21 percent cut in staffing, and a 20 percent drop in funds for materials.[2] Part-time staff were the first to go in many libraries, reducing scheduling flexibility and forcing reduction in hours and closure of outlets. Children's story-hour programming was reduced or eliminated, and audiovisual desks were closed. Outreach and special services were curtailed. People found that their libraries and the materials that they counted on were just not as good as they once had been. The excitement and innovation which had characterized California public library development was gone.

Libraries were not the only local government services hit. Parks, recreation, and other "nonessential" local government services also suffered. The most telling example of the loss of local control was the counties' costs of programs, required or mandated by the state, compared to the growth of local revenue. According to the state's legislative analyst, county general purpose revenue between 1983–1984 and 1985–1986 grew by 13 percent. In the same period, health and welfare program costs grew by 27 percent; trial court costs by 61 percent; and jail costs by 30 percent.[3] The result is that the discretionary "pot" of money from which many libraries and other services were funded was significantly reduced. Through 1986–1987, the legislative analyst indicates that the total amount of state and local tax relief granted since June 1978 is a mind-boggling $178 billion.[4]

Proposition 13 created changes that have reached far beyond just public libraries. School and community college libraries have also felt a tremendous impact. Many elementary and junior high school libraries no longer exist. Some high schools libraries are run by parent volunteers, and book collections are replenished by bake sale revenues.[5] Community college libraries facing bulging student counts are hampered by flat revenues and shrinking collections. Even with recent initiatives[6] to provide a dedicated portion of the state's general fund budget in each year for K-14 education, libraries are seeing little relief.

The University of California and the California State University system likewise have seen flat revenues and very slow growth for staff and collections. Although formula driven, the allocations to the two systems have not kept pace. Growth in population has not been reflected by growth in enrollment in higher education because of capped enrollment. New campuses in each system are needed, but funds have yet to be allocated. There is also a lack of dollars for preservation of deteriorating collections in spite of the vast growth in the amount of information that must be processed, stored, and made available. Although the importance of university library research collections to support economic growth and development of the state is recognized, these collections receive limited funding.

The story of the California State Library is no different. In five years, no cost-of-living adjustments have been provided to state operations budgets or to the public library systems. Inflation has more than curtailed growth and the ability to respond to the needs of libraries for support services.

MAJOR LEGISLATIVE INITIATIVES

In the era of funding initiatives which have restricted the ability of governments to meet the needs for services of their constituencies, a number of major legislative initiatives have strengthened library services. Each of these innovative and very strong efforts has required the attention and collaborative efforts of the State Library, the state library association, and trustees and friends of libraries. While public attention has shifted in favor of support for education, libraries have not always been included in this change. But progress has been made.

The Blind and Physically Handicapped

For a number of years, services for the blind in the ten southern counties of California were provided by the Braille Institute of Los Angeles with no reimbursement from the state. In 1978 the legislature passed legislation[7] which provided partial funding to the Braille Institute from state general funds to serve those eligible for services in partnership with the State Library. The Braille and Talking Book Library, a branch of the California State Library serves the blind and physically handicapped in northern California. This funding has been appropriated to the State Library's budget in each year since. To provide more ready access to the services from the two regional libraries, the legislature passed legislation directing the State Library to provide toll-free telephone access for patrons.[8]

California Library Services Act

In 1978 the legislature passed the California Library Services Act[9] (CLSA) which replaced the Public Library Services Act.[10] The CLSA provided funding to encourage universal access to the library resources of all types of libraries through inter-library loan for people through their local pubic libraries and by direct loan from any public library. The legislation created the California Library Services Board composed of thirteen members, nine appointed by the Governor, two by the Speaker of the Assembly, and two by the Senate Rules Committee. This statutory body provides a state level forum for the determination of resource sharing policy and context for the interaction of public libraries on behalf of their users.

The most critical provision of the CLSA encouraged public libraries to open their resources to all residents of the state through universal borrowing and equal access provisions. Under these sections, libraries allow any person, regardless of residence, to borrow materials and to receive services from any public library in California who agrees to participate. In turn, the state reimburses the libraries for all items loaned by inter-library loan and for the net imbalance of services rendered. In this past year, over 15 million books were borrowed by people under the provisions of the CLSA (total circulation from public libraries was 125 million volumes).

The 15 cooperative public library systems provide reference services and communication and delivery; they work with advisory boards representing each member library jurisdiction. The creation of this second level of public library services has significantly enhanced the ability of public libraries to work together and open resources and information to users. While a number of systems had emerged as a result of the Public Library Services Act, the CLSA provided for the creation of systems to serve public libraries across the state. Today, fewer than ten public libraries choose not to participate under CLSA.

The state-level components of the Act—system level planning, coordination, and evaluation; statewide reference services; statewide communications and delivery; and the special services programs—have never been funded. Proposition 13 dealt its blow to the CLSA when immediately after passage, the governor mandated a ten percent cut in appropriations. The first Board found itself having to make immediate and difficult trade-offs with the new CLSA. The Board made an attempt to fund information and referral centers under the special services component in 1979, but was restricted by the legislature from doing so in subsequent years.

Statewide Database Program

At the state level, the CLSA database program has enabled the development of a statewide public library database now totalling more than 8 million items added to public libraries since 1978. The State Library coordinates the collection of holdings information for new acquisitions for all CLSA public library participants. Through a precedent setting contract with OCLC, these holdings are either directly entered by OCLC participant public libraries or tape-loaded under the state's system level access agreement. The CLSA funds the access fee and member libraries are responsible for covering the costs of their use of the inter-library loan system.

Special Services Programs

When funding from the State general fund was achieved for the California Literacy Campaign in 1985, it was administered through the Special Services provisions. The Board recently identified the area of "Youth-At-Risk" as the next phase of program development under the special services component.[11]

Public Library Finance Act

In 1981, the legislature acknowledged the need for direct assistance to individual public libraries when it passed SB 358, the Public Library Fund[12] (PLF). The California Library Association and the California State Library worked hard to secure the first direct per capita assistance to public libraries. The first funds were distributed in 1983–1984 in the amount of $6 million. PLF uses a formula that establishes a per-capita amount needed for the foundation program of local library service and awards one state dollar per capita for each nine dollars of local appropriation. The PLF has never been fully funded, but achieved 53.7 percent of the amount needed by 1987–1988 with an allocation of $20.2 million. Full funding of PLF remains a high priority for the Association and the State Library.

California Literacy Campaign

When the California Literacy Campaign received its first state general fund appropriation in 1985, the legislature made a significant commitment to the learning role of public libraries. More than $25 million has been appropriated to support public libraries participating in the CLC since that first appropriation. Thousands of Californians[13] have learned to read in programs now offered in over 81 public libraries through hundreds of reading centers and learning sites across the state. Additional public library jurisdictions are scheduled to come into the Campaign in this and future years.

Recognizing the success of the California Literacy Campaign, Senate President pro tem, David Roberti introduced legislation creating the Families for Literacy Program[14] and calling for the addition of a consultant for children's and youth services at the State Library. The bill failed passage the first year and was reintroduced the next session. This time favorable consideration moved the Act to the Governor's desk. He signed the legislation but vetoed funds to support the program. Working closely with the Department of Finance, the State Library achieved a budget augmentation to fund the Act the next year. In 1989–1990, the second year of the Families program, 20 public libraries with

CLC programs are offering Families For Literacy programs, the children's consultant has been hired, and first year programs served over 900 families.

An attempt to create a legislative program for students for literacy[15] was introduced in 1985 by Assemblywoman Teresa Hughes who chairs the Assembly Education Committee. The bill would have established the Students for Literacy Program, which would create a work-study type program designed to bring eligible post secondary students together with public library literacy programs. The students would have provided tutoring and other literacy related services. To be administered by the State Librarian, the proposal drew immediate fire from the various student aid offices in the respective college and university systems who thought it was their "turf." After many long meetings they reached agreements, which cleared the way for support from the student aid officials. But the bill was caught up in the battle over budget allocations and failed passage in the final hours of each session. While not totally successful, many public library literacy programs have developed work-study relationships with colleges and universities locally to accomplish the goal.

Public Library Construction and Renovation

Based upon data collected by the California State Library, it was apparent that an incredible gap existed to fund needed costs of construction for public libraries[16] across the state. With a need nearing one billion dollars, Senator Barry Keene took up the challenge and called for a ballot issue to be placed before the voters to provide funding for public library construction and renovation. Proposition 85[17] was approved by the legislature for placement on the November 1988 ballot. After much negotiation, conferees settled on $75 million, far short of what was initially discussed. The voters, in the first library ballot measure to be offered for statewide consideration, passed the measure by 52 percent of those casting votes—a major success for public libraries.

Other Initiatives

Recognizing the role that public libraries could play in bridging the gap in the emerging electronic age, Assemblywoman Gwen Moore has championed legislation to provide tax credits (Assembly Bill 274 in 1989) for donations of computer equipment and other services to public libraries. The key stipulation is that the computers and services must be for the direct use and benefit of public library users. Even with support from IBM and Apple, the legislation fell short of success in the final days of the session.

Members of the blind community began work to draft legislation that would provide for funding of a statewide radio reading service for the blind and physically handicapped. Preliminary estimates developed by the proponents of the legislation were far short of amounts determined necessary to initiate the program in at least three sites and to provide administrative cost support to the State Library. It is expected that legislation will be introduced once again to establish this program.

LIBRARY SERVICES AND CONSTRUCTION ACT

No discussion of California library politics can be complete without a brief note on the way in which the State Library has used funds received under the Library Services and Construction Act (LSCA).[18] The State Librarian is responsible for administering the funds received from the federal government under the LSCA. Most of the funds are administered to encourage change and innovation in public library services under Title I. Over the past ten years, the State Library has taken the initiative to fund ongoing program commitments from state or local funding. For example, the administrative cost of public library systems was once funded entirely from LSCA allocations. In 1989–1990, a phase-over plan was achieved and these costs are now fully supported by state and local revenues.

By facilitating the transition of these long-term commitments to other funding sources, the State Library makes the commitment to retain what works well and to cut loose those programs which may not have met the challenge of competition against other programs. This shift has allowed the State Library to focus on program innovation and development in the light of Proposition 13. With one-time funding from LSCA, the State Library launched the California Literacy Campaign. The following year, based on the incredible success and acceptance of the program, the California legislature appropriated funds and the Governor agreed to continue this program.

State-level reference service has always been important in California. BARC (the Bay Area Reference Center) and SCAN (the Southern California Answering Network) pioneered such service and built strong programs over twenty years of support. As a result of the passage of CLSA, system reference centers provided a regional level of reference service which provided a narrowing filter for questions being funnelled to the two statewide centers. In 1986, the State Library began to examine the restructuring of the two reference centers (BARC and SCAN) and to fund state-level reference service from LSCA funds. The report[19] issued was extremely controversial and created an upheaval within the library community.

Numerous statewide meetings and further studies have moved the public library community toward a new direction in supporting system and state-level reference service. The California Library Services Board has approved the reference service framework which now moves forward for funding by the legislature and the Governor.[20] The concept encompasses the need to address the strengthening of existing services and the addition of important services for ethnic and racial groups for specialized local, regional, and state-level reference and information resources. Question answering, resource building, training and staff development, and public relations and publicity are major components of this consensus-built initiative.

Under Title III, the State Library has assisted in the planning for a multi-type library network to serve California libraries. Based on 20 years of discussion and several successful projects such as the Total Information Exchange (TIE) and the Cooperative Information Network (CIN), the library community is now moving into the second year of a three year planning cycle to establish the basis for the network. The State Library continues to facilitate the interaction among the many library interests in the state. A task force of 134 people, working in focussed subgroups, is moving the planning forward to ensure that the breadth of interests and concerns are addressed.[21]

Partnerships for Change is the State Library's newest initiative supported under the LSCA. Based on a report and findings of the RAND Corporation,[22] the State Librarian announced the partnerships program during the conference of the California Library Association in November of 1988. In the ensuing year, the Library has begun its Community Library Grants Program. Twenty public libraries are working at the community/branch level to initiate change in library services based on careful analysis of community expressed needs. Coalitions made up of citizen groups at the local level support each branch effort. LSCA funds will provide the assistance to sustain the changes.[23]

THE STATE LIBRARY DEVELOPMENT ROLE

The California State Library has taken a strong leadership role in assisting public libraries in stabilizing their service programs in the wake of Proposition 13. Moreover, it assists libraries of all types in planning together to support resource sharing. It is evident that the State Library must work in close coordination with the California Library Association, the California Media and Library Educator's Association, and the legislative committee of the California Library Services Board. In addition, most other library and library-related organizations have legislation committees who work to further library concerns.

Groups like the California State PTA, County Supervisors Association of California and the California League of Cities have also proven to be important allies. Another paper on these groups would describe and document these important linkages and relationships.

The importance of citizen support cannot be underestimated. Citizens compose a large percentage of people attending the California Library Association's legislative day held in May of each year in Sacramento. Drawing more than 500 people in 1989, this effort has contributed much toward building tremendous credibility within the legislature. Delegations meet with every legislator and her/his staff for an annual briefing and call for assistance. Progress has been made each year, but the agenda is far from complete.

The politics of a state like California are difficult. The pull of various programs, libraries, and people often test skills of negotiation and persuasion. To succeed, many interests, needs, and concerns must be balanced. Californians are now preparing for state elections in 1990. Hopefully, another window of opportunity to enhance the condition of library services in the nation's most populous state will open.

At the risk of leaving something out, the State Librarian offers the following agenda for the 1990s as California counts down to the year 2000:

Public Library Finance Act, $20–25 million (est.):
The amount would fully fund the state's commitment of 10 percent of local public library expenditures. Funds are allocated on a per capita basis against a foundation level of local support.

Funding for Distressed County Libraries, $2–5 million (est.):
Legislation to be developed would provide relief funding to some 20 to 25 county libraries whose funding base ranges from minimal to nothing. This provides the basic public library service in California, which ensures citizen access to information and library services. The State Library maintains that without basic county library services, residents of the state will be unable to access the knowledge and information they need to be productive people.

California Library Services Act

Transaction-Reimbursement Program, $800,000 (1990–1991 est.):
This augmentation would cover reimbursements for direct and interlibrary loan supported by provisions of the Act. These programs depend upon usage.

System Level Services, $1–2 million (est.):
The public library systems have not received a cost-of-living adjustment in the last five years, and no adjustment is expected in 1990-91. Workload and population levels continue to increase. These increases drain the ability of

the public library systems to respond to demands from member institutions for reference, communication and delivery, and system advisory boards.

State Data Base, $500,000–$750,000:
This program is currently under study to examine possible applications of newer technology. The monographic database resides on OCLC and the union list of periodicals is maintained by CLASS.

California Literacy Campaign, $1–3 million (est.):
While the current baseline includes continued funding, the Governor has vetoed support to public library literacy programs, which have completed their five-year establishment period. The California Library Services Board has recommended that the state and local libraries equally share the cost of ongoing literacy services under the California Literacy Campaign. Continued support for the Families for Literacy Program is expected. A legislative task force on workforce literacy is currently working and will propose initiatives for the 1990–91 legislative session. It is expected that part of this legislation will address the library role in workplace literacy.

State Reference Centers, $5 million (est.):
The program calls for support in four areas: 1) Reference Service Enhancement and Improvement, to expand the capacity and capability of local public libraries and CLSA Systems to respond to the informational needs of people within their service areas (25% of funds); 2) Ethnic Resource and Research Center/Centers, to expand access to multilingual, multicultural information resources for people and for libraries and to increase the statewide capacity to meet the information needs of a pluralistic, multicultural society (30% of funds); 3) Ethnic Reference Service Enhancement and Improvement, to expand the capacity and capability of local public libraries to respond to the specific information needs of multilingual, multicultural groups (20% of funds); and 4) Reference Referral/third-level reference, to provide access to highly-specialized or complex information, requiring resources and expertise beyond those possible at the System Reference Resource Center level (25% of funds).

Special Services Program, $2–3 million (est.):
The California Library Services Board has designated its Youth-At-Risk initiative to be the next program component to be developed. No staff is available to support the development of the component.

California State Library, $2.5–4 million:
No cost-of-living adjustments have been provided to the state operations budget for the past five years. None are recommended for 1990–91. The loss in the buying power for library materials alone is alarming. This situation prevents the State Library from acquiring new formats of information and from fully participating in linking the library with other libraries and networks on behalf of state government and the libraries of California. While workloads increase, staff levels have remained virtually static since 1980.

State Library Annex Building, $900,000 for working drawings, $22–25 million (est.):
This project has been awaiting funding since 1984. Schematic drawings and preliminary plans were completed in 1988. Meanwhile valuable collections are exposed to uneven temperature and humidity conditions, and staff members work in cramped quarters scattered over several locations in Sacramento. The annex will provide space to relieve shelving problems in the Library and Courts Building. Many books and periodicals are now being stored on the floor between the stacks.

Library and Courts Building, $8–10 million (est.):
The fire and life safety and environmental control for the state library's current building must be updated. The central stack tower is open between each of its 13 floors endangering both collection and staff to the rapid spread of fire. Several mold and insect infestations have further jeopardized the collection.

Partnership for Change, $3 million (est.):
The potential for this program's components to be developed for funding from the state general fund is great. Elements of the program are being developed and tested during 1988–89 and 1989–90. Many local communities require assistance in retooling their programs, collections, and services to respond adequately to the growing diversity of the state's populations.

Multitype Library Networking, $15 million (est.):
The California Library Networking Task Force is in the second year (1990) of planning for the design of a multitype network. It is expected that funding proposals will be complete in 1991 and be ready for legislative consideration during the 1992 legislative session.

Public Library Construction and Renovation, Phase II, $300–500 million:
When the Public Library Construction and Renovation Bond Act of 1988 passed, it was already determined that the $75 million would be insufficient to meet the demand for funds for public library facilities. Initial surveys have indicated that the need may be as high as $1 billion. If Phase I is successful, it seems logical to attempt a second statewide bond issue. Proposition 85 (Phase I) passed with a 52 percent vote.

State Institutional and Agency Libraries, $3 million (est.):
These libraries fall under the various state agencies and number in the hundreds. The State Library attempts to monitor the condition of institutional and agency libraries but does not have a current estimate of their needs. Most are poorly funded, especially hospital libraries.

School Library Funding, $10–15 million (est.) to supplement local appropriations:
School library services are in critical condition. Unless funding is allocated soon, little basic school library service will remain in elementary schools across California. Junior high and secondary school libraries seriously need resources and certified staff to prepare students for higher education and a demanding job market. While legislation was passed during the last session (AB 2026 Eastin),

the Governor vetoed it. The Superintendent of Public Instruction has jurisdiction over school library services.

Community College Library Funding, $10–15 million (est.):
As is the case with school libraries, community college library services have been neglected since the passage of Proposition 13 in 1978. The condition of the collections and levels of staffing have reached a crisis. The Chancellor of Community Colleges has jurisdiction over initiatives to support community college library services. A new office for libraries has been established following a successful grant under the Library Services and Construction Act.

California State University Libraries and the Libraries of the University of California, No estimate:
These libraries fall under the jurisdiction of the respective campuses and state systems. Generally, the libraries have fared better than others in the state but are still under tremendous strain to keep pace and support the research and graduate programs being developed.

Library Education and Continuing Education for Librarians, $1–2 million (est.):
There are no estimates of the need for support and funding for library education in the state. A task force on continuing education has been appointed (December 1989) to consider needs and will report in the fall of 1990 to the California State Librarian as a part of the work of the California Networking Task Force activity.

This agenda is by no means complete or comprehensive. Several of the estimates are based on legislative attempts to provide new funding. It does illustrate that the job of library development and program support for the libraries of California is far from finished. The agenda will continue to grow and will serve as an inventory upon which discussion can center. The library service we have in the year 2000 will be conditioned on our success in making progress.

Notes

1. J. Fred Silva, "California's Great Tax Revolt; 10 Years Later—Where Has All The Power Gone?" *California State Library Foundation Bulletin.*, no. 24 (July 1988): 3.
2. Collin Clark, "The Best Year Libraries Had." *California State Library Foundation Bulletin*, no. 24 (July 1988): 13.
3. Silva, *op. cit.*, p. 4.
4. Silva, *op. cit.*, p. 3.
5. Barbara Brandeis, Comp. *Crisis In California School Libraries; A Special Study* (Sacramento, California: California State Department of Education, 1987).
6. Proposition 98, amends the California Constitution and adds provisions to the Education Code.

7. California Statutes of 1978: 2765, Ch. 880.
8. California Education Code Section 19325.
9. California Library Services Act (CLSA). California Education Code Sections 18700–18767.
10. Public Library Services Act (PLSA). Former Education Code Sections 27111–27146.
11. California Library Services Board. Minutes. August 16–18, 1989.
12. Public Library Finance Act. Education Code Sections 18010–18031.
13. The California State Library conservatively estimates that more than 42,000 adults have received instructional services in California Literacy Campaign programs since 1984, 21,000 adults have been referred to other instructional programs that can more readily assist their learning need, and 30,000 individuals have volunteered to tutor in local public library CLC programs.
14. Families For Literacy (part of the California Library Services Act). Education Code Sections 18735–18735.4
15. Assembly Bill ;718 (1985) and Assembly Bill 2621 (1986).
16. *California State Library Newsletter.*
17. Proposition 85. California Library Construction and Renovation Bond Act of 1988. Education Code Sections 19950–19981.
18. For a complete list of projects funded under the Library Services and Construction Act consult Collin Clark's *Projects Funded Under the Library Services and Construction Act, 1966–1988* (Sacramento, California: California State Library, 1989).
19. James H. Henson, Comp., *Staff Report On Third Level Reference Referral* (Sacramento, California: Library Development Services, California State Library, 1985).
20. California Library Services Board. Minutes. May 10–11, 1989 and August 16–18, 1989.
21. For background, consult *The California Conference On Networking. Proceedings.* September 19–22,1985. Kellogg West Conference Center, Pomona, California; *The California Conferences on Networking. Proceedings.* September 22–27, 1988; *California Library Network Retreat,October 23–25, 1988. Summary and Outcomes.* 1989; and *California Library Network Retreat, December 6–8, 1989.* To be published in 1990.
22. Judith Payne et al., *Public Libraries Face California's Ethnic and Racial Diversity.* Prepared for the Stanford University Libraries with a grant from the California State Library. (Santa Monica: The RAND Corporation, 1988).
23. For further information consult the *California State Library Newsletter*, no. 96 (December 1988): 7; no. 98, (February 1989): 1–2; no. 101 (May 1989) 2–3; and no.106 (October 1989) 2–4.

References

Library Services

Allen, Barbara, and O'Dell, Lorraine. *Bibliotherapy and the Public Library: The*

San Rafael Experience. San Rafael, California: San Rafael Public Library, 1981.

Campbell, Barbara J. *Library Services for Shasta County: Final Report to the Shasta County Board of Supervisors, July 11, 1989.* Prepared by the consultant under a grant from the California State Library, 1989.

"A Diverse California: Partnerships for Change." *California State Library Foundation Bulletin.* 27 (April 1989): 1–12.

Green, Marilyn V. *Intergenerational Programming in Libraries: A Manual.* San Jose: South Bay Cooperative Library System, 1981.

Introducing Public Library Services To ESL Students: Ready To Use Classroom Lessons for Teachers. Library Awareness Project. San Jose, California: South Bay Cooperative Library System, 1986.

Liu, Grace F. *Promoting Library Awareness in Ethnic Communities: Based on the Experience of the South Bay Cooperative Library System, 1984–1985.* San Jose, California: South Bay Cooperative Library System, 1985.

McGovern, Gail, and Holtslander-Burton, Linda. *Arts Programs: Ideas for Libraries.* Sacramento, California: California State Library, 1988.

Newspapers in California. Compiled as part of the U.S. Newspapers Projects. Sacramento, California: California State Library Foundation, 1985.

Rubin, Rhea Joyce, and McGovern, Gail. *Working With Older Adults: A Handbook For Libraries.* Third Edition. Sacramento, California: California State Library Foundation, 1990.

Talking Buildings: A Practical Dialogue on Programming and Planning Library Buildings. Proceedings of a Building Workshop, sponsored by the California State Library, October 1985. Edited by Raymond M. Holt. Sacramento, California: California State Library, 1986.

Literacy Services

"Adult Learning Services in Libraries." *California State Library Foundation Bulletin.* 26 (January 1989): 5–15.

"Families for Literacy." *California State Library Foundation Bulletin.* 28 (July 1989): 6–22.

Goldberg, Lenny, and Associates. *Literacy, Employment and the California Literacy Campaign.* Oakland, California: Goldberg and Associates, 1985.

Handbook for CALPEP, California Adult Learner Progress Evaluation Process. Sacramento, California: California State Library, 1988.

Joint Committee on the State's Economy and Senate Select Committee on Small Business Enterprises. *Joint Hearing on Workforce Literacy: Growing Disparity Between Worker Skills and Employer Needs, March 10, 1989.* Sacramento, California: The Joint Committee, 1989.

Lane, Martha A. *A Summary and Evaluation of the California Literacy Campaign Retreat held February 25–27, 1987 at Asilomar Conference Center, California.* Submitted to Gary E. Strong, State Librarian. 1987.

Lane, Martha A.; McGuire, Jean F.; Yeannakis, Christine H.; and Wurzbacher, Mark P. *California Literacy Campaign Program Effectiveness Review.* Sacramento, California: California State Library, 1984.

Literacy for Every Adult Project (LEAP). Report of Learning Center Component. Richmond, California: Richmond Public Library, 1986.

Ruby, Carmela. "It's Bad When You Can't Get Your Dreams: The California Literacy Campaign." *Public Libraries* (Winter 1984), pp. 116–118.

Senate Office of Research. *Invisible Citizenship: Adult Illiteracy in California*. A special report on adult illiteracy to Senator David Roberti. Sacramento, California: Senate Office of Research, 1986.

Solorzano, Donald W. *Analysis of Learner Progress from the First Reporting Cycle of the CALPEP Field Test: A Report to the State Librarian, February 15, 1989*. Pasadena, California: Educational Testing Service, 1989.

Solorzano, Donald W. *Analysis of Learner Progress from the Second Reporting Cycle of the CALPEP Field Test: A Report to the State Librarian, October 11, 1989*. Pasadena, California: Educational Testing Service,1989.

Solorzano, Donald W. *California Adult Learner Progress Evaluation Process, Phase II: Final Report to the State Librarian*. Pasadena, California: Educational Testing Service, 1988.

Solorzano, Donald W. *Study of Adult Learner Progress Evaluation Practices in the California Literacy Campaign*. Pasadena, Educational Testing Service, 1987.

SRA Associates. *Illiteracy in California: Needs, Services and Prospects*. Submitted to the California State Department of Education, 1987.

Strong, Gary E. "Adult Illiteracy: State Library Responses." *Library Trends* (Fall 1986), pp. 243–261.

Strong, Gary E. "Public Libraries and Literacy: A New Role to Play." *Wilson Library Bulletin* (November 1984) pp. 179–182.

Wurzbacher, Mark F., and Yeannakis, Christine H. *California Literacy Campaign: Program Effectiveness Review II*. Submitted to Gary E. Strong, State Librarian and Chief Executive Officer, California State Library. 1986.

Networking and System Services

Black Gold Regional Telecommunications Network Plan. Volume One: Main Report. Volume Two: Appendices. Ventura, California: Black Gold Cooperative Library System, 1988.

California Conferences on Networking Proceedings, September 22–27, 1988. California Library Networking Task Force and California State Library. Sacramento, California: California State Library Foundation, 1988.

The California Conference on Networking Proceedings, September 19–22, 1985. Kellogg West Conference Center, Pomona, California. Published by the Peninsula Library System, Belmont, California. Edited by Diane E. Johnson, Consulting Librarian, 1985.

California Libraries in the 1980s: Strategies for Service. Prepared by Claudia Buckner under the direction of Gary E. Strong, California State Librarian. Sacramento, California: California State Library, 1982.

California Library Network Retreat, October 23–25, 1988. Summary and Outcomes. Sacramento, California: California State Library, 1989.

CLSA Statewide Data Base: Status Report. Prepared for Gary E. Strong,

California State Librarian by Kathleen Low. Sacramento, California: California State Library,1989.

Cortez, Edwin M., and Epstein, Susan Baerg, *A Study of Future Directions for the California Library Services Act Bibliographic Data Base Program.* Prepared for the California State Librarian. Sacramento, California: California State Library, 1982.

Final Report of the Network Serials Steering Committee. Presented to Gary E. Strong, California State Librarian. Sacramento, California: California Library Networking Task Force, 1989.

Gibson, Liz. *System Level Access Project: Evaluation Report.* Sacramento, California: California State Library, 1982.

Report on CD-Rom Technology in Relation to the CLSA Data Base Program. Prepared for Gary E. Strong, California State Librarian by Kathleen Low. Sacramento, California: California State Library, 1989.

System Service Alternatives: A Study of the Santiago Library System. Prepared by the Library Development Services Bureau. Sacramento, California: California State Library, 1982.

Policy Studies

The Black Family: Are Our Youth At Risk? Legislative hearing, October 6, 1989. Sacramento, California: State Assembly. 1989.

The Crisis in California School Libraries: A Special Study. Prepared by Barbara Brandeis. Sacramento, California: California State Department of Education, 1987.

Dervin, Brenda, and Clark, Kathleen. *ASQ: Asking Significant Questions: Alternative Tools for Information Need and Accountability Assessments by Libraries.* Belmont, California: Peninsula Library System for the California State Library, 1987.

Dervin, Brenda, and Benson, Fraser. *How Libraries Help.* Stockton, California: University of the Pacific, Department of Communications, 1985.

Dervin, Brenda, *et al. The Information Needs of Californians—1984.* Davis, California: Institute of Governmental Affairs, University of California, Davis, 1984. Report # 1: Technical Report. Report # 2: Context, Summary, Conclusions, Implications, Applications.

Hayes, Robert M., ed. *Libraries and the Information Economy of California: A Conference Sponsored by the California State Library.* Los Angeles, California: A GSLIS/UCLA Publication, 1985.

Jacob, Nora, ed. *A State of Change: California's Ethnic Future and Libraries. Conference and Awareness Forum Proceedings.* Presented by the planning group for "A State Of Change." Published by the planning group for the "State of Change" project. 1988.

Payne, Judith *et al. Public Libraries Face California's Ethnic and Racial Diversity.* Prepared for the Stanford University Libraries with a grant from the California State Library. Santa Monica, California: The RAND Corporation, 1988.

Policy Analysis for California Education. *Condition of Children in California.*

Berkeley, California: PACE, School of Education, University of California, Berkeley, 1989.

Proceedings of the Second Binational Conference on Libraries of the Californias, October 11 and 12, 1985. Calexico, California and Mexicali, Baja California. Institute for Border Studies, San Diego State University, Imperial Valley Campus. 1985. (Published in both English and Spanish)

Promote The Profession: Recruitment Handbook For Librarians and Information Professionals. Compiled by the California Library School Recruitment Project. 1987.

Proposition 13, a special issue of the *California State Library Foundation Bulletin.* No. 24, July 1988.

Scarborough, Katharine T.A., *The Need for Librarians in California: Report on a Survey of the State's Libraries.* Funded by a Library Services and Construction Act Grant Award to the California Society of Librarians, a constituent group of the California Library Association. April 1987.

Strong, Gary E. *Local/State Support for Public Libraries, 1976/1978 to 1980/ 1981.* Sacramento, California: California State Library, 1982.

Reference Services

CLSA: Prospectives for Statewide Reference Services: Background Paper. Sacramento, California: California State Library, February, 1989.

Design Priorities for a Statewide Reference Service Program. Sacramento, California: California State Library, January 1989.

DeWath, Nancy Van House. *California Statewide Reference Referral Service: Analysis and Recommendations.* Rockville, Maryland: King Research, Inc., 1981.

Discussion of Alternatives for a CLSA State Reference Centers Program. Sacramento, California: California State Library, 1989.

Field Responses to the Reference Referrral Study Report: Summary/Analysis. Compiled by Jim Henson. Sacramento, California: Library Development Services Bureau, California State Library, 1987.

Framework for Public Library Reference Service. Sacramento, California: California State Library, May 1988.

Greenberg, Marilyn W., and Tarin, Patricia. *Ethnic Services Task Force Collection Evaluation Project.* Submitted to the California State Library, July 31, 1982.

Issues: State Reference Centers Program. Sacramento, California: California State Library, February 1989.

Mick, Colin K. et al. *Evaluation of the California Minority Information Services Network.* Palo Alto, California: Decision Information Services, Ltd., 1981.

Robinson, Barbara M. *A Study of Reference Referral and Super Reference in California.* Volume One: Main Report. Volume Two: Appendices. Sacramento, California: California State Library, 1986.

Staff Analysis of Barbara Robinson's A Study of Reference Referral and Super Reference in California. Prepared by Cy Silver for the California State Librarian. Sacramento, California: Library Development Services Bureau, California State Library, 1987.

Staff Report on 3rd Level Reference Referral. Prepared by Jim Henson. Sacramento, California: Library Development Services, California State Library, 1985.

Trustee Education

Proceedings. CALTAC-WILL 1983–1984; 1984–1985; and 1985–1986. Regional Workshops in Library Leadership. Petaluma, California: California Association of Library Trustees and Commissioners. 1986.

Proceedings. CALTAC-WILL 1986–1987; 1987–1988; and 1988–1989. Regional Workshops in Library Leadership. Petaluma, California: California Association of Library Trustees and Commissioners. 1989.

Trustee Tool Kit For Library Leadership. Prepared in Cooperation with the California Association of Library Trustees and Commissioners. Sacramento: California State Library, 1987. (Distributed by the California State Library Foundation)

State Policy in Florida

Barratt Wilkins
Director, State Library of Florida

In many ways, library policymaking in Florida has accomplished a great deal. Usually participatory and by consensus, policymaking involves a variety of participants: the Secretary of State; the chief elected library officer; the State Librarian in consultation with various appointed library councils and committees; the Governor and Cabinet, sitting as the State Board of Education; and, ultimately the State Legislature. Because Florida has a strong legislature, my discussion will center on the role of librarians in the legislative process.

Shortly after I arrived in Florida, I attended the first state budget conference for writers responsible for writing agency legislative budget requests. I will never forget the state budget director explaining that "you can write an airtight, closely argued, irrefutably proven budget request for additional resources—indeed, prove beyond a shadow of a doubt that your agency needs more money, people, and space to do the job—and still be ignored." The reason was: "You forgot the political process." Likewise, he explained that sometimes you could write a broadly argued, vaguer budget request initiative and, if you had the right political backing, you could secure at the very least an appropriation of major planning money, if not the establishment of the program.

Another event also happened shortly after I arrived in Florida. My good friend, Cecil Beach, then serving as State Librarian, noted with some frustration during a legislative session that he could not be expected to lobby alone for the statewide library program as the library community seemed to expect.

What I learned from those two unforgettable events has become part of the collection of general principles that I have used during my twelve-year tenure as State Librarian. Other principles which I have taken to heart, sometimes with great pain, are the following:

- The legislative process is unpredictable. It is a constant system of rewarding and punishing, and you can never know all the players. Legislators tend to have long memories; it may be years before the opportunity arises for a legislator who has been defeated on one issue to repay or get even with the former winner. Even though you may think you have all the library support bases covered on a library issue before the legislature, the issue may get defeated for an entirely different reason. On a positive note, I remember one Florida representative securing a library construction grant for his locality because he voted for a sales tax issue on two previous sessions. That particular library construction grant was a total surprise to all of us, since the local library community had not previously established a record of need.
- It is important to keep the message before a legislative body or a legislator as simple as possible and in everyday language. I have seen legislative committees lose complete interest in a project when the explanation became too technical or long-winded.
- It is important to remain as accurate as possible when presenting a program to a legislative committee. Our State University System library program was put in a perilous position some years ago when several legislative staff members caught considerable discrepancies in statistics given in support of the libraries' budget requests. The system suffered two very lean years in library materials budgets until uniformity in statistics could be achieved and confidence restored.
- Try not to be a fence sitter. One prominent public librarian was quoted saying about a library taxing initiative: "When I go home a look at my tax bills, I say we don't need any more taxes, but, then I go to work and see a need for books for Mary Smith and her children and know we don't have the money to buy them." I have found there are no free lunches—you either support the taxes to pay for the services or you do not have the services. I also remember one state librarian who used to write long philosophical arguments against federal aid for libraries, but, nevertheless, he continued to spend those federal funds over a twenty-two year period.
- In the legislative process, it is important to lobby an issue aggressively once you have decided upon a position. In lobbying the position, leave the "fairness doctrine" at home in your library. I have found librarians too fair in listening to the opposition and even in providing a forum for the opposition to present their case to your supporters. If you have adequately researched a position and have good support for that position, then "battle" the opposition until you win, lose, or compromise. We are still paying for a lack of support of a library initiative sponsored by a friendly legislator, because the state association president could see both sides and would not take a position in support of what a majority in the library community wanted. That legislator, a state senator, is now firmly indifferent to library issues and, unfortunately, sits on the Senate Appropriations Committee.
- As a private citizen, be as active as you can be in local and state politics. Elected officials will respect you for supporting a candidate—particularly

if they are the candidate. A number of Florida librarians who are active on local and state party executive committees exercise influence in finding and supporting candidates friendly to library issues.

- Finally, above all, keep a sense of humor. One who can use humor can often disarm tense situations and maybe win points in favor of a library position or issue. While the legislative process is a serious business, remember libraries have been around for 4,000 years, and they will even survive our legislators.

In putting my thoughts together for this discussion, I did not intend to present Florida as a shining example of a state that has its political act together as a library community. For we have experienced both successes and failures. Fortunately, however, Florida has rapidly grown in population and wealth. Indeed, because our state's growth and natural expansion of wealth and tax income have made life rather easy, I sometimes find our library community has become a bit too complacent. For some library directors, it is easy to get in the "tin-cup" habit, passively waiting for the money to flow to their program. To encourage librarians to participate more actively in securing funds, I will provide an outline of the role of Florida's librarians in the legislative process and suggest the pitfalls to be avoided.

Florida's approach to the legislative process is three-pronged: It involves the State Library Association, its paid lobbyist, the State Library agency, and a strong, statewide Friends and trustees group. When I became State Librarian, I knew that any success we were going to have in our state would result from a broadening of the library lobby and less reliance on the State Library agency to be the sole spokesman for library interests in the state.

Over the years, the State Library Association has matured and expanded its role in lobbying for library interests. Since 1970, the association has sponsored in the legislature an annual Library Day, which brings 700 library supporters annually to the Capitol to lobby the legislature. For most of the 1970 s, the association relied almost totally on the State Library for logistic support for sponsoring the day— selecting the theme and the food for lunch with the legislators; securing the space; registering participants; stuffing packets; and looking after other important details. It took State Library staff weeks to prepare for the event. In the past few years, an almost complete shift back to the association for logistic support has occurred, and the association can now view the event with pride and independence as their event. I think the library community is stronger for assuming this responsibility.

Certain traditions have continued. The evening before Library Day, the State Library's Chief of Library Development hosts a reception for all Library Day participants who arrive the night before. The reception draws nearly 300 people. On the afternoon prior to Library Day events, rum cakes for special legislators and for the appropriations committees are distributed. The State Library promotes the sense of continuity by filling in gaps in emergencies when last minute details have been overlooked.

For many years, our Secretary of State, who serves as our state's chief elected library officer, viewed the Florida Library Association as being run by the State Librarian. In the late 1970 s, at my insistence, the library leadership began mapping a careful long-term strategy to ensure Association independence in the minds of elected officials and in reality. The Association retained an excellent lobbyist and, from the beginning, an outstanding rapport has developed between the lobby and my office. The cornerstone of this rapport has been a mutual understanding of our roles and an *agreement to disagree without malice,* while understanding that our goals are the same, but the methods to achieve them may differ.

It is understood that the lobby takes its direction from the Association on all legislative matters. The State Librarian serves as an ex-officio member without vote of the Association's legislative committee, and the president-elect of the Association serves a one-year ex-officio term on the State Library Council. Thus, both the Association and the State Library agency are able to provide continuity in the state's library legislative program.

I suspect the area where the State Library continues to exert its greatest influence among the three major forces in the legislative process is in its work with trustees and Friends groups. The agency maintains a full-time senior consultant to work with the 300 Friends and trustee groups representing 43,000 citizens in our state. The agency has put much effort into providing manuals for guidance, films for education, and a series of high-powered workshops for continuing education on topics such as lobbying, alternative fund raising, the role of boards and Friends groups, and library public awareness. The State Library devotes one of its three major publications entirely to issues that concern trustees and Friends.

An important part of the statewide public awareness program for libraries that has raised the image of librarians in the legislative process has been the establishment of the Council for Florida Libraries which grew out of the Florida delegation to the first White House Conference. Although it did not achieve its original goal of drawing its membership from the major corporate leadership in Florida, nevertheless, the Council did sponsor and continues to sponsor a number of public awareness programs which have helped draw attention to the library by the business community.

All of these efforts have drawn library supporters in Florida into effective networks. I mention networks because there are several: a Friends and trustees network operated by the president of the state organization; a public library directors network activated by either the State Library or the state association's Legislative Committee chair; and a network of former and current members of the state association's Legislative Committee activated by the current committee chair. Although some supporters want a greater explanation of an issue than others, when properly utilized, the networks can place considerable pressure on legislators in support of various library issues.

Now, I would like to share with you two case studies in working with the legislature—one was a success, while the other was a disaster.

The first case involves how we made major changes to our State Library law in less than one year from inception to passage and signature by the Governor. In June, 1982, the State Library convened a small group of representative librarians to explain the needs for a possible change in the law and to ask for recommendations for other changes. The principal changes were necessary because of a growing confusion with respect to: the eligibility requirements for libraries to receive state aid; the need to put qualifications for the State Librarian into law; the need to strengthen the State Documents Depository Program; the need to add a regional incentive to the state aid program; the need to provide a substantive definition of "free library service"; and, the need to strengthen the agency's law to encourage interlibrary cooperation and networking.

Such an omnibus bill would be difficult to get through the legislative process without developing a strategy for moving the proposed legislation quickly. After the bill had reached nearly final form by the library community, it was decided to secure as many House and Senate leaders as sponsors as possible. Thus, three House appropriations subcommittees, chairs of several other committees, as well as a dozen others sponsored the House bill. In the Senate, the minority leader was the prime sponsor along with the Senate president-designate; half of the Senate signed on as cosponsors. One of the reasons we needed to secure such broad support is that the year before, the legislature had been elected for the first time from single-member districts, and we were concerned that legislation would increasingly reflect parochial interests rather than statewide issues. The strategy worked. The bill went through quickly, mainly because the leadership of both the House and Senate wanted it, and the library community was united and aggressive in encouraging passage.

My good friend and Florida colleague, Bill Summers, likes to tell the following story. Some time ago, when a particularly bad hurricane hit Florida and laid waste to the central part of the state, then Governor Haydon Burns went on the radio to thank everyone who had helped with disaster relief. He began by thanking the Red Cross, the National Guard, the Boy Scouts, and the Kiwanis Club. As the list grew longer, he must have become concerned that he might leave out somebody or a group. Thus, he said, "In conclusion, I just want to thank everyone for the best-managed disaster we have ever had."

Now for the library's "best-managed disaster." For a number of years, the state's library community had been looking for a stable source of funding for the state aid to libraries law to generate enough income to keep up with the growth in the formula, which is based on 25 cents of state money for each dollar of local expenditures. Finally, in early 1986, the then president of the Florida Library Association convinced his representative, who was chair of the House Appropriations Committee, to devise a creative dedicated tax which could be applied to state aid to libraries.

Thus was conceived our 2 percent book tax scheme. It was a privilege tax that involved a 2 percent tax on the first-time sale or transfer of books, magazines, and spoken-book audiotapes in Florida. Thus, a Florida publisher would have to pay a 2 percent wholesale tax as a privilege for doing business in the state, as would a retailer or wholesaler who first sold the books, magazines, or tapes in Florida. There were certain exclusions, such as K-12 textbooks, religious books, social printing, and newspapers.

You can imagine the uproar we heard from bookstores, book jobbers, and Florida publishers. You would think that we had struck at the heart of the constitutional guarantee of free speech. One bookstore manager accused me of relegating books to the category of sin taxes on liquor, cigarettes, etc. The newspapers came out against us, as well as the Catholic Church. The ultimate blow came from a sharply divided library community. Academic libraries were against the tax because they would not benefit from it. Small libraries said the tax would raise the price of books and reduce their buying power, while the Board of Trustees of one public library resource center came out against it because they were philosophically opposed to taxes.

Obviously, the legislation failed. It didn't make it out of a House finance and tax subcommittee. It was indeed a disaster! And, we are still looking for a dedicated tax source.

I cannot think of any more exciting times than these for librarians to get involved in the legislative process. But, they should be prepared—nobody in the process always wins. However, I have found that unless you are willing to take risks—unless you are willing to accept a less than perfect outcome—little progress will ever occur, and we will be reduced to holding out our "tin cups."

In conclusion, I can only state that librarians can play an important part in the legislative process if they follow the numerous guides that have been written concerning community activism and lobbying; show common sense in approaches to issues; keep a sense of humor; develop long-term strategies for reaching goals with the assistance of elected officials; and, demonstrate aggressive energy in working in the political process.

The challenge is with you!

State Policy in New York

Joseph F. Shubert
State Librarian of New York

When Bruce A. Shuman's article on "Effort and Regionalism as Determinants of State Aid to Public Libraries" appeared in *Public Libraries* in 1989,[1] it was gratifying to people from New York State to see New York listed as number one in state aid for public libraries in 1987. But the article also reported that New York's rank, when measured per capita, was third. And, at the same time, New Yorkers know that in 1987 state aid for libraries fell nearly $30 million short of what was actually needed, as documented in the Regents 1987 legislative proposal for libraries. These observations in part sum up a political reality: number one in library aid is not good enough when the need is so great. There is more than one way to look at the same number of dollars.

New York has always had a strong commitment to education. Taxes are high, public services are good, and education is important. New York's library systems program in the 1960s drew the support of legislators and remains a basic part of the state's library policy. The 1970s were not easy years for libraries seeking state aid. In 1978, however, the Governor's Conference on Libraries marked a watershed for aid, providing the first in a series of increases, and substantially broadening aid for multiple library services. The late 1980s proved to be difficult years, but the 1990 Governor's Conference on Libraries and Information Services may again be vitally important in raising awareness of the need for library aid and other legislation.

TWO DECADES OF LIBRARY AID LEGISLATION

Although Shuman dealt only with public library aid, his bench marks in two decades are useful because they illustrate the results of both public policy and cycles in the state's fiscal health. In those twenty years, the state experienced severe fiscal crises in the years 1971–1972, 1975, 1982–1983, and 1988–1989. The two decades were also marked by such major library developments as:

1966–1971

- Completion of the 1963–1966 evaluation of the New York State Public Library System and publication of *Emerging Library Systems.*
- Organization of nine Reference and Research Library Resources Systems, completed in 1967.
- The 1967–1970 Commissioner's Committee on Library Development.
- Central Library aid initiated in 1966.

1972–1977

- Major study of library services needed by blind and visually handicapped people, 1972.
- State aid for the Schomburg Center of The New York Public Library, 1973.
- Indian libraries aid, 1977.
- Aid to county correctional facilities, 1974.
- First professional Certified Association Executive (CAE) appointed as New York Library Association (NYLA) Executive Director, 1974.

1977–1981

- Assembly and Senate Subcommittees on Libraries established in 1977.
- New York State Governor's Conference on Libraries, 1978.
- First comprehensive library bill enacted including statutory status for reference and research library resources systems and funds for pilot school library systems and regional networks, 1978.
- Legislation and aid to place a Kurzweil reading machine in each public library system, 1980.
- Second comprehensive library bill enacted, largest dollar increase to date, annualized to $10 million aid increase for 1982, including rural hospital library services program and coordinated public library outreach aid, 1981.
- The 1980–1981 Commissioner's Committee on Statewide Library Development, included recommendations for school library systems and regional automation programs.
- Peat, Marwick, Mitchell and Co. evaluation of school library system and regional network pilot projects, 1983.

1982–1986

- Position of Director of Library Development Division reinstated after ten-year hiatus, 1983.
- Third comprehensive library bill enacted, a $13.5 million increase,

annualized to $15 million in 1985, establishing new programs for regional automation bibliographic database and resource sharing, conservation/ preservation aid, school library systems, public library construction, public library system service to inmates of state correctional facilities, and expanded the hospital library services and coordinated outreach programs, 1984.

- NYLINE, an electronic message system, based on ALANET launched, 1985.
- Major study of interlibrary loan, 1985.
- Fourth comprehensive library bill enacted boosting state aid from $57.2 million to $73 million including funds for public library-based literacy programs, 1986.

1987–1989

- NYLA engaged lobbyist and sponsored its own omnibus bill, 1988.
- State Library commissioned the first external study of library systems since Emerging Library Systems, 1988–1989.
- The 1987–1989 period has not included a major enactment of library aid increases, although the need for an increase has grown steadily.

Against this backdrop of events, the legislature increased state aid for libraries from $14 million in 1967 to $33 million in 1977, and to $73.9 million in 1987. Major increases (usually reflected in aid payment data for the following year) were enacted in 1973, 1976, 1978, 1981, 1984, and 1986.

Throughout this paper I will refer to "Regents bills." The New York State Constitution established the Board of Regents for the University of the State of New York. This is a 16-member board whose powers are established in the constitution and whose members are elected by the legislature.[2] The University of the State of New York encompasses all educational institutions in the State, and the Regents determine broad policy and standards for all educational institutions in the State: the elementary and secondary schools (public and private); institutions of higher education (public and independent); libraries; public broadcasting; historical societies; and other cultural institutions.

The Regents appoint the Commissioner of Education, who is responsible for the operation of the State Education Department. The New York State Library is part of the State Education Department. The State Library is composed of two major divisions: the Research Library and the Division of Library Development (DLD). The DLD administers state aid and LSCA programs, prepares library legislative proposals for the Regents, provides leadership and technical assistance to library systems and libraries, and carries out other library development services. The DLD, therefore, is an important part of the library legislative picture in New York State.

A BROADER LEGISLATIVE AGENDA AND MORE
COMPREHENSIVE AID

A chronology of major New York State library legislation (including both bills and enactments) prepared by Anne E. Prentice and Jean L. Connor for the 1978 Governor's Conference on Libraries shows that 13 bills were introduced in 1973.[3] Of these, twelve were bills to increase or establish general or special aid, and one dealt with tax levies for school libraries. For 1989, the Legislative Bill Drafting Service list shows 40 bills, including 26 relating to other library issues.

The legislative agenda is broader today because it increasingly includes intellectual freedom issues, technical bills relating to retirement systems, book sales and library districts, and other matters which do not relate exclusively to library aid.

The aid agenda is also more comprehensive. The Prentice-Connor list shows separate Regents and NYLA bills, and separate bills for public library systems, reference and research library systems, and other purposes. By 1978 most library advocates were working together on a single comprehensive bill. The $28.7 million 1989 comprehensive bill includes, for instance, aid to public library systems, reference and research library resources systems, school library systems, public library construction, outreach and literacy services, parent and child services, conservation/preservation, automation and databases, hospital library programs, coordinated collection development, and aid to the Research Libraries of the New York Public Library.

The agenda is also much broader. As the scope of aid for resource sharing has broadened, there has been increased cooperation in lobbying by statewide organizations, particularly as a result of comprehensive (or "omnibus") library bills.

THE NEW YORK STATE LIBRARY AND THE REGENTS
ROLE IN LEGISLATION

Every year since 1976, comprehensive legislative proposals which take a systematic approach to strengthening all kinds of library service have been introduced at the request of the Regents. In the several years preceding 1976, NYLA and the Regents each submitted several legislative proposals. Often, several of the bills covered the same purpose. In 1974 and 1975, for instance, the Regents and NYLA each introduced library legislation to increase state aid to libraries. The Regents proposed a more comprehensive approach in the 1976 legislative proposal. In 1987, the Regents' first comprehensive legislative proposal was enacted and from 1977 to 1987, NYLA did not introduce separate bills.

As more organizations have become involved in legislation, the Regents bills since 1978 have become the vehicle for compromise. Amendments to the Regents legislative proposals are expected. As the single bill, the Regents bill is predictably the focus for demands of all sorts—to increase, modify or delete parts of any proposal. Initiatives suggested in one year may be debated for one or two years before being reshaped into legislation which is finally enacted. Examples include: coordinated academic collection development aid, first proposed by the Regents in 1980, and modified and enacted in 1981; regional bibliographic databases and resource sharing, proposed by the Regents in 1982, and enacted in 1984; and local library services aid, proposed by the Regents in 1987, but not yet enacted.

With the approval of the Governor, the legislature sometimes provides funds for pilot programs, rather than fully launching a Regents proposal. In 1978 the legislature provided public library aid and intersystem cooperation funds considerably below the levels recommended by the Regents but appropriated funds for pilot school library systems (which they made permanent and statewide in 1984). To move the program ahead when funds were limited in the last decade, the legislature has also enacted increases phased over two years.

The development of Regents legislative proposals is a continuous process that builds on legislative accomplishments over successive years. Key points in the process are: a Regents Legislative Conference at which education and library organizations present their legislative recommendations to the Regents; Library Development Division staff work on specific proposals after preliminary discussions with the Regents; and the Regents formally adopt the proposal and transmit the bill to the leaders of the legislature in December or January.

The Regents Legislative Conference is important in providing to the Regents and the State Education Department the points of view of interested constituencies. During the course of the day representatives of statewide organizations testify on legislation related to cultural education, elementary and secondary education, higher education, the professions, and vocational rehabilitation. In 1989, 61 organizations, including the New York Library Association, presented testimony, representing all types of libraries. Other organizations testifying included the New York State Association of Library Boards, the Medical Library Association chapters, the Public Library System Directors Organization, and the Reference and Research Library Resources System Directors Organization.

The recommendations of the library organizations are used by DLD staff in completing a draft proposal for Regents action in November. As they develop the library proposal, the staff relies on a number of information sources: the Regents Advisory Council on Libraries; information gained at regional conferences; studies; and reports. In 1988 and in 1989, the Regents also established a Task Force on Library Aid Legislation composed of Regents to work with staff on developing the aid proposal.

Once the Regents adopt a library legislative proposal, DLD staff work with the Department's Office of Counsel in preparing bill language and a memorandum of support detailing the proposal and reasons the legislation is needed. The proposal is formally transmitted to the leadership of the Assembly and the Senate. The Speaker of the Assembly and the President-pro-tem of the Senate decide upon sponsors, and the bill is introduced.

During the course of the legislative session, the Department and library organizations work with legislative committees and the governor's office to develop compromises that permit important library legislation to be enacted.

LEGISLATIVE SUBCOMMITTEES

The presence of library subcommittees in both houses of the legislature distinguishes the New York legislative picture from that of many other states. In most states, library legislation is considered by education, local government, or other committees with a concern for several related fields of interest. Since 1977, New York has had subcommittees concentrating almost exclusively on libraries (the Assembly Subcommittee on Libraries reports to the Assembly Higher Education Committee; the Senate Subcommittee on Libraries reports to the Education Committee).

These subcommittees have been instrumental in developing increased and continuing legislative expertise in library matters and greater commitment to library services. Their continuing interaction with library organizations, professional leaders and State Education Department representatives has produced new partnerships in developing and reshaping legislation. Public hearings on library legislation and library concerns, legislative "town meetings" at New York Library Association conferences, and other contacts provide a forum for librarians and trustees to discuss needs and (occasionally) to debate differing points of view.

The chairs of both subcommittees issue press releases. Since 1987, the Assembly Subcommittee on Libraries has occasionally issued a newsletter. More important, the chairs exercise leadership in speaking and writing for both state and national audiences. The chairs were delegates to the 1979 White House Conference on Library and Information Services, and the governor appointed both chairs to the 1990

Governor's Commission on Libraries, which was responsible for planning the 1990 Governor's Conference on Library and Information Services.

How Library Aid Operates

Library aid bills adopted by the legislature and signed by the governor are formally incorporated into permanent education law. Consequently, the bills automatically drive an appropriation each year thereafter. For instance, once the public library aid formula is established to drive $56 million, the governor must budget that amount each year (unless population or other factors change the amount generated by the formula) until the law is changed. Public library construction aid (enacted in 1984) is the major exception to this condition: permanent law authorizes the legislature to appropriate funds for construction and requires an annual report on the need for construction funds, but it does not require the governor to include construction aid in his budget. As a result, construction aid has been available only two out of the last six years.

Special Member Items

The inclusion in the state budget of special line items for library projects within a legislator's district has become more frequent in the last ten years. Such "member items" are part of a tradition that in 1989 saw the legislature add $80 million to the State budget including monies for library projects.[4] In 1978, there were three such special budget lines for libraries; by 1984 the budget included 23 library special lines; and by 1989 the number had grown to 75 lines totaling $1.4 million. These ranged in size from $2,000 to $187,000.

Member items, such as funds for a new roof for a public library, an integrated library system for a high school library, or a Holocaust collection are important to individual libraries. In some instances, legislators work together to provide automation for a library system. In some cases a member item for a reference service project or demonstration in one library or library system suggests the need to establish a permanent program in library law. At the same time, pursuit of member items for local purposes may lessen advocacy for the comprehensive library aid bill which benefits all libraries.

The NYLA Legislative Committee has urged other organizations to join in its year-round efforts to influence legislation. The Committee includes several "associate group" members such as the New York State Association of Library Boards, the Citizens' Library Council of New York, the Public Library System Directors' Association and the Library Association of the City University of New York. These organizations strengthen NYLA's annual "Library Day" in Albany. In recent years they have also extended the number of capitol contacts earlier in the session, as the Public Library Coalition and other groups come to the legislature in February.

Annually since 1978 the New York State Library has produced a *Fact Book on the Regents Legislative Proposal for Libraries* which provides information on aid proposal and the need for legislative action.

RECENT DEVELOPMENTS

The NYLA has had a well recognized and effective legislative program for many years.[5] In the fall of 1987, the NYLA decided to undertake a more vigorous legislative program. It retained a professional lobbyist, introduced its own "omnibus" library bill in 1988, and sponsored higher profile legislative events and advertisements urging legislative action. In 1989, the NYLA decided to move its headquarters from New York City to Albany and to appoint its new executive both to the position of executive director and lobbyist.

The NYLA Legislative Committee has also been reorganized several times in the last few years. It currently has 15 voting members. Of these, nine at-large members are appointed by the president and six specifically represent the NYLA sections. At-large members appointed by the president (with approval of the NYLA Council) serve three-year terms. In addition to its section representative, each section can appoint a section intern who can vote in the absence of the representative.

The committee also includes seven non-voting ex-officio members. The ex-officio members are the NYLA President, Vice President and the Executive Director, and four people from the State Education Department: the State Librarian, the Director of the Division of Library Development, the Chief of the School Library Media Programs Bureau, and the State Archivist. The committee also includes eight representatives of "Associate Groups and Institutions" (organizations are invited annually by the NYLA Council to be advisors to the committee because their "interest in and support of legislative work makes their active participation in NYLA's legislative work vital to its success"). In addition, the NYLA encourages members with a special interest in legislation to become legislative associates. For $10, associates receive special mailings that keep them completely informed on legislative developments. The Legislative Committee has a six member executive committee.

THE FUTURE

Library aid advocates are entering the 1990s with some frustration and a sense of expectation. Library aid has not increased since 1986, and the 1988–1989 falloff in state revenues has not reversed. The Governor's Conference and the White House Conference should help focus attention upon library needs. Moreover, the presence of both the NYLA and NYSALB offices in Albany (the trustees' association moves its office from New York City to Albany in 1990) should be helpful in securing legislative action, particularly if the associations are successful in engaging more members in legislative activity.

The accomplishments of the services which state aid helps to make possible, however, may prove to be more substantial than these initiatives. A 1989 study of library systems, commissioned by the New York State Library and conducted by King Research, Inc., documents the impact of the aid program and the need for an increase. King's report, which is based upon extensive data on costs and member library evaluations of system services, shows that if there were not library systems in New York, it would cost member libraries at least 3.5 times more than it now costs to provide the services currently offered by the library systems.[6] The state library participated in the Federal-State Cooperative System (FSCS) for public library data, in which 40 states in 1989 shared public library statistical data with the National Center for Education Statistics after agreeing to use common definitions for 41 data elements. The results should, over time, enable library advocates to deal with more assurance as they discuss public policy questions on public library services.

Congressional support for reauthorization of the Federal Library Services and Construction Act, as shown in action by both houses after the April 1989 hearings on the act, is also encouraging to library legislation advocates. LSCA and state aid have complemented each other in several instances in breaking new ground in library services in the state, and legislators are interested in the ways state and federal programs are coordinated. At times, LSCA funds have fostered innovation that is subsequently incorporated in state aid, as in the case of the various LSCA Title I outreach projects that demonstrated the need for continuing state aid for coordinated library outreach aid in 1981, and the LSCA Title III computer-based union list of serials project that paved the way for the 1984 state aid for regional bibliographic databases and resource sharing program.

On the other hand, New York State innovations have anticipated LSCA changes. State aid for Indian Libraries (which started in 1977) was noticed by advocates for Indian library services in the course of the 1979 White House Conference on Library and Information Services, and in 1984 Congress enacted a program similar to LSCA Title IV, Indian Library Services. The 1984 New York State legislation establishing the program for conservation/preservation of endangered library research materials anticipated the 1989 federal bills to authorize preservation as a part of a reauthorized LSCA.

The legislature in 1984 and 1986 recognized that an effective state aid program requires an effective Division of Library Development in the state library. In both years the library aid bill included some funds for staff to administer new or expanded programs. Library leaders recognize that division planning, evaluation and reporting functions are important in advancing aid proposals, providing the accountability expected by state government, and serving as a reliable government source of information on other library legislative matters.

Library legislation in the 1990s will continue to deal with state aid and will probably more frequently include proposals affecting local support of library services, governance of libraries and library systems, telecommunications and other indirect support of library and information services. We won't wait until 2007 for Mr. Shuman to measure the effects of legislative action and state aid to public libraries but when the measurement is taken, we want to remain first because state aid is an important factor in assuring library services to people in New York State and to the economy and quality of life in the state.

References

1. Bruce A. Shuman, "Effort and Regionalism as Determinants of State Aid to Public Libraries," *Public Libraries* 28, no.5 (September–October 1989): 301–307.
2. Joseph F. Shubert, "The Regents and Library Aid Legislation in the 1970's and 1980's," *The Bookmark* 42, no. III (Spring 1984): 188–196.
3. Ann E. Prentice and Jean L. Connor, *Library Service Now in New York State, a Background Paper Prepared for the Governor's Commission on Libraries* (The University at Albany, 1978), p.99.
4. Elizabeth Kolbert, "Cuomo's Budget Strategy: Sticking to Some Issues, Giving in on Others," *New York Times*, 21 April 1989, Section B, p. 3.
5. Patricia H. Mautino, "Support of Library Services in New York," *Libraries in the Political Process*, E. J. Josey, ed. (Oryx Press, 1980), pp. 17–27; Robin Herman, "Thousands Join in Quest When It's Lobbying Day," *New York Times*, 11 March 1981, Section B, p. 1.
6. Jose-Marie Griffiths, *Library Systems in New York State* (Rockville, MD: King Research, Inc., 1989), p. 26.

The Politics of the State Budgetary Process and Library Funding

David Shavit

The state budget is the most important policy statement that a state government makes each year. The state budget is a representation in monetary terms of state government activities, because it provides insight into the state's purposes and priorities. Since state funds are limited and have to be divided among many competing activities, the budget becomes a mechanism for making choices among alternative expenditures.[1] State budgeting, therefore, requires a balancing of competing demands against a relatively fixed pool of resources.

The budget lies at the heart of the political process. If politics is regarded in part as a conflict over the allocation of funds among various activities and in part a decision about which policies will be implemented, then the budget records the outcome of this conflict. The process by which a budget is negotiated is often as important as the end product of that process. In the words of one authority,

> A key point to remember about budgets is that they are *political* documents. Although budgets have the appearance of accounting ledgers with columns of numbers and a bottom line that balances, they are really expressions of deeply held political values and ideological preferences. Programs that pursue goals that governors or legislators care about, or that benefit politically powerful interest groups, will be generously funded. Those that do not, will not.[2]

No universally accepted budgetary procedures are followed in the fifty states, but certain common features are found in most of them. The budget-making authority in most states is the governor who has the primary responsibility for preparing the budget.

Governors realize that implementing any real change in state policy either requires a change in current allocations by the legislature or new taxation when the policy change requires a level of expenditures that is higher than current revenues permit.[3]

In each state, there is an executive agency, subordinate to the governor, commonly known as the bureau of the budget, which is responsible for preparing the budget document. Departments and agencies of state government submit their requests to this agency. The bureau of the budget holds hearings, analyzes the requests based on the governor's priorities and spending guidelines, and makes recommendations to the governor as to the amounts and priorities to be included. The governor then submits a formal budget to the legislature. The governor's budget message is a policy document of considerable importance because it is used to highlight many of the policy changes which the governor wishes to enact.[4]

In many states, copies of the departments' and agencies' submissions to the bureau of the budget are sent simultaneously to the legislature. The legislature often becomes involved in the bureau of the budget's analysis of these submissions. Rosenthal notes: "Frequently individual legislators—especially leaders, committee chairmen, and members of appropriations committees—intervene, and intervene successfully, to shape an agency's budget request to their liking."[5]

The budget is then reviewed by one or more legislative committees commonly known as either a committee on appropriations or a committee on appropriations and revenues. The legislative committee reviews and refashions the governor's budget. There are often separate committees in the house and the senate but some states have a joint appropriations committee. The committee on appropriations often operates through subcommittees, which make possible more extensive hearings and greater specialization by committee members.

In recent years, the appropriations process has become more open than in the past, when control of the process was held by a few legislators. Now control is more evenly distributed among legislators. The manner of budget preparations is related to influence. Where more information is available to legislators, the likelihood of their having an impact on the budget is increased. The relative impact of the legislature on the appropriations process, in turn, may affect legislative emphases on efficiency, effectiveness, and district concerns.[6]

The strength of the state legislature depends on the knowledge and experience of its members and on the availability of professional staff.

The modern legislature is equipped to challenge the governor at every point. As a result, the state's budgeting system is one of the institutions of state government that is changing in significant ways.[7] Indeed, "[o]ne of the most consistent and most important trends over the last twenty years in American state legislatures has been the growing scrutiny of the executive budget and increasing influence over budgetary decisions."[8]

The "power of the purse" is a state legislature's greatest power, and the appropriations process is the most important source of legislative power. Fenno writes: "The power of the purse is the historic bulwark of legislative authority. The exercise of that power constitutes the core legislative process—underpinning all other legislative decisions and regulating the balance of influence between the legislative and executive branches of government."[9]

Rosenthal elaborates in this point:

> Probably the most important bills taken up by the legislatures are the budget bills that appropriate funds for the operations of state government. Money is the critical ingredient of government, largely determining whether abstract policies get translated into concrete services and action. Insofar as the legislature can exercise control over the flow of funds . . . it exercises power. At the very least, it can command attention. "If you've got your hands on the money," an appropriations committee chairman from Ohio declared, "that's the only language anyone understands in state government." In almost the same vein, an appropriations chairman from Kentucky said: "If you grab them by their budget, their hearts and minds will follow."[10]

The legislature's role in the budgetary process and its impact on the budget has grown for a number of reasons, most of which are related to the greater capability and independence of the appropriations committees. The committees have larger and better staffs, their membership has greater stability and thus more experience, and they have gained political independence from the governor.

In order to be able to devote more careful attention to budgetary review, state legislatures have established and developed a budgetary office composed of an expert staff of analysts, many of whom have extensive budgetary experience. State legislatures have come to rely heavily on this professional staff. Although the legislative fiscal staff is involved in the political struggle within the legislative system, its influence increases as the legislation under consideration becomes less political, less controversial, or less partisan. The staff is more likely to reinforce existing opinions of legislators than to change them. The more salient the issue, the less likely it is that the judgment of the staff will prevail.[11]

The budget bills are among the most important and contentious bills taken up during a legislative session. After passing one house, the budget bill will go to the other house. Differences between versions are resolved generally in a conference committee. After the two houses agree, the enacted budget is sent to the governor for a signature.

State legislatures today are very different places from the state legislatures of twenty years ago and even from the legislatures of ten years ago. Today, state legislatures are more political and more partisan; they are more fragmented, with power dispersed among leadership, standing committees and individual members, each with their own agenda; and they are more aggressive, particularly in relations with the executive branch. Legislatures participate forcefully in making policy and shaping budgets.

While the executive branch formerly controlled the budgetary process by virtue of having a near monopoly on staff and information and, therefore, on the ability to estimate revenues, the legislature today habitually challenges the governor over the budget. Both the legislature's own spending agenda and tougher rein on executive allocations are unsettling to the governors.

A state budget is the product of a *chain of delegation*, whether conscious or unconscious. Delegation represents a strong incremental force in budgetary decision making. Legislative participants are willing to delegate choice in the budgetary process to the governor or line agencies for the less important decisions. But for the most important decisions, the participants are much less inclined to delegate their choices and exercise their authority where it counts.[12] Jewell and Miller summarize these points as follows:

> Extensive review of the executive budget by the appropriations committee and its staff does not, of course, guarantee that there will be major changes in the budget passed by the legislature and enacted into law. The governor has extensive political resources that can be used to defend his budget, including promises and threats regarding projects in particular districts. In most states the governor also has the item veto over appropriations. But in all states the final budget is now a product of careful scrutiny and joint decision making by both branches of government and not merely by the executive.[13]

While most state legislatures have unlimited power to change the budget, there are certain limits on legislative control of the state budget. These limits include legal restrictions (such as constitutional restrictions dealing with debt and tax limitations), balanced budget requirements, restrictions against running deficits for current or operating expenditures, and requirements for extraordinary majorities to enact appropriations. Other restrictions include legislative commitments. In many states, the majority of the state's income is derived from revenues earmarked for predetermined purposes. Thus, these commitments impose limitations on the legislative power to modify the executive budget and the ability of most governors to veto items in the budget approved by the legislature.

Furthermore, legislative review of the budget does not often result in major changes in spending priorities because governors have substantial political support in the legislature, and there is often a fundamental agreement between the governor and a majority of the legislature on spending priorities. In some cases, both the governor and the legislature are responding in similar fashion to demands from interest groups. The legislature, however, can make a real difference because it can change items in the budget. While these items seldom amount to a large proportion of the total, they do matter to the specific agencies and programs involved. Legislators can also easily become program advocates, especially if members of the appropriations committees also serve on various policy or substantive committees. If legislators themselves are not already inclined to promote programs by increasing their funding, client groups will help to incline them in such a direction.

Regardless of the importance of the state budget and the budgetary process, in most states "the budget document seldom reaches the high goals set for it as a policy device."[14] Indeed, the states have lost effective control over expenditures. The budget actually covers only a part (in some states as little as one-fourth), of the state's expenditures. Complex structures of special funds that are difficult to understand and more difficult to change, coupled with heavy investment in existing activities that must continue, make up an expenditure base that leaves extremely little room for maneuver. There may, in fact, be relatively little over which the legislature can exercise control.

A consequence of this situation is that the battles over state expenditures are fought only on the margins. A combination of factors such as earmarked taxes, the prohibition against deficit spending, restricted federal funds, limited time and knowledge, and commitments to interest payments and retirement programs, massively reduce the amount of actual discretion left to decision makers. Furthermore, utilizing an incremental budgeting mechanism means that current expenditures will vary only slightly from past expenditures. By accepting the legitimacy of established programs and agreeing to continue the previous level of expenditure, governors and legislators limit their task: they consider only the increments of change proposed for the new budget and the narrow range of goals embodied in the departures from established activities. This means, Treadway observes, that,

[i]ncrementalism is at the heart of the budgetary process in the states. When reviewing agency budgetary requests, executives and legislators are most concerned not with the size of the request but rather with the increment of change. Those concerned with shaping the budget tend to work at the margins. What is of greatest concern is what is new or what is to be significantly increased from last year. Such proposed expenditures must be justified. What was in the budget last year and is being continued with only a modest increase in funding typically escapes intensive scrutiny. Last year's budget is perceived as legitimate. Last year's budget, or at least most of it, becomes the base for this year's budget. Attention, then, is focused on the deviation from the base.[15]

In nearly all the states, the governor has authority to item veto appropriations bills, striking out certain appropriations while leaving others intact, and in one-fifth of the states the governor has the power to reduce items in the appropriations. The line item veto permits legislators to increase the governor's budget, comforted by the knowledge that the governor can item veto or reduce an appropriation if he feels strongly that spending is too high. The legislature can override a governor's item veto but seldom does. The line item veto, however, does not significantly affect the outcome of the budgetary process, except in states in which the governor faces a legislature controlled by the opposition party and has, therefore, political incentives to exercise such a veto.[16]

Libraries in most states do not generate political issues because they are still in the stage of consensus politics. Thus, although library policies are seldom controversial, at the same time, they are seldom fiscally significant. A peripheral issue on the state level, libraries are seldom dealt with by the governor or the legislature.

State expenditure for libraries is a marginal item in the state budget. In 1987, for example, only 0.09 percent of the state government expenditure was allocated to libraries.

Once a library program is funded, however, it will generally continue to be annually funded on the same level as state expenditures in general or even on a higher level. The annual increment of state government expenditure for libraries in 1987 over 1986 (6.6%) was close to the annual increment of total state government expenditure (7.4%), but in previous years the increment of the expenditure for libraries was larger than the increment of the total expenditure. (It more than doubled between 1983 and 1984, rose by two-thirds between 1984 and 1985, and almost doubled between 1985 and 1986).

Libraries are seldom an issue of concern to governors. (State library agencies generally do not come under the purview of the governor's appointed power.) Based on their particular character and interests, governors only sporadically take a leadership role in library policy. In addition, libraries are generally of limited interest to legislators.[17] But legislators are more influenced by pressure and are more responsive to it. The fact that libraries, librarians, and library trustees are part of almost all legislative districts has been an important factor. Legislators may also have relatives or friends who are library board members.

State library associations and state library agencies still function as the most important library pressure group. Despite the fact that this lobby is small and has little power, political activity by these groups is crucial to achieving better funding of libraries by state governments. Library pressure groups must overcome the fact that in recent years many state governments have not generated new revenues. Moreover, competition for state revenues has increased, and many state governments have continued to be reluctant to fund library services and programs.

It is a difficult challenge to increase the budgetary base to implement new policies promoting libraries. Furthermore, funding new programs often requires a significant increase in the state government allocation for libraries. Only rarely and under unusual conditions (e.g., a governor who favors libraries or state revenues that dramatically increase) will state governments implement new library policies and increase the budget allocation for libraries above the incremental amount.

References

1. Aaron Wildavsky, *The New Politics of the Budgetary Process* (Glenview, Ill.: Scott, Foresman, 1988), p.2.
2. Michael J. Ross, *State and Local Politics and Policy: Change and Reform* (Englewood Cliffs, N.J.: Prentice-Hall, 1987), p. 206.
3. Coleman B. Ransome, Jr., *The American Governorship* (Westport, Conn.: Greenwood Press, 1982), p. 128.
4. Ransome, *op. cit.*, p. 128
5. Alan Rosenthal, *Legislative Life: People, Process, and Performance in the States* (New York: Harper & Row, 1981), p. 286.
6. Glenn Abney and Thomas Louth, "Perceptions of the Impact of Governors and Legislators in the State Appropriations Process," *Western Political Quarterly* 40 (2) (1987): 335–342.
7. Robert P. Kerker, "The State of the Executive Budget," *New York State Today: Politics, Government, Public Policy.* Peter W. Colby and John K. White, eds. (Albany, N.Y.: State University of New York Press, 1989), pp. 205–218.
8. Malcolm E. Jewell and Penny M. Miller, *The Kentucky Legislature: Two Decades of Change* (University Press of Kentucky, 1988), p. 131.

9. Richard Fenno, *The Power of the Purse: Appropriations Politics in Congress* (Boston: Little, Brown, 1966), p. xiii.

10. Rosenthal, *op. cit.*, pp. 285–286

11. Alan P. Balutis and Daron K. Butler eds., *The Political Pursestrings: The Role of the Legislature in the Budgetary Process*, (New York: John Wiley, 1975).

12. James J. Gosling. "Patterns of Influence and Choice in the Wisconsin Budgetary Process," *Legislative Studies Quarterly* 10 (4), (1985): 477–479.

13. Jewell and Miller, *op. cit.*, p. 132.

14. Ransome, *op. cit.*, p. 129.

15. Jack M. Treadway, *Public Policymaking in the American States* (New York: Praeger, 1985), p. 111.

16. Douglas Holtz-Eakin, "The Line Item Veto and Public Sector Budget: Evidence from the States," *Journal of Public Economics* 36(30), (1988): 269–92.

17. David Shavit, *The Politics of Public Librarianship* (Westport, Conn.: Greenwood Press, 1986), p. 94–95.

The State University Library and Its Political Environment

Benjamin F. Speller, Jr.

Dean, School of Library and Information Sciences
North Carolina Central University

INTRODUCTION

State universities are institutions of higher education that carry out their missions, goals, and objectives as a result of substantial financial support from the legislatures of the states where they are located. These institutions usually derive their legal authority from legislative mandate or from provisions in the states' constitutions. Most state universities are governed by a board whose duties, responsibilities, and authority are established by the state legislature.

By the very nature of their establishment and governance structures, state universities are part of—and in some instances—at center stage of the political environment of the state. State university libraries, as major academic support units of their parent institutions, are also a part of the political environment of their states.

State universities and their libraries must seek to maintain their support within the context of two basic political issues: (1) the state hierarchy for higher education and (2) the state budget. The purpose of this chapter is to provide a concise overview of the state hierarchy of higher education and of the state budget as a political force in supporting state university libraries.

The literature of academic librarianship has focused primarily on the internal political environment for support of libraries, especially in times of retrenchments and on the politics of budget allocation.[1] This chapter is therefore limited to an examination of the external political environment and to strategies that librarians should use in the local environment to ensure support of their libraries at the state level.

STATE HIERARCHY FOR HIGHER EDUCATION

One of the political issues that most state universities have to face is where they fit within the state hierarchy for postsecondary and higher education. The most widely recognized method of determining the rank of an institution in this hierarchy is by use of the classification scheme for colleges and universities developed by the Carnegie Foundation for the Advancement of Teaching.[2] The legislatures place most state colleges and universities into one of the following categories:

1. *Major Research Universities:* Often, these institutions are called "flagship" state universities, and are named "The University of the State's Name." They maintain many graduate and professional programs, have large student enrollments, and are noted for being the state's major recipient of substantial research grants from the corporate world as well as the federal government. These institutions are usually considered to be the major providers of research scientists, lawyers, doctors, and business leaders.

2. *Major Comprehensive Universities:* These institutions are usually known as "State's Name University." They normally contain a number of professional schools and graduate programs, as well as a large undergraduate program. These institutions are usually the recipient of a large number of external grants, primarily from the federal government and, to a lesser extent, from corporations.

3. *Regional Comprehensive Universities or Colleges:* These institutions are often named for a region of the state or for a location (usually a town or city) within a region of the state. These institutions usually emphasize their undergraduate program. Some may have a very small number of graduate and professional programs. There is usually very little external funding for research activities.

THE STATE BUDGET AS A POLITICAL FORCE

The major driving force in the political environments of states is the budget. Nearly all political activity centers around state budget appropriations; namely, who gets how much. State universities are able to get a political advantage as a result of the prestige that they have nationally and within the state. Financial support and allocation of resources depend essentially upon whether an institution is considered elite or not.[3] Understanding the political system (the organization and the people in it) is essential in state higher education budgeting.

The Systems Context of State Budgeting of High Education

A state system of higher education is usually considered a subsystem of the total system of state government. The budgeting system for higher education operates in this same context. The subsystem for budgeting usually consists of at least four components: (1) the state executive budget office; (2) the state legislative committees and staffs; (3) the state higher education agency (a few states do not have this unit); and (4) the institutions of higher education.

The state higher education budgeting model presented as Figure 1 shows the relationship of the statewide budgeting process to state higher education and state government in the broader political context. This model is based on a 1977 version which was originally developed by Schmidtlein and Glenny.[4]

Institutions in various categories produce a variety of products that are of value to society. Societal groups make their preferences for these products known to the state-level agencies and the producing institutions. At the same time, these institutions make their preferences known through budget requests to the state-level agencies. The institutions base their budget request justifications on previously agreed upon quantitative and qualitative criteria and measures. The state-level agencies conduct the budget review process and make decisions subject to the constraints of available resources, available information, and legal regulations.

The Political Aspects of Statewide Higher Education Budgeting

The state agencies engaged in budgeting assess and articulate societal preferences through budget recommendations and appropriations. The staffs responsible for preparation of budgets for higher education are usually part of a unit in a larger agency of state government. While their primary goal is to provide resources for institutions of higher education, they also produce their own products—policy decisions and information—which they must share with other subsystems to obtain the inputs that they require to perform effectively their functions. An exchange cycle model for budgeting in higher education developed by Schmidtlein and Glenny [5] has been adapted to illustrate the levels and numbers of inputs and products which are usually involved in the budgeting process. (See Figure 2)

FIGURE 1. The State Higher Education Budgeting System.

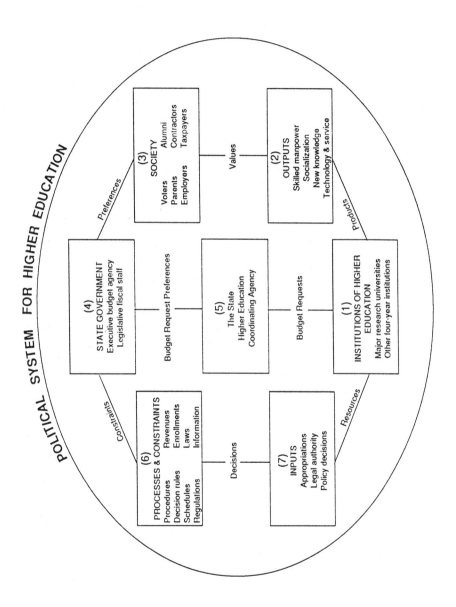

Source: Schmidtlein and Glenny. *State Budgeting for Higher Education: The Political Economy of the Process.* Revised by B. F. Speller, 1989.

FIGURE 2. The State Higher Education Budgeting Subsystem.

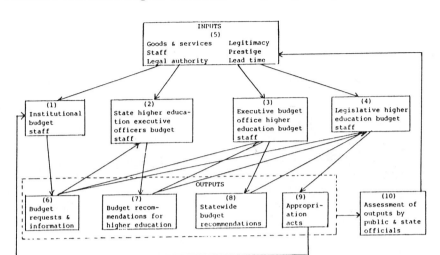

Source: Schmidtlein and Glenny. *State Budgeting for Higher Education: The Political Economy of the Process.*

Budget staffs receive resources so that they may prepare requests for recommending funds. Institutional budget requests go to one or more state-level budget staffs depending on state policy. The executive budget staffs receive these institutional requests and incorporate them into a state budget recommendation, referred to as the governor's budget or executive budget. The governor's budget is transmitted to the legislative budget staff members responsible for higher education. The legislative budget staffs help develop recommendations that eventually lead to appropriations. During this process, assessments of the results of the various budget staffs are made by public constituencies, and state and institutional officials.

Political bargaining takes place over these assessments. This bargaining process usually results in new resource inputs. The budget cycle is complete when the budget staffs incorporate the new resource inputs into the final appropriations.

The state-level budget agencies compete with each other for needed resources to give them maximum influence during the budget formulation process. All groups involved in the budgeting process need to watch the level of competition very closely because changes in allocations of resources to units can result from imbalances among the perspectives brought to bear on budgets, in addition to assessments of the effectiveness with which units carry out current functions.

The Librarian and State Budgeting for Higher Education

A librarian should understand a number of dimensions of state budgeting. Those that are of strategic importance are:

1. The environmental trends that affect the demand for higher education and act as constraints on the budget process, on both the state and national levels.

Librarians should constantly monitor the external environment for potential changes in demographic and economic trends that tend to have significant implications for higher education. Librarians should develop skills in environmental scanning and forecasting. They may have learned some of these skills in management courses and in information resources courses when they were students in library and information science programs. In these programs, the information-seeking behavior of users is monitored to determine current and future needs in collection development and in provisions for information services.

A more sophisticated system of monitoring the external environment is needed to plan and prepare for state-level support for libraries. A scanning/forecasting model developed in the corporate world to address the problem of collecting and evaluating information from the external environment has been modified by Morrison and others for use in higher education institutions.[6] Librarians should review this model for possible use in their organizations. Librarians should also become familiar with the uses of environmental scanning in forecasting changes, especially changes in the external political environment.[7]

2. The sources of inputs into the budget process.

Librarians should know what revenues are generally available for allocation to higher education, what the costs of higher education resources are, and whether there are measurable benefits.

3. The structure, resources, and processes that are involved in the act of budgeting.

4. The sequential phases of the budget process from formulation through administration to retrospective performance evaluation.

Librarians should become thoroughly familiar with the budget cycle and when retrospective performance evaluation is scheduled. Timing of budget requests and indirect negotiations of potential allocations is a critical factor in gaining support at the state levels especially within state legislatures.

5. The resource allocation and policy outputs of the budget process.

The major issue that surfaces during resource allocation is how the structure of the budget relates to the organization of the agencies or organizations. The real politics of budgeting relates to perceived or actual changes in the hierarchy for state higher education, especially where formula allocations have been historically linked to the existing structure.[8] Librarians should be ready to support the officials responsible for budget preparation and negotiations when allocations for new degree programs are being considered at the state level.

Politics of Budgeting in the Local Environment for State Support

Librarians should provide support to their local budgeting officers who prepare and defend the state budget requests through use of the following strategies in their local environments:

1. involve all constituents in the budgetary development process;
2. provide as much documentation as possible to justify current and expansion budget requests. The current emphasis on effectiveness assessment for accreditation self-studies and evidence of goal achievement should be especially useful as documentation to support funding requests;[9]
3. provide the officials who prepare and defend the library budget requests at the state level with alternative budget requests in advance;
4. inform all constituencies of how each alternative budget request will best help their programs achieve their institutional goals;
5. ensure that the budget requests equitably support the various constituencies of the library; and,
6. ensure that the constituencies of the library have a positive attitude about how previous budgets were allocated.

In summary, librarians should know their local environments and structure the budget development process to ensure that cooperation and support will be forthcoming when needed to support budget allocations or recommendations at the state level.

CONCLUSION

The political environments of state university libraries are identical to those of their parent institutions. Support for state university libraries is generally affected by the defined place of parent institutions in the state hierarchy of higher education. State support for state universities may also be affected by historical roles, by statewide constituencies' support, and by the national prestige of a significant number of its instructional and research programs.

The state budget is generally the driving political force in a state higher education environment. Librarians will generally ensure better support for their libraries if they know the major dimensions of state budgeting and are able to provide support to the local officials responsible for preparing budget requests and for negotiating state budget allocations.

References

1. Judith Niles, "The Politics of Budget Allocation," *Library Acquisitions: Practice and Theory* 13 (1989): 51–55; F. William Summers, "The Use of Formulae in Resource Allocation," *Library Trends* 23 (April 1975): 631–642.
2. *A Classification of Institutions of Higher Education* (Princeton, N.J.: Carnegie Foundation for the Advancement of Teaching, 1987).
3. Sheila Slaughter and Edward T. Silva, "Toward a Political Economy of Retrenchment: The American Public Research Universities," *The Review of Higher Education* 8 (Summer 1985): 295–318.
4. Frank A. Schmidtlein and Lyman A. Glenny, *State Budgeting For Higher Education: The Political Economy of the Process* (Berkley: The University of California, Center for Research and Development in Higher Education, 1977), p. 16.
5. *Ibid.*, p. 18.
6. James L. Morrison, "Establishing an Environmental Scanning/Forecasting System to Augment College and University Planning," *Planning for Higher Education* 15, no.1 (1987): 7–22.
7. W.P. Neufeld, "Environmental Scanning: Its Use in Forecasting Emerging Trends and Issues in Organizations," *Futures Research Quarterly* 1, no.3 (Fall 1985): 39–52.
8. Richard John Meisinger, "The Politics of Formula Budgeting: The Determination of Tolerable Levels of Inequality Through Objective Incrementalism in Public Higher Education" (Ph.D. dissertation, University of California, Berkeley, 1975).
9. Nancy A. Brown, "Assessment Perspectives: How To Make The Case For Better Library Funding." *Library Administration & Management* 3 (Spring 1989): 80–83.

III
Local Politics and the Support of Libraries

Funding for Public Libraries in the 1990s

Arthur Curley
Director, Boston Public Library

Public libraries in the United States are struggling to emerge from a decade and more of crisis. The most obvious manifestation of that crisis has been severe revenue shortages, leading to major reductions in services and resources development. Financial strategies for the 1990s must begin with an assessment of that crisis, for its roots lie deep in the history of the public library movement and in conflicting forces within the nation's framework of values.

The public library is something of an anomaly in American society: revered as fundamental to the nation's values, yet without mandation or secure fiscal niche at any level of government in most areas of the country. In the spontaneous nature of its origins, and the voluntary basis of its continuance, are rooted both the strengths and weaknesses of this remarkable institution as well as the causative background to the financial predicament we confront as we enter the final decade of this century.

That the birth of the public library movement occurred in the United States, in the mid-nineteenth century, is a matter of some irony. The decision to serve a universal audience hardly sprung from a super-abundance of private resources. By 1850, the oldest and largest library in the country, that of Harvard University, contained only 84,000 volumes; the Library of Congress merely 50,000. In fact, only five libraries in the country held over 50,000 books, and the entire national composite amounted to barely 2,000,000.[1] The inadequacy of the young nation's library resources was dramatically underscored by the provocative charge of Fisher Ames that ". . . we have produced nothing in history. Our own is not yet worthy of a Livy; and to write that of any foreign nation where could an American author collect his materials and authorities? Few persons reflect, that all our universities would not suffice to supply them for such a work as Gibbon's."[2] Charles Coffin Jewett, who would set about to correct this assessment upon his appointment in 1858 to the Superintendency of the Boston Public Library, maintained at mid-century that "not one American library could meet the wants of a student in any department of knowledge."[3]

On the other hand, the fallow soil of a new nation would prove particularly receptive to the zealous idealism which was the principal motivating force behind the movement to create the public library. New England in the 1840s was a still fervent disciple of the Enlightenment, committed to the concepts of humanism, of human perfectability, of democratic promise, the center of the universal free education movement and of the growing Abolitionist cause. As Sidney Ditzion summarized,

> "the main currents of nineteenth-century American thought, no matter what their origin or direction, supported the foundations and growth of the free public library movement. That such a confluence of diverse ideologies, meeting on the common ground of a system of free schools and libraries, was at all possible is to be attributed to the adjustability of the American mind to shifting forces and changing conditions. It was this flexibility which could start with a common heritage—the democratic premise—and could modify, distort, or even pervert it to suit the requirements of widely varying points of view. The tax-supported public library not only answered the criteria inherent in the democratic premise but also offered an instrument as responsive to varying social requirements as democracy itself.[4]

The idealistic origins of the public library have remained a force to shape its mission and philosophy for nearly a century and a half; unfortunately, the naivete so characteristic of an idealistic movement placed greater reliance on noble inclinations than on a rational legal and financial framework to insure support for the infant institution, and this too continues as an operative force to our present time. The famous Act of Authorization to Establish a Public Library in the City of Boston, enacted in March of 1848 by the legislature of the Commonwealth of Massachusetts, represented the culmination of a fervently idealistic movement, but the statute also contained the provision that "no appropriation for the said library shall exceed the sum of dollar 5,000 in any one year."[5] The cautious solons need not have feared: the initial appropriation by the Boston City Council, and that after a delay of three years, was the princely sum of dollar 1,000.[6] Edward Everett, the first President of the Library Trustees, had become the major colleague and catalyst in the ultimate success of George Ticknor's twenty-year struggle to establish a public library; yet, the uncertainty in the minds of even these determined founders of the proper relationship between public mission and public support is evident in Everett's 1850 letter to the Mayor, in which he pleads that "if the city government would provide a suitable building for a public library, it would be so amply supplied from time to time by donations, that only a moderate annual appropriation for books would be wanted."[7] The first report of the Trustees of the Boston Public Library, issued in July of 1852, has been cited on innumerable occasions for its visionary articulation of the philosophy which would influence the mission of public libraries everywhere; but, again, the visionary confidence seems to falter on the matter of public financial support:

> If it were probable that the City Council would deem it expedient at once to make a large appropriation for the erection of a building and the purchase of an ample library, and that the citizens at large would approve such expenditure, the Trustees would of course feel great satisfaction in the prompt achievement of an object of such high public utility. But in the present state of the finances of the city, and in reference to an object on which the public mind is not yet enlightened by experience, the Trustees regard any such appropriation and expenditure as entirely out of the question. They conceive even that there are advantages to a more gradual course of measures. They look, therefore, only to the continuance of such moderate and frugal expenditure, on the part of the city, as has been already authorized and commenced, for the purchase of books and the compensation of the librarian; and for the assignment of a room or rooms in some one of the public buildings belonging to the city for the reception of the books already on hand, or which the Trustees have the means of procuring. With aid to this extent on the part of the city, the Trustees believe that all else may be left to the public spirit and liberality of individuals.[8]

The faith of the Trustees in private philanthropy was soon rewarded by the great generosity of Joshua Bates, as was the case in New York with that of John Jacob Astor, and universally through Andrew Carnegie's gifts of public library buildings to over 1,500 communities in the United States alone a half-century later. To be less than grateful for such generosity would be boorish, indeed; private philanthropy was both an important predecessor, and at times a stimulant, of tax support. But a case may also be made that philanthropy discourages communal responsibility, even unto the present time in which many a beleaguered library has been urged by public officials to seek private funds in lieu of additional tax support.

The shift from private to predominantly public support was a matter of considerable gradualism; there were, after all, nearly 700 private academic and subscription lending libraries in the United States in

1850, many of which would become the basis of future public libraries. Getz contends, in fact, that "for more than their first one hundred years the line between private and government support of libraries was never crisp."[9] This is much more than a matter of historical curiosity, for the long identity crisis which it signifies continues to complicate the legitimate search of public libraries for a rational support structure.

Another characteristic of the challenge we confront as we plan for library funding in the 1990s is the great diversity of taxation structures throughout the country. The principal source of support for financing public libraries in the United States is local taxation; but, as Robbins-Carter concludes: "local government financing varies from state to state and within states there are usually a number of local government financing options open to communities and/or counties; thus, it is not possible to present an accurate picture of a 'typically' financed public library."[10] Most major urban public libraries are, either legally or *de facto*, departments of municipal government, in competition with police or fire or sanitation for scarce funds distributed at the discretion of elected officials; a very few have power to seek special levies by referendum; the New York Public Library is a private corporation. Libraries in some parts of the country are creatures of county government, some are local but receive supplemental services or funds from county sources, others have separate district status with tax millage formulas determined by state statutes and voter referenda. Such diversity presents a serious obstacle to funding strategies based on comparative research or to effective lobbying on a nationwide, or even statewide, basis.

The traditional concern of state governments was service to rural and unincorporated areas; by the 1980s nearly all fifty states provided some form of support for library service, but the pattern varied widely from support for cooperative or regional services to direct per-capita aid. In a few states, modest aid to major urban libraries has been achieved, in recognition of service beyond local borders or resources of more than local importance; but by far the prevailing pattern has been small support to virtually all communities rather than significant aid for the special few. The role of the national government in library affairs, beyond support of the splendid libraries of the national government, has been extremely limited, in large part precisely because the initial library movement sprung from local initiative; and continued resistance to national support and coordination reflects the lasting effects of that historical identity crisis, for the appropriate role of government in the development and support of library resources remains unresolved. As Wedgeworth has noted, "inconsistencies in public library financing are only the superficial manifestations of the confusion that exists over public support for libraries."[11]

As we devise financial strategies for the nineties, however, the confusion we confront goes beyond that of the library's place in the public sector to a national crisis of confidence toward the public sector itself. For most of this century, following the demise of spectacular personal philanthropy in the wake of progressive tax legislation, local public support remained modest but healthy, even during the Depression years, reflecting a comfortable relevance to the values and aspirations of most American communities. As one library administrator remarked recently,

> For over one hundred years, public library funding was a consensus decision made by public officials. The message was clear: Libraries—no matter how large or small—must be supported. Taxpayers willingly financed library services . . . Then, along came the 1970s . . . Suddenly, libraries didn't appear quite so high on the priority list as public works projects, governmental infrastructures, water and sewer facilities, streets, or public safety. Once regarded as an essential service and birthright for every American . . .libraries were forced into budget-cutting positions.[12]

The response of the library profession to this undeniable crisis was essentially defensive, at least initially. The mid-seventies ushered in a virtual obsession in the library profession with cost-accountability, cost-benefit analyses of services formerly deemed essential, market research, performance measurement, and back-to-basics redefinitions of mission. Professional management techniques are certainly useful to effective budget development and presentation; too often, they merely masked a crisis of confidence. An institution which is largely the embodiment of intangible values can be only diminished when a material monetary standard is applied to every function, when only that which is tangibly measurable is valued. Planning, managerial, and political skills will be essential to the development of effective funding strategies for the nineties; but they are not enough. It was not so much such skills, as it was the ideals of visionary founders and early champions, which launched the library movement. It is not libraries which have fallen out of favor in America, it is the larger public sector, itself. Small comfort, this, but we can ill afford a flawed analysis of our crisis.

A skeptical attitude toward the public sector and a distrust of government have long been latent in American society. The reactionary swing in the national consciousness, reflected in the political balance of power, began as a corrective to excesses of the explosive 1960s. Traumatic national frustration with the debacle of military failures in Southeast Asia soon led to anger and distrust toward government, as did the scandals associated with the Watergate incident. Simultaneous disenchantment with the great expense yet miniscule apparent success of governmental efforts to create an ideal "great society" virtually free of poverty or injustice unleashed a backlash which has not yet abated. The 1980s continued to witness the triumph of political campaigns based on promises to do less, to dismantle government, to enhance the private sector at the expense of the public.

Yet the 1980s also saw several stunning reaffirmations of popular belief in the importance of the public library, particularly in instances (such as bond issues) when the electorate could vote directly on library issues.[13] California was the scene of the most influential tax limitation referendum of the 1970s, the infamous Proposition 13, which sent a shock wave of retrenchment across the country; but, in 1988, the people of California approved a $75 million bond issue for library construction and renovation, and the citizens of both Los Angeles and San Francisco have voted over $100,000 million each for new central libraries. Similar successes, by direct popular vote, have occurred in Detroit, Cleveland, Atlanta, Miami; extensive revitalization programs are underway in New York, Boston, Chicago, Philadelphia. That very degree of separateness from the center of government, that uncertain status in the public sector, which so contributes to the fiscal instability of the public library serves also as a buffer in this era of antagonism toward government.

Strategies for public library funding in the 1990s must include legislative efforts to increase the ability of libraries to go directly to the public; creation of a national public library network; establishment of direct support for major research-level public library resources as a basic national responsibility; full federal funding of the depository library system; special state legislation incorporating equalization and compensation factors for urban public libraries serving multi-community metropolitan areas and population concentrations with high degrees of special needs. But, more than all else, these strategies must be based on a reassertion of the fundamental relationship of the public library to the cultural, educational, civic, and economic health of the nation. Strategies based on a diminution of mission, on fees for access to information in any format, on the privatization of public responsibilities can only be counterproductive. E. J. Josey, in his 1984 Presidential address to the American Library Association, urged that "Librarians . . . need to integrate their goals with the goals of greatest importance to the American people . . . We need to foster and to reaffirm the inseparable relationship between libraries and democratic liberties."[14] That relationship, so confidently assumed for over a century, helped shape the noblest goals of the public library movement; reasserted, it offers the best hope for revitalization of the public library—and of the humanistic values it represents—in the 1990s and well beyond.

References

1. Malcom Getz, *Public Libraries: An Economic View* (Baltimore: Johns Hopkins University Press, 1980) p.3.
2. Fisher Ames, *Works, Vol. II*, (Boston: Little, Brown, 1954) p. 440.
3. Jesse H. Shera, *Foundations of the Public Library* (Chicago: University of Chicago Press, 1949), p. 205.
4. Sidney H. Ditzion, *Arsenals of Democratic Culture: A Social History of the American Public Library Movement in New England and the Middle States from 1850 to 1900* (Chicago: American Library Association, 1957), p. 51.
5. Commonwealth of Massachusetts, *Statutes* . . ., 1848. Chapter 52.
6. Walter Muir Whitehill, *Boston Public Library: A Centennial History* (Cambridge: Harvard University Press, 1956), p. 22.
7. *Ibid.*, p. 21.
8. Boston Public Library, *Report of the Trustees of the Public Library of the City of Boston, July 1852* (Boston: City Document 37, 1852).
9. Getz, *op. cit.*, p. 3.
10. Jane Robbins-Carter, *Public Librarianship* (Littleton, Colorado: Libraries Unlimited, 1982), p. 329.
11. Robert Wedgeworth, "Prospects for and Effecting Change in the Public Library," *Library Quarterly* 48 :4 (October 1978): 534.
12. Suzanne Walters, "Funding Strategies for Survival," *The Bottom Line*, 1:3 (1987): 4.
13. Betty Turock, "A Fiscal Agenda for the 1990s," *The Bottom Line* 2: 4 (1988): 3.
14. E.J. Josey, *Libraries, Coalitions, and the Public Good* (New York: Neal-Schuman, 1987), p. 2.

Politics and the
Public Library:
A Management Guide

Marilyn Gell Mason
Director, Cleveland Public Library

As I was preparing for this presentation, a colleague in Cleveland asked what I was going to say. "I think I'll try telling the truth," I responded. She looked at me for a long moment and finally commented. "Well, you might be able to get away with it. You'll be out of town."

Those of us who operate libraries, or other public institutions for that matter, are not accustomed to getting away with much of anything. In fact, most of us find that our jobs are not well understood by many people either inside or outside the library profession.

Just recently my mother finally worked up the courage to ask, "What exactly is it that you do? I know what your title is, but what do you do when you go to work?" It's a sensible question. Nevertheless, it made me think in a different way about the job of a public library director and I have come up with the following explanation.

STEADY AS SHE GOES, MR. SULU

I fight the Klingons. After all, if you remember your *Star Trek*, Scotty actually runs the ship. Captain Kirk sets the direction and fights the Klingons. Of course, he also keeps Dr. McCoy and Spock working

Reprinted from *Library Journal*, March 15, 1989. Copyright 1989 by Reed Publishing, USA, Division of Reed Holdings, Inc.

together, and communicates with Star Fleet Command, but his primary job is to keep the ship on course and moving toward its goal in spite of problems that may arise.

In a political environment there seem to be plenty of Klingons to deal with. Funding obstacles, governance issues, personnel limitations, and press relations are chief among them. When I was hired to run the first White House Conference on Library and Information Services some years ago, a colleague took me aside and gave me some friendly advice. "The job is impossible," he said. "You have no control over your budget, you can't hire or fire your employees, and your goals are set by elected officials. It's like walking into a boxing match with a blindfold and one hand tied behind your back. Survival is about the best you can hope for."

My experience then, and since then, has convinced me that while my advisor's caution may have been justified, he was overly cynical in his conclusion. It is true that public institutions operate within a world of especially challenging constraints and relationships. But it is equally true that these same conditions and relationships can be managed productively, for the good of the institutions and in the best interests of the people the institution serves.

Politics in this context refers not to partisan politics but to the more generic art of influencing government policy. While the management of any organization is political to the extent that one must try to influence decision makers, and I trust that some comments will resonate with colleagues in academic and private sector environments, public libraries deal directly with government. Indeed, one might argue that public libraries are part of government.

This governmental context brings with it some special conditions. Governance of a public library is most often through a Board of Trustees; funding is typically a function of the political process and as such it is neither constant nor predictable; employment practices are regulated either by Civil Service rules or union contracts; and the press is an ever-present factor in day-to-day operations. In addition, goal setting must be done in conjunction with local elected officials and negotiating skills provide the glue that holds it all together.

GOVERNANCE AND THE BOARD OF TRUSTEES

There are a number of governance structures for public libraries. Some public libraries are departments of city or county government and have no Board of Trustees at all, or only an advisory board. Other public libraries are departments of city or county government and have a policy-making board as well. A third type of public library governance occurs when the library operates as an independent, not-for-profit corporation, with or without independent taxing authority. Finally, there are a few public library systems that are part of state government.

The power of a Board of Trustees varies enormously, depending on the role of the board within the governmental structure and the strength of the individuals on the board. An advisory board has little direct power. It cannot set policy. It cannot allocate resources. It does not hire or fire the director. Indirectly, such a group can bring terrific pressure to bear on policy makers, and many advisory boards are fine advocates for libraries, but they are limited by their inability to set policy directly. Still, an advisory board is better than no board at all.

A policy-making board for a library located structurally within government has the toughest and most ambiguous role of all. Charged with setting policy, a board in this situation is constrained by its inability to generate and allocate funds. Without this implementing capability, the board is restricted realistically to making policy decisions about nonfiscal library programs and activities. This type of board is more powerful than an advisory board. It can hire or fire the director. It can take definitive stands on issues of intellectual freedom. It can approve long-range plans and recommend budgets to elected officials. It cannot, however, prevent the governing body from freezing staff, closing facilities, or reducing funds available for the purchase of materials.

Library boards governing libraries that are independent, not-for-profit institutions have the highest level of power. This type of board exercises power comparable to that available to the board of a corporation. It can hire or fire the director. It can make policy on nonfiscal issues. It can even allocate resources. Within budgetary constraints it can open or close facilities, expand or contract the staff, increase or decrease the budgetary allocation available for materials. Financial resources available to the library remain within the library. They are not vulnerable to reallocation to other city or county departments.

There are two secrets to the development and maintenance of a productive working relationship with a Board of Trustees: clear role definition and the communication of adequate and appropriate information.

A public library is just that, the public's library. It belongs to the citizens of a given community. It does not belong to the library director. Trustees are selected as representatives of the community to govern the library. The library director is hired by those trustees to manage the institution and to carry out policies established by the board. The board makes policy. The director carries out policy.

As straightforward as this principle may seem, many of the problems that arise between directors and boards are a result of a confusion of roles. Either the director tries to set policy or the board tries to manage the institution. The scenario that most often develops is one in which the director begins to feel that he or she is better able to make policy decisions than the board. A series of conflicts develops. The board, deprived of its ability to make policy, begins to try to control the director by managing the institution. By moving too far into the establishment of policy the director creates a vacuum that is filled by trustees who are frustrated in their attempts to perform their own jobs.

The director's job goes beyond the simple implementation of policy. It is also the responsibility of the director to make sure that trustees have all the information they need to make informed decisions. This includes background information about the community, board information about national library trends and issues, and specific information concerning the issue under discussion. With respect to information needed to make specific decisions, bulk is not necessarily better.

Appropriate information may be an analysis of cost and benefits or a comparison of options clearly and concisely presented. It may also be a phone call to let an individual trustee know about a pending problem or a possible call from the press. At the most fundamental level, good decisions are based on complete, comprehensive, timely information.

FUNDING

The operating budget for all public libraries (with the partial exception of the New York Public Library's Research Libraries) comes from tax-generated revenues. Sometimes, as in the State of Ohio, library support is a combination of state-collected income tax and local property tax. Most often public libraries receive a portion of local property tax that is collected and allocated on a year-to-year basis by city or county government.

No matter how revenues are collected or allocated public libraries are constantly confronted with the twin political realities of the public's aversion to taxes and the need to compete with other public agencies, many of which do good, for a reasonable share of the pie. The goal, then, is to find effective ways to get and keep an adequate budget in a volatile, pressure-filled environment.

The political strategies for achieving this goal include the provision of the highest quality service possible, the effective presentation of budget requests, an understanding of political pressure points, and the ability to mobilize an effective demonstration of power.

In poll after poll across the country, citizens rank public libraries at or near the top of all public agencies in the importance of the service they provide and their success in providing it well. Nevertheless, budgets continue to be inadequate. That reality indicates that there must be more to the decision-making process than logic would suggest. Still, libraries must continue to make every effort to maintain that level of performance. It is a necessary, but insufficient, condition for achieving adequate support.

The first point at which showmanship comes into play is at the initial presentation of the budget. Many of us have learned that a picture is indeed worth a thousand words and have come to rely on graphs, charts, and cartoons from *The New Yorker*.

I remember several years ago making a budget presentation during a year of austerity. The mayor had directed all departments to reduce their budget by some percentage. The library board directed me to go forward with a proposed budget that was an increase. When we appeared before the appropriate committee we presented a pie chart with the library's slice of one-half of one percent of total revenues indicated. As you can imagine it looked a lot like a straight line. What we said was, "Where are you going to make a reduction, and, if you do, what difference will it make anyway?" We got our increase.

I don't mean to suggest, however, that a flashy presentation will solve all your financial problems. I have made equally splendid presentations with the opposite result. Presentation is, after all, only a continuation of a logical process and politics is a function of power. The elements that are most useful in acquiring political support for the library budget are an understanding of political pressure points, and the willingness and ability to lean on them.

If the library budget is to be approved by seven elected officials you need four votes. The way you get those votes may vary. Individual telephone calls from a few well-placed supporters may persuade some, while others may be more affected by the two hundred library supporters who pack the hearing room. No one strategy is always right. The point is you have to know the pressure points and develop a strategy that is appropriate to the situation.

PERSONNEL MANAGEMENT

Just as with the section on funding, this is not meant to be a full discussion of personnel management. Comments are restricted to those issues that have some political component.

Conventional wisdom tells us that public agencies have limited control over personnel, that civil service rules and regulations and union contracts make it impossible to manage.

In fact, just the opposite is true.

Civil service was instituted to counteract the abuses of patronage. Its goal was the establishment of a system in which individuals would be hired and promoted on the basis of merit. In fact, what civil service has accomplished is the removal of personnel issues from the political process.

Unions representing public employees have done much the same thing. By focusing on the development of fair labor practices and adequate levels of compensation, they have served to protect staff from the more damaging aspects of politics. While we must acknowledge the fact that unions are themselves political in a broader sense, and may in fact assist libraries in funding strategies described above, their goal is to depoliticize the workplace.

The largest remaining political issue in the personnel area is the achievement of adequate compensation for library employees. Although this issue surely has a large impact on library staff, it can most appropriately be seen as a funding issue.

THE FOURTH ESTATE

Contrary to public opinion, the press is not the enemy. Successful press relations depend on a recognition of the fact that an organized approach to press relations is an important part of management's job and an understanding of how the press operates and what reporters are trying to achieve.

At the most basic level, a reporter is trying to write—or film or record—a good story. Print reporters have a designated number of column inches to fill while television or radio reporters fill time segments, generally very short time segments. You can help reporters do their job better by providing quotable quotes and good photo opportunities. If you are trying to increase media coverage of the library, sensitivity to what is considered newsworthy will build credibility with working journalists.

In conjunction with this, an understanding of how the press and media operate will also contribute to good press relations. Everyone has a deadline. For most morning dailies that deadline is generally around 7:30 p.m. While pressing stories can come in later, library items are usually not that urgent. If you want press coverage of board meetings and major announcements, it makes sense to schedule them at a time when they can be covered. Some libraries have even been known to change the time of their board meetings to fit in with press deadlines.

Timing is important with TV news also. If you want to be on the 6 p.m. news you should schedule your events between 11 a.m. and 3 p.m. Noon is always good. You might begin to notice how many news events seem to happen around noon. Sometimes a TV station will arrange for live coverage, but unless you have a real emergency on your hands such coverage would be scheduled in advance.

The 11 p.m. news on Sunday has the highest ratings of the week. In addition, there is often little hard news available. Many libraries are open on Sunday, and are often quite busy. You might consider showcasing a program or making an announcement early on Sunday afternoon. Just make sure that it's more than talking heads. You will reach a lot of people and make some TV reporters happy in the process.

Don't wait until you have a problem or a message to deliver to establish good press relations. Open communication, which is the basis for trust and rapport, should be developed early on. I remember one time in Atlanta when we were generating a long-range plan for the Atlanta Public Library. At each stage in the planning we met with members of the editorial board of the *Atlanta Journal Constitution* to explain what we were doing and to answer any questions the board members might have.

When the time came for citizens to vote on the $38 million bond referendum we once again packed up our charts and graphs and answers and went down to ask for the endorsement of the newspaper. The group of editors asked us a single question: Is this the same plan you've been talking about for the last two years? When we said yes, they agreed to endorse the referendum with no further discussion.

CHOOSING A SPOKESPERSON

Who should speak to the press? While there is no single answer to the question, there are some principles upon which I have come to rely. In Cleveland, our public relations officer handles most of the day-to-day contacts with the press. She had developed her contacts, and in many instances real friendships, over a period of years. Newspaper and media representatives have come to know and respect her. She is the first person to be called if an issue arises. She fields the questions and refers them to appropriate individuals for response.

If the question or story is about a library service, the staff member most knowledgeable is asked to respond. We feel that the most knowledgeable person is the best representative of the library and do not try to restrict press contact. Thus, a children's librarian will discuss the latest children's program, the head of special collections answers questions about our rare book acquisitions, and branch librarians talk about service in their neighborhoods.

If the issue is a broad one, or a highly sensitive one, the director talks with the press. Some examples of such issues are: increases or decreases in service, library policy regarding privacy of library records, long-range plans, or the impact on the library of an increase or reduction of the library's budget.

There are some situations that are so sensitive that it is usually in the best interests of the library for the president or chair (titles vary) of the board to respond to the press inquiries. Major changes in service, policy, or direction fall in this category. The closing of a branch or the initiation of a major capital campaign are some examples of this type of issue.

In all dealings with the press there are several things to keep in mind. There are three rules of press relations: 1) always tell the truth; 2) never volunteer information; and 3) never speculate.

The first rule is obvious. You simply must deal honestly with the press if you expect them to be fair and honest with you. This includes, by the way, notifying the press about newsworthy items in a timely fashion.

Obviously, rule number two does not apply to those instances when you are trying to generate press coverage. What it does refer to is the management of a crisis situation. If a branch has been closed and the newspaper, radio, and television have all sent out reporters to cover the events, they might ask a staff member how the public is reacting. Staff members should answer the question honestly, but should not go on to compare this problem with one they experienced two weeks ago. That kind of thoughtless response can lead to stories that might be damaging. Moreover, they are irrelevant to the story being covered.

Speculation can generate exciting copy but it is almost never factual and can be gravely misleading. Questions that begin, "How do you think Mr. Jones feels?" or "What do you think Mrs. Smith thinks?" or "What do you think will happen next?" all lead the responder into a line of speculation that may indeed have no basis in fact. None of us really knows what someone else thinks or feels. We can only report on actions.

A final word about the press. I will always remember what I call the Kissinger Doctrine (having first been enunciated by Henry Kissinger). It states that whatever is going to come out eventually should be disclosed immediately. Most of us don't deal with state secrets, but occasionally encounter a situation that we'd rather not disclose to the press. Remember, if it's that big a problem, it's probably going to come out anyway. If you disclose the potentially embarrassing information, it is less likely to be embarrassing.

CARE OF ELECTED OFFICIALS

Elected officials often get a bad rap. While it is true that some politicians use public office for private gain or abuse the public's trust in some other way, it is equally true that there are numerous elected officials who take their responsibilities seriously and work long and hard to improve government and the services government provides. In working with elected officials it helps to begin by assuming that most are competent and committed. It also helps to understand the goals and constraints that influence their decision-making processes.

Elected officials, without exception, have a broad agenda and numerous constituents. Libraries are seldom at the top of their list of concerns. Libraries are, however, well thought of in most communities and elected officials are happy to support them, especially if they become a part of a larger agenda. Since most public libraries have a great many needs it is usually not difficult to tie one or more into the overall agenda of the community.

A few examples may help illustrate this point. If a given community is deeply concerned with neighborhood development or redevelopment, the library might want to emphasize its branch services and the contributions that branch libraries make to the neighborhood. If, on the other hand, the community is focused on downtown development, it would be an appropriate time to examine the role of the main library in supporting business growth and to propose needed improvements of the main library facility. Some elected officials are interested in bricks and mortar programs while others are more concerned with services. In any event, most will be more likely to support the library actively if it is sensitive to the overall directions of the community.

That is not to say the library is not an important force in itself. Anyone who has had to close a branch library knows that libraries are one of the most important positive elements in any community. Not only do they provide important services on a regular basis, but they are also a symbol of knowledge, of wisdom, and the possibility of progress for individuals and for the community. However an individual elected official may feel personally about the contributions of the library, few can ignore the importance of this institution to voters.

Rules for working with elected officials are similar to those suggested for working with the press. Relations should be developed early on, before a situation arises that requires political assistance, and formal and informal channels of communication should be developed and maintained. In Cleveland, we send a personal letter and report on library activities every month to all elected officials in the area, whether we think we will need their help or not. In addition, we make a point of notifying appropriate elected officials when any important library-related activity is planned for a specific district.

If you do need help in a specific situation don't assume that the individual you are approaching is fully aware of the details, no matter how many times they may have been in the newspaper. Be prepared to provide a clear, straightforward briefing. If you want help, be prepared to ask for the specific action you need. "We just want your support on this issue" is too vague. If you want a vote, ask for it. If you want an individual to make a phone call, have the number ready. Most elected officials have limited time for any one issue. Use the time you have with them effectively.

For elected officials, timing is a critical element in any decision. Remember that elected officials are *elected*. If you can avoid it, don't ask one to take an unpopular position in an election year. Libraries want to avoid any kind of involvement in partisan politics, but that does not mean that we should be naïve about the conditions under which elected officials work.

NEGOTIATING STRATEGIES

Negotiation is the glue that holds everything together in a political environment. Negotiating strategies include timing, pacing, and presentation. Negotiating skills are more specific than simple communications skills and are useful in all of the relationships described above. In this section I will simply list some strategies and observations that I have found useful over the years:

- Pacing in organizational development is critical. Typically, there should be a pushing forward followed by an easing off. This gives both the community and staff the opportunity to assimilate change. No organization can sustain the stress of unremitting progress. Sawtooth development is natural and healthy.
- It is almost impossible to expand and contract an institution at the same time. The strategies and rhetoric are different. Unfortunately, many public libraries have had far more experience with contraction than they have had with expansion. Still, there are benefits that can be gained in lean times. Cutting from one area to add to another, however, may be good management, but it is political quicksand.
- One goal of management is to make whatever happens an asset. Anyone can play a good hand; it takes skill to play a mediocre hand. Nowhere is the imperfection of life more obvious than in the falling apart of well-laid plans. Examples are numerous. The situation may involve the starting up of a new service, increase in the operating budget, or the negotiation of a major contract. In any case you may have planned carefully only to be confronted by some change or obstacle. You may lose the vote of a key elected official. Perhaps your Board of Trustees voted differently from the way you expected. Your project will fare far better if you incorporate the change or unexpected action into your overall approach than if you bemoan the loss of your original plan of action.
- Never overlook the possibility that they may be right. In conflict situations most of us assume that our position is the correct one. That is not always

the case. Sometimes a different perspective brings with it an important insight.

- Timing is crucial. Don't try to rush things; let the situation mature. Remember it takes nine months to have the baby whether you have one woman or nine working on the project. Process is important. Let the situation fully expand before trying to solve the problem. A quick solution is not always the best solution.

- Always control the space of a debate, the context in which decision making will take place. Most people will decide among alternatives presented to them. If you present alternatives, any one of which is satisfactory, you will be likely to achieve your goal without alienating needed support.

- Stick to facts, not an interpretation of facts. Try to avoid assigning motives to people, especially elected officials, staff, and the press. You will almost always be wrong, and it won't help your cause anyway.

- Reduce the debate to a few, easily understood points. This is especially important if a crisis becomes public. Examples include the closing of a branch, a strike by a union, or an attempt to pass a levy or bond referendum.

- There are four stages in a negotiation: 1) posturing; 2) smoke; 3) personal attacks; and 4) resolution. Pumping smoke is a strategy that is usually used by an individual when their case is weak and not supported by the facts. Personal attacks, though distasteful, are usually a sign that the end of a dispute is near. They represent an act of desperation.

- Pacing in negotiations is like a marble in a sink. The tempo quickens as the solution nears. Contract negotiations are classic. They generally begin with interminable discussions that appear to accomplish very little, but end with a great deal concluded in a limited amount of time.

- Remember the rule of three: when an individual has a list of problems or issues, the third is always the most important one.

- Share the glory. When there is credit, there is always plenty to go around.

- "I understand how you feel." These words are magic, but only if you really mean them. By affirming the emotional response of an individual to a given situation, you can often move on to a discussion of the facts of the matter. Without the initial affirmation, progress is often impossible.

FUNCTIONS OF A PL DIRECTOR

Running a library in a political environment is a challenging but not impossible task. Fortunately there are many skilled library directors in communities of all sizes that thrive on the conditions described. While there are many definitions of leadership, I like to think of it as a combination of vision, courage, stamina, and the ability to communicate effectively.

Vision is needed to set the goals. Courage is needed to fight the Klingons. Communications skills are needed to get and keep needed support. But stamina is the quality that makes it all possible. After all, when you go back to City Council for the sixth time on the same issue, it isn't vision that keeps you going.

After reviewing this document, a colleague noted that my observations are too upbeat. He said that I appear to overlook the possibility that some members of the press might really distort the news, that elected officials are sometimes hostile, and that trustees are occasionally unsupportive.

While all of that is true, managing in a political environment is nothing more or less than working with people. Each individual has different sets of goals and values but most try to accomplish good, as defined in very personal terms. These goals and values may not duplicate our own but they are not necessarily in conflict with them. We are more likely to achieve respect and understanding for ourselves and our institutions if we begin with respect and understanding for the people with whom we come in contact.

As we lead our libraries through the forcefields of competing interests, it is important for us to keep in mind that all aliens are not enemies, some are allies. Our goal is to work with trustees, elected officials, the press, and others in our communities to find a shared path to the public good.

Funding of Public Libraries: A Case Study

Paul J. Fasana
Andrew W. Mellon Director
of the Research Libraries
The New York Public Library

INTRODUCTION

The New York Public Library (NYPL) is unique and complex. It is a private institution dedicated to public service. Each year its Board of Trustees must secure an annual operating budget of more than $136,000,000 from a combination of sources, including city, state, and federal governments, in addition to the private sector (i.e., foundations and individuals).

Though the library is a single institution, it is made up of two complementary, but separate systems—the Branch Libraries and the Research Libraries. The Branch Libraries system comprises 82 branches serving three of the five boroughs of New York City, while the Research Libraries is comprised of four research centers. The Branch Libraries receive more than 95 percent of their operating budget from public funds, primarily the City of New York. By contrast, the Research Libraries rely primarily on private sources of revenue (i.e., grants, gifts, private philanthropies, endowment income, etc.). The library thus depends on a public/private base of support, which is complex and unusual. This public/private partnership has proved to be both a source of strength for the library in recent years and a weakness. From its origin in 1895 with the consolidation of the Astor and Lenox Libraries, the NYPL has been forced to seek operating funds from all possible sources, public and private. This has required that the library be innovative and entrepreneurial in seeking sources of funds, while at the same time being acutely aware of its efficiency and effectiveness. When asking for money, one must be able to be clear about needs and be able to advance compelling arguments to the various funding sources.

Cultural institutions in the United States are facing increasing pressure to become more fiscally responsible and independent. As cultural entities in a public environment, public libraries have to compete for public funds against urgent social programs, such as drug abuse, medical care, etc. The problem has intensified during the past eight years as a result of the Reagan Administration's program of reducing government support of cultural and educational programs, and the requirement that private monies be raised to match government monies.

In this paper I describe a fundraising effort undertaken by the NYPL to deal with its crucial fiscal needs, and address the issue of a public/private partnership for funding. This description includes a brief review of the planning that was required to evaluate the library's needs, the solution adopted by the library to address those needs, and finally an assessment of how successful this fundraising effort has been. The experience of the New York Public Library may be useful to other libraries planning major fundraising campaigns.

BACKGROUND

During the 1970s, the NYPL was beset with major fiscal problems, a reflection of the New York City budget crisis and a depressed financial market. The library was forced to adopt a variety of strategies to cope with these budgetary problems. A guiding principle during this period of "negative planning" was to define and implement strategies that were reversible, that is, no permanent or irreversible damage would be imposed upon the institution or its collections. The theory was that if and when funds were to become available, the library would then be able to reverse a decision or an action implemented during a period of financial exigency and repair any damage done to the library's collections or services. The strategies adopted by the library during this period ranged from delaying maintenance of the physical plant, shortening hours for all units rather than closing libraries or individual collections, and continuing to acquire materials but backlogging them rather than curtailing acquisitions. Each of these decisions could be reversed with no lasting harm being done to the integrity of the collections or continuity of service. We learned, however, that this strategy was time dependent. If negative decisions are allowed to stay in place too long, lasting damage can result.

By the end of the 1970s, these problems had a severe impact on the well-being of the institution. The library's primary mission—service—was severely threatened. Management was no longer able to state that basic policy would not be adversely affected. At this point, management made a decision that it must assess the situation critically to determine what needs were most urgent, what measures were most necessary and appropriate to address those needs, and what level of resources would be required to continue to fulfill the library's mission without sacrificing collecting, service, or access in such a way as to alter radically the nature of the institution.

THE NEEDS ASSESSMENT

The library began by instituting a planning effort which lasted almost two years and involved staff at all levels. The effort came to be known as the "Needs Assessment." The result of this intensive, broadly scaled effort was a detailed report which was presented to and reviewed by the Library's Board of Trustees. The Needs Assessment was a structured, phased, intensive self-examination of the condition of the library measured against its mission. The results led to a consensus about the institution's most important needs and priorities.

The assessment began with a survey of current activities, costs, and requirements for providing good "basic service." It also elicited new ideas and proposals for new initiatives, examined long-range budgetary and financial implications, and summarized capital and technological needs. It was a synthesis of information gathering and sharing without parallel in the history of the library. It challenged middle management, strengthened communication at all levels and forced librarians at all levels to focus on priorities and mission.

One of the earliest and most important conclusions of this effort was that the library needed a plan to raise money. The critical analysis of the Needs Assessment indicated that the library needed a lot of money and that it would have to be raised from a variety of sources. The planning group tentatively decided that the only realistic solution was to plan and conduct a large-scale fundraising effort. The Needs Assessment analysis provided both the impetus for the fundraising effort and also an array of prioritized specific projects. In effect, the Needs Assessment provided the substance of what eventually became a five-year fundraising effort which set as its goal $307,000,000 to be raised from a combination of public and private sources.

THE CAMPAIGN

The library's fundraising campaign was initiated in 1985 and continued through 1989. The goal of the campaign was to raise $307,000,000, half from public sources and half from private sources. Among the several specific objectives were the following: an examination of current programs and possible new directions and initiatives for the library; an estimate of the amount of new operating, capital and endowment funds which would allow the library to plan for stability and development during the campaign and beyond; and the creation of a presentation that would establish a convincing case for government and private funding sources, both current and future.

In brief, the campaign had to attempt not only to remedy past problems, but also to form a base for future programs and fundraising efforts. (One of the more significant accomplishments of the campaign has been its ability to increase the number of individual contributors from a few thousand to more than 40,000 individual annual contributors.)

A second important result of the Needs Assessment effort and the campaign was that institutionalized planning was recognized as a process that is continuous and draws on the experience and expertise of staff and management.

THE CASE STATEMENT

The planning and prioritizing of the Needs Assessment effort produced a massive document entitled "Rebuilding the New York Public Library: A Plan for Recovery, Consolidation and Progress,"[1] which included concise statements describing hundreds of discrete projects and efforts and their costs. These ranged in scope from capital projects costing millions of dollars, endowed chairs for specific collections, funds to support term projects (e.g., cataloging backlogs), and funds for new initiatives (e.g., enhanced conservation services). The cost of the complete package of identified needs was enormous, totalling more than a billion dollars.

This amount obviously was far beyond the library's ability to fundraise; therefore, a consultant was hired to help assess the level of giving which the library could realistically expect to achieve from the various funding sources. He advised that with a five-year project, the maximum expectation would be about $300,000,000. The task then became one of reviewing and reordering previously established priorities to reduce the overall size of the campaign. This proved not to be as difficult as was initially thought, primarily because of the thorough and very detailed data gathering and analysis done during the Needs Assessment phase. An interesting and important result of this phase of planning was the definition of the types of funding that would be included in the campaign since, to a large degree, the types of funds sought determined the most appropriate funding source. Four distinctive types of funds were identified:

1. *Endowment*
   - Unrestricted endowment—to secure the financial base of the Library's operations generally.
   - Restricted endowment—to guarantee current levels of operations or funding for specific activities, e. g., collection development.
2. *One-time or term projects*—e. g., eliminating cataloging arrearages in Roman alphabet.
3. *Annual needs*—funds to support essential ongoing operations during the campaign, e. g., hours of service.
4. *Capital needs*—e.g., the renovation of a branch library.

The next step was to create a campaign budget which would identify the discrete projects and efforts included in the campaign with an indication of the most probable source of funds for each project. As stated earlier, the campaign was designed to be an effort drawing on both public and private sectors. Eventually, the planning process yielded the allocations of fund types by source, as shown in Figure 1.

The final step in this campaign planning process was the preparation of a document entitled "The Campaign for the Library: Rebuilding the New York Public Library—A Future for Our Past."[2] (1985) This document has been distributed widely to potential funding sources. It describes in simple terms the significance of the library on local,

FIGURE 1.

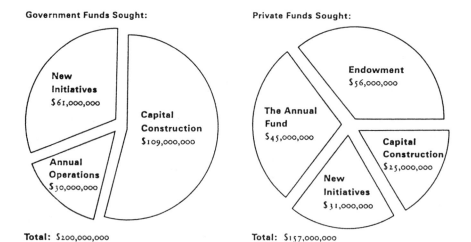

Government Funds Sought:

New Initiatives $61,000,000

Capital Construction $109,000,000

Annual Operations $30,000,000

Total: $200,000,000

Private Funds Sought:

Endowment $56,000,000

The Annual Fund $45,000,000

Capital Construction $25,000,000

New Initiatives $31,000,000

Total: $157,000,000

national and international levels, the reasons for undertaking a campaign, a listing of all projects that the campaign will attempt to fund, and instructions on how to contribute to the campaign for the library. This document has been invaluable in introducing individuals, corporations, and foundations to, and informing them about the library and the campaign.

THE CAMPAIGN EXPERIENCE

Conducting a campaign requires special planning skills and an unknown degree of luck. The first challenge in implementing a campaign effort is to assemble staff who have the necessary experience and training. Such staff members are difficult to find, expensive, and hard to hold, since they are in short supply and eagerly sought after by other institutions. The NYPL created two separate offices to coordinate its fundraising. One, the Government Affairs Office, deals exclusively with governmental bodies and was charged with raising $150,000,000 from government sources. The second, the Development Office, deals with all other initiatives and was charged with raising $157,000,000. The cost of both of these offices was included as part of the total cost of conducting the campaign. During the course of the campaign, the Government Affairs Office was staffed at a level of three to five persons. The Development Office had a staff that ranged from a low of 20 to a high of 32. As a general rule of thumb, a campaign should cost about 10% of the stated goal. The cost of the campaign described herein was less than 3 percent. It must be remembered, however, that the direct costs of the campaign are only a part of the overall or real costs of conducting a campaign.

PRIVATE FUNDRAISING

Private fundraising is an art requiring a wide array of skills and talents: understanding and interpreting the needs of the library; writing about them in an eloquent and convincing manner; organizing and orchestrating a wide range of affairs (e.g., dinners, tours, receptions, etc.) ; and matching donors and needs.

Much of this work has to be done by the professional fundraiser. Staff participation is critical but also quite costly. The demands on staff, especially senior staff, are significant and, more often than not, these responsibilities are added on to already busy schedules. The range of additional duties includes: briefing campaign staff (because of turnover, this almost becomes an ongoing effort); assisting in the preparation of proposals; giving tours to prospective donors; and attending what sometimes feels like an endless round of receptions, dinners, and parties.

In 1988 more than $104 billion dollars was given by private individuals and philanthropic organizations in the United States. During the past eight years, there has been a steady and very impressive growth each year in charitable giving. However due to revisions in the U.S. tax law in 1986, the annual growth in the amount given has leveled off. Additionally, because of the squeeze on charitable organizations by the government, the competition for funds has become increasingly competitive. This does not bode well for the future of private giving.

All of this organized effort may be fruitless. A potential donor, who may have been extensively cultivated with the expectation that a large contribution would be forthcoming, may decide without warning or reason not to give. One's only recourse is to smile and go on to another potential source.

PUBLIC FUNDRAISING

Raising money from public sources (e.g., city, state, or federal governments) is quite different from raising funds from private sources. In one sense, it is less expensive and less time-consuming. Generally, one prepares a proposal, submits it, and then waits for a response. The long period of cultivation, typical of private fundraising efforts, is avoided. However, when approaching government sources, one usually works within very strictly defined guidelines controlling the type of effort that the agency will consider. These guidelines greatly influence the nature of the project to be submitted. Proposals usually must include a great quantity of detail about what is to be done, how it is to be done, and the cost of doing the work. This requires detailed planning and documentation well in advance of project submission. Proposals are usually reviewed by panels of experts who take great pride in their ability to ferret out of proposals minor ambiguities, which the proposing institution often must explain.

Government agencies prefer to fund proposals which fall into two general categories. The most popular are proposals seeking funds to be used as "seed money" for new initiatives or for term projects. Almost without exception, funding for ongoing operations will be rejected. Government agencies are also good sources for money for capital construction.

IMPLEMENTING AND INTEGRATING CAMPAIGN RESULTS

Ultimately, one of the most difficult aspects of fundraising is doing what one has proposed or set out to do. In the NYPL Campaign, for example, the time that elapsed between defining and prioritizing needs and actually being able to start working was several years.

In the following paragraphs are descriptions of some of the more important experiences gained in conducting the campaign.

Stability and Dynamic Planning

Over time, circumstances change; therefore, previously identified needs may change, thus requiring a reevaluation and possibly a reassessment of priorities.

For example, during the early 1980s, processing of books into the collections was an urgent library need given high priority. By the mid-1980s, funds to acquire library materials became an urgent need which required a reevaluation of campaign priorities. Though it is essential that planning be dynamic during the course of the campaign, changes in needs and priorities can have an adverse impact on fundraising efforts. Cultivating fundraising sources is arduous, time-consuming, and risky. Therefore, one should avoid changing or altering defined, prioritized needs. Fundraisers should generally maintain stability in terms of campaign objectives.

The lesson that should be noted here is that the definition of needs should be done at a fairly general level to allow for maximum flexibility for later planning and implementation. Needs statements, however, must be specific enough to avoid the temptation for fundraisers to be totally opportunistic in terms of fundraising approaches. Stated somewhat differently, fundraising staff should be given a fairly strict, stable focus for their fundraising activities. If allowed to solicit monies without these limitations, funds may be accepted for projects which do not fit an institutions's priorities. The first objective for a fundraiser is to ensure that the institutions's needs are matched to donors' interests. If there is no clear match, then the fundraiser should attempt to cause the donor to change, not the institutions's priorities. To do otherwise inevitably ends up with the institution receiving funds to work on projects which do not contribute toward its objectives and may, in fact, work against the institutions's objectives and mission.

Projects that Appeal

Raising money for specific purposes also poses problems. Donors in general are not terribly knowledgeable about libraries and how they operate. It is difficult for them, for example, to understand the need for and cost of adding a book to the collection. Therefore, donors are rarely eager to give money for unglamorous activities such as checking in books, or binding books for the shelves.

Donors want to give money for something that they know and understand, and for efforts that they can be proud of and for which they receive recognition. These desires do not necessarily coincide with the library's objectives. A common way to interest a donor in an unglamorous project is to offer the donor a naming opportunity, that is, to name a room, a collection, a chair or position. Naming to acknowledge a gift, however, is fraught with problems and probably should be avoided if at all possible. There are only a finite number of rooms, collections, and positions that can be offered for naming. And, since naming is usually permanent, an institution soon runs out of naming possibilities. Of greater potential importance is the fact that a named entity, such as a collection, cannot be merged, eliminated, or reorganized. This restriction can seriously hinder future planning efforts.

The "Term" Project

Many efforts appropriate to a campaign are temporary and project-oriented. This means that temporary staff must be hired and space located and prepared to carry out the project. Planning a special project is never exact or entirely predictable. In the case of a major campaign effort, attempting to define and plan a variety of projects which are to be implemented at a later date can greatly complicate matters.

If at all possible, campaigns should be kept simple; they should focus on capital projects. But, needs go beyond simple capital projects. Thus, other kinds of projects will have to be planned. A word of advice is in order here. Campaign funds almost never match a project's scope precisely. Often, several sources of funds must be pooled to make up a special project budget. In addition, monies are pledged and received on different schedules, making it difficult, if not impossible, to plan and conduct the project efficiently. And finally, projects almost always require more work than was anticipated. But perhaps the most vexing problem connected with a term project is how to deal with what we have come to call the "Cliff Problem." Once a project is completed or project funds depleted, what does one do with the special staff that was hired? There is no simple and certainly no satisfactory solution to this problem.

CONCLUSION

By all standards, the campaign has been a success. The campaign goal of $307,000,000 has been achieved. The effort has been beneficial in ways that we had not been able to predict in advance. The needs assessment that preceded the effort forced the library to review critically its mission and to assess its needs. The campaign itself involved staff at all levels in interpreting the library and its services to funding sources and, in so doing, caused the library to have to identify its users and to evaluate their needs. This has, in turn, allowed the library to rethink many of its services and policies.

Library staff have developed a different attitude toward the future. Too often, in the past, the staff simply assumed that funds would be found to support library programs. They now are aware that they must become involved in the effort to raise those funds. This new attitude has caused the staff to evaluate more the range and quality of services the library offers, and to become more aware of users' needs.

The trend in the United States towards pressuring cultural institutions to become more self-supporting and to compete with other social programs for funding will continue. Public libraries, if they are to remain vital and responsive, must realize this, aggressively find ways to promote their importance, and actively cultivate new and innovative sources of funding.

References

1. The New York Public Library, "Rebuilding the New York Public Library: A Plan for Recovery, Consolidation and Progress," New York, 1984.
2. ———, "The Campaign for the Library: Rebuilding the New York Public Library—A Future for Our Past," New York, 1985.

The Multitype Library System and Its Political Environment

Janet M. Welch
Executive Director, Rochester Regional
Research Library Council

INTRODUCTION

On an otherwise sunny June morning in 1988, librarians in New York State paused to consider another cloudy report on the state's financial situation. "Facing Up To State Budget Pain" was the apt title of the *New York Times* editorial that morning. By the time the editorial appeared, library advocates knew that the sufferers would include their libraries and their users. Those library organizations most dependent on state funding, including multitype library systems, would be among the first to feel the pain.

The *Times* editorial was not the end of the story. In a sequence of events typical of the drama, complexity and uncertainty of the political environment in which multitype library systems (and other types of library systems) obtain their funding, the situation in New York continued to deteriorate. The headlines which followed the editorial highlighted the story: "Tax Receipts Fall Short"; "Additional $400 Million Shortfall Is Found"; "$900 Million Shortfall Leads To Finger-Pointing"; and, finally, perhaps the most descriptive headline, "Capitol Mirages."

The pursuit of adequate funding by library system advocates in the halls of local or state legislatures (and Congressional office buildings) is among the most visible and important activities of multitype networks. Efforts to obtain enabling legislation, service improvements and increased funding from local, state, and federal sources are an aspect of the external political environment of multitype systems.

This article examines the politics and support of multitype library systems. It will review the external political forces which surround and influence multitype library organizations—ranging from the political policy agenda to categorical funding. It will also review their internal political characteristics—ranging from representation to fragmentation.

Definitions, Goals and a Common Vision

The dramatic growth in the number and activities of multitype library organizations since the 1960s necessitates a review of definitions. Over 7,000 libraries and library systems belonged to at least one network in 1987. A 1986 report by the Association of Specialized and Cooperative Library Agencies, American Library Association, identified 731 organized cooperative groups; 36% of these groups were multitype cooperatives. Multitype library cooperatives have experienced a 164% growth, from 102 reported cooperatives in 1979 to 269 reported in 1986.[1]

The definition of multitype system or network employed in this chapter will be the definition used in *Standards for Multitype Library Organizations*: "A formal organization that has more than one type (i.e. academic, public, school and special) of independent and autonomous libraries working together for their mutual benefit."[2] This article will not focus on large bibliographic utilities such as OCLC; instead, it will emphasize the political environment of the numerous multitype cooperatives serving member libraries in states, sections of states, and metropolitan areas (which often cut across state boundaries).

While multitype organizations vary widely and are difficult to characterize within a single definition, they share some common attributes. Establishment of most multitype organizations has been driven by complex user demands and financial pressures within individual libraries. All multitype library organizations seek to improve access to information and library collections, all draw on a rich and unique history of cooperation in the library community, and all have responded to the needs of their members to bridge the "natural, economically-driven gap between what librarians feel is right for their own institution and what promotes the greater good."[3] To meet these needs, multitype library organizations establish member services which often include: interlibrary loans; coordinated reference services; shared access to electronic databases and automated library services; union lists of library materials; delivery; common interest groups of staff members from different libraries; coordinated collection development; and continuing education for librarians.

Local participation and membership governance are viewed as

essential ingredients in the provision of these cooperative library services, particularly when network members are individually responsible to a wide variety of institutions, corporations and public agencies. The result has been the establishment in the United States of a large number of diverse multitype library organizations, each of which is responsive to the service needs of its own membership. The distribution of federal funds for multitype library cooperation (LSCA Title III) through each of the fifty states has also fostered this diversity.

The large number and wide variety of multitype library organizations, coupled with limited public resources, have tended to preclude the establishment of a single national multitype network. According to the Library of Congress Network Advisory Committee's "Library Networking: Statement of a Common Vision," ". . .the diversity among libraries and other information providers, and the variety of political factors influencing them is so great as to make impractical a monolithic nationwide network."[4] Instead, in the absence of a single national network, most multitype library organizations subscribe to a common vision, which includes the national goal of a diverse but coordinated structure of networks, based on "active research, rapidly developing technology, collaborative leadership, common standards, and shared communications. . ."[5] These factors, it is hoped, will provide the means by which an interlocking series of local, state, regional, and international relationships will be capable of serving the nation's information needs.

Multitype library organizations function within this broad context of goals and common visions. The support needed to achieve these goals is dependent upon and closely related to the political forces, both internal and external, which surround and characterize the organizations.

EXTERNAL POLITICAL FACTORS

To survive and flourish, multitype library organizations must operate successfully in a complex external political arena. In the United States, political power is very broadly distributed. Interest groups such as librarians must try to influence both the legislative and the executive branches of national, state and local governments. The separation of power among the three branches of the federal government and the division of power between the federal government and the states are precautions taken against the concentration and abuse of power. However, the broad distribution of power in the American system has also fostered and reinforced the growth of many independent and competing interest groups. It has made the task of influencing legislative priorities a time-consuming and difficult one, particularly for multitype library organizations, which often cross traditional political and geographical boundaries.

The Political Policy Agenda

Many multitype library organizations obtain at least part of their financial support from members and users; usually controversial, fees for services are not uncommon. However, ongoing funding from local or state tax revenues is often needed to provide organizational continuity, basic administrative services, and flexibility in serving a diverse group of libraries and users.

To achieve stable support from the public coffers, the multitype library organization must begin with the problem of getting on the political policy agenda of lawmakers on the local, state, and federal levels. Only a few items of the many proposed to legislators actually become part of the political agenda; still fewer are enacted. Multitype library organizations get on the political agenda by presenting to legislators an easily understood solution (cooperative effort) to a real problem (access to information resources) faced by large numbers of people.

Unfortunately, the services of multitype library organizations may seem distant from the everyday needs of legislators because many services are provided to member libraries rather than directly to users. The problems multitype library organizations seek to address may not seem as urgent to legislators as those involving crime, drugs, and other "high-profile" issues. According to Robert Preston of the U.S. Department of Education, "Libraries should be dandelions living on the land with the rest of the weeds rather than orchids needing classy loam and climate control."[6]

Convincing legislators and other decision-makers of the value of cooperative library services is an important external political activity of the multitype organization's board, staff and members. Testifying at hearings, issuing press releases, and formally visiting legislators are only the visible surface of this legislative effort. Multitype library organizations must also understand and use the informal, invisible network of pressure, control and power in state and local politics.

For example, at the state level, informal agreements between legislators in both houses and between the legislature and the governor are common and may establish the general outlines of resource commitments for an entire legislative session. It is vital to know about and gain access to the informal network of legislative leaders (and their aides) who will help to develop general state policy favorable to libraries and who will actively promote library legislation. Membership in this informal network often crosses party lines. Contacts in the informal network must be developed and nurtured so that legislators will consult trusted library leaders in developing a legislative package favorable to libraries.

Problems of Funding: Categorical Aid

Legislative advocates for multitype library organizations who gain the trust of legislators and are able to influence the contents of library legislation soon encounter additional questions involving the types of library programs to be funded. Most librarians and trustees in multitype library organizations (and in other types of library systems) prefer general organizational support which allows the organization to set its own priorities and choose its own services. However, legislation often focuses on easily described solutions to particular problems. The result can be "categorical" funding which is limited to one aspect or category of the multitype library organization's service program (such as delivery of library materials to the elderly). Project grants, which fund short-term programs or start-up costs, are another type of categorical funding.

Categorical funding presents numerous problems. Project grants tend to favor those well-established organizations which are adept at grantsmanship, and single-service grants tend to skew local priorities by diverting organizational resources into what may be low priority (but well-funded) services. Categorical funding may sap an organization's strength with the red tape involved in applying for, administering and documenting numerous, separate and, sometimes, short-term service programs.

The problems of categorical funding are compounded by ambiguities in the definitions and the implications of such programs. The definition of a "narrow" or "categorical" program depends on the context of the legislation—and the viewpoint of the legislator. When librarians propose a bill, they often do not wish to have legislators add or substitute their own categorical programs for broad-based, general support of systems and networks. However, when library supporters try to get library programs included in comprehensive educational or cultural legislation, they may find themselves accused of promoting "categorical" or narrow programs.

In *Governing America*, Joseph Califano, Jr. (former Secretary of the U.S. Department of Health, Education and Welfare) states: "The proliferation of narrow programs, however well-intentioned, each with its own legislative authorization or separate funding, has gone too far."[7] Many librarians and administrators of cooperative programs would agree with this part of his statement. However, he goes on to note that: ". . .metric education, homemakers' courses, ethnic studies, environmental courses, and various literacy and library programs, for example, symbolized the ability of each group to get from a pliant Congress what they weren't able to get from a state legislator. . ."[8] In this context, library programs were viewed as narrow, categorical intrusions by a special interest group.

In fact, categorical funding is often a necessary component of legislative success in the multitype library organization's political environment, particularly for establishing and maintaining popular services when no other source of funding is available. Legislators may use categorical programs to promote their own political interests or to address their own social concerns in a bill originally created by professional librarians or state agencies. Categorical programs are used in negotiations between different parties or houses of a legislature and may become part of the legislative compromises needed to obtain passage of a bill which benefits multitype library cooperation.

INTERNAL POLITICAL FACTORS

These external political forces and realities must be balanced and integrated, in the multitype library organization, with another series of political forces—the internal issues of coordination, representation, equity, governance and administrative power. The development of organizational support, the formulation of organizational policy and the exercise of organizational power are political activities which characterize all organizations including multitype library organizations.

Structure: Coordination, Centralization and Dismemberment

The competing internal forces of consolidation and fragmentation are an inescapable characteristic of multitype library organizations. In the more colorful terms of Alexis de Tocqueville, ". . .single nations are led toward centralization and confederations toward dismemberment."[9] Multitype library organizations are subject to these same forces of centralization and dismemberment as they seek to achieve a balance between individual library interests and common goals achieved through shared services. For example, the current trend in libraries toward purchasing cataloging data from vendors and loading it into stand-alone systems threatens to dismember resource sharing programs which depend on shared bibliographic and holdings data.

Historically, attempts to merge individual libraries into a single large unit to achieve greater efficiency, economies of scale, collection strength and visibility have succeeded only in a very limited number of locations.[10] However, it also became apparent in recent decades that self-sufficiency could not be attained by any single library. Technological advances and the flood of print and non-print materials fostered new patterns of library organization. Instead of merging libraries, larger service units were achieved through cooperative systems, comprised of separate individual member libraries.

In these cooperative library systems, each participating authority continues to operate its own library. The system is created and governed by the participating authorities; the system, in turn, depends on the participating authorities to carry out its programs.

The cooperative structure is used to foster a sense among its participants of common interest in the affairs of the group and of individual responsibility to see that the common activities are efficiently and fairly administered. Multitype library organizations, in pursuit of the common good, rarely have the funds to purchase all shared services needed by participants. Usually they depend heavily on a sense of common interest and agreement of participants to commit their own institutional resources to achieve common goals. A governance structure which is close to and responsive to the participants is an important characteristic of successful multitype library organizations.

However, the cooperative, participatory structure which characterizes most multitype library organizations is a mixed blessing. Despite its advantages and assets, the cooperative participatory method of governance carries a price tag. Many individual institutions must consent and cooperate before the multitype organization can function at all. Often prolonged deliberations and negotiations precede any action. The organization relies heavily on compromise which sometimes inhibits rapid action and delays or prevents the emergence of necessary standards of uniformity. Insoluble disputes within the participatory governance structure may even lead some members to withdraw entirely from the organization.

Despite the forces of fragmentation, most multitype library organizations have survived, many have thrived, and new ones have been established (primarily through state-level legislative action) in recent years. However, whether they function at anywhere near the optimal level has continued to ignite controversy. One of the most enduring subjects of dispute has been the fair and equitable representation of member interests in the governance structure of the multitype library organization.

Governance: Representation, Equity and Power

A basic component of organizational power in multitype library systems is found in the organization's governance structure. The ideal governance mechanism for these organizations has been clearly established: "The Multitype Library Organization shall have a formal governance structure that provides for representation of all types of libraries that are members of the organization."[11] However, achievement of the ideal to the satisfaction of all members is a difficult task.

Libraries participating in multitype organizations have widely varying missions, goals and responsibilities within their own institutions. Type-of-library differences (academic, school, public and/or special) are further complicated by issues of public and private, profit and not-for-profit. Size, organizational structure, and geographic location of members may also vary considerably. These differences are part of the strength of the multitype library organization, but they also make it particularly difficult for individual members to achieve fair and equitable representation in the organization's governance structure.

Representation of particular library interests and resolution of conflicts of interest among members of the governance structure are also thorny issues. Decisions made by the governing board are seldom neutral. They almost always benefit some interests, libraries or services more than others, entailing costs that are rarely equally distributed among the organization's participants. Ideally, multitype library organization governing board members should represent the cooperative interests, not the libraries from which they originate. However, the internal needs of a governing board member's own library versus outside network responsibility is a conflict not easily resolved. Often a dual role for governing board members, representing both the organization as a whole and their constituent groups or libraries, is accepted.

Relationship Between Governance and Administration

Another potential political conflict involves the division of organizational power between the governing board and the administration of a multitype library organization. The relationship between governing board and administrator is always difficult to define precisely and takes many forms in multitype organizations.

In theory, the board sets the policy, and the administrator and staff implement the policy. However, in many situations it is impossible to make a sharp, clear distinction between policy formulation and administration. Often the board and administrator implicitly limit the types of issues defined as "policy" and expand the types of issues defined as "administrative." In practice, decision-making is often dominated by the administrator of the multitype organization who has the power to control information, has extensive technical expertise, and is charged with educating the board. Unlike board members, the administrator devotes to the issues at hand his or her entire occupational attention. Although multitype library organization administrators are legally subordinate to the boards which are responsible for hiring them, they exercise considerable de facto power through greater expertise in systems issues, longer tenure than most board members, control of issues to be placed on the board agenda, and full-time involvement in their work.

Indeed, the success of the multitype organization administrator in securing and maintaining financial support depends largely on an appreciation of and ability to function in the context of the political process. As Oliver Garceau stated in *The Public Library and The Political Process* more than 40 years ago: ". . .public administration at every level is a political process, operating within a matrix of political forces, adjusting to and building on dynamic political change in the community."[12]

When governing or advisory groups are comprised of member library administrators and technical experts, the tendency toward dominance by politically astute administrators in multitype library organizations is curbed. Another and very common pattern of multitype library board composition, a mixture of professional librarians and lay people, tends to reduce conflict of interest problems but may increase the dominance of the administrator because lay board members may not be well-versed in library issues.

Regardless of the particular composition of its governing board or the sagacity of its administration, the success of a multitype library organization in gaining support depends on a diverse but cohesive group of members actively seeking equitable means to solve common problems. De Tocqueville captured these essential elements in *Democracy in America*: "For a society of nations, just as for one of individuals, there are three main elements which give it lasting power: the wisdom of those associating, their individual weakness, and the smallness of their numbers."[13] Multitype library organizations continue to be influenced by these same forces.

CONCLUSION

The budget predicament in New York State described at the beginning of this chapter has yet to be resolved. This situation is not unusual in the political world of multitype library system funding where "politics and economics are but two sides of the same coin."[14] Complex and politically-based funding dilemmas are an inevitable characteristic of the quest for support of cooperative library services.

To date, multitype library organizations, along with the rest of the library community, have managed only to nibble at the fringes of public resources. The central question of how to get the public to allocate the resources needed to meet the library and informational needs of our citizens remains unanswered not only for multitype library organizations, but for the entire library community.

There is no reliable flowchart for the complicated and untidy political process in which multitype library organizations operate. However, it is clear that participation in the intricate legislative ballet, along with attention to the closely related internal political issues of governance and equity, are essential to the survival and success of multitype cooperative services.

References

1. Dottie Hiebing, *Regional Library Cooperative News* (Winter 1989) p. 2A.
2. American Library Association, Association of Cooperative and Specialized Library Agencies, Standards for Multitype Cooperatives Ad Hoc Subcommittee, *Standards for Multitype Cooperatives and Networks, Draft,* (December 1988) p. 3.
3. Pat Molholt, *Library Networking: the Interface of Ideas and Actions* (June 1988), p. 10.
4. Library of Congress, Network Advisory Committee, *Library Networking: Statement of a Common Vision,* 1987.
5. *Ibid.*
6. Ronald Preston, "Defining A Federal Role For Libraries," *The Bottom Line,* 2:3 (1988): 14.
7. Joseph A. Califano, Jr., *Governing America* (New York: Simon and Schuster, 1988), p. 274.
8. *Ibid.*
9. Alexis de Tocqueville, *Democracy in America* (Garden City, New York: Anchor Books, 1984), p. 366.
10. David Shavit, *The Politics of Public Librarianship* (New York: Greenwood Press, 1986), p. 84.
11. American Library Association, *op. cit.,* p. 4.
12. Oliver Garceau, *The Public Library in the Political Process* (New York: Columbia University Press, 1949), p. 239.
13. Alexis de Tocqueville, *op. cit.,* p. 376.
14. Michael Parenti, *Democracy for the Few* (New York: St. Martins Press, 1977), p. 4.

The Community College Library and Its Political Environment

Ngozi Agbim
LaGuardia Community College

The community college library, like its parent institution, is created to be all things to all persons. In its most comprehensive form, this type of library is usually called the Learning Resource Center ("L.R.C.") which comprises several elements in various combinations depending on its local circumstances. "No other type of educational institution in this country is asked, indeed expected, to provide so much diversity in programs and resources for so many different demands."[1] Today, the L.R.C. is faced with the challenge of providing more and more programs and services with less and less funding. To deal effectively with this unenviable situation, the director and his or her staff must wake up to the fact that their library is no longer a passive, service-oriented social institution, but is now a political animal which must devise strategies for dealing with the various elements in its obviously political environment. For the sake of convenience, these elements can be collapsed into internal and external forces.

Internal elements of the community college library environment include the library faculty and staff, the classroom faculty, the administrative officials of the college, students and other users. Externally, the L.R.C.'s political environment consists of businesses, organizations and community groups served by the parent institution, the appropriate governmental and other funding agencies, professional associations including those residing within the university system or the district to which the library and/or the parent institution belongs, among others. The library faculty members, led by the director, should always be mindful of how they and the library are perceived in their political environment. Critical factors include their ability to perform a service, to communicate and cooperate effectively with others, to create good will, to generate income, and, most importantly, to be accepted as professionals.

It is common knowledge to most academic library directors that in times of financial crisis, the library is one of the first to get the axe. Why? Most college officials do not quite understand the role of the library. "College presidents support the educational program as it creates enrollment and graduates. They recognize the athletic program as enhancing enrollment, creating school pride and recognition, and winning trophies. They value the registrar's office for reporting college enrollment as either up or down and the business office for reporting college affairs as either in the red or black. . ."[2] Some perceive the library as a black hole which swallows all investments made in it and generates little or no tangible returns. This unfortunate image of the L.R.C. must be avoided or reversed where it already exists.

The L.R.C. director's role as the chair of an important academic department is a leadership role. The director devises and implements mechanisms for effective representation of the L.R.C., its programs and its faculty, to the college administration including the deans and the other department chairpersons, all of whom constitute the chief policy-makers of the college.

The library director should never tire of explaining and reiterating, as needed, the role of the library in the college. Nothing should be taken for granted, because many of our colleagues do not understand what we do. But they do know that the academic library is mandated by law and therefore cannot be eliminated altogether. It behooves us then to keep proving our value.

Just as the heads of other departments/divisions of an institution constantly make known achievements, goals and aspirations in their areas, the L.R.C. director should never miss an opportunity to present appropriate library programs to the administration. In this way, the library is seen as a real partner with other academic areas of the college.

In addition, the library director must insist (tactfully of course) on library representation in the development of all new programs, masterplans, task forces, etc. Thus, the library representative not only learns firsthand the activities planned by other parts of the institution, but is afforded the opportunity to give input regarding necessary funding for library resources and services required for the implementation of the new program or project. In most community colleges, the L.R.C. has, or should have, a mandatory seat at the institution-wide curriculum committee. This library position, if creatively filled, should afford the L.R.C. the opportunity to work closely with the creator of each new course or program, thus promoting faculty dependence on the library.

Furthermore, the L.R.C. must watch out for, and be prepared to participate fully in, such important regular college events as the annual goal-setting and budget request process. It is incumbent upon the director to ascertain where the college is headed each year, both from the administration's perspective as well as from the academic chairpersons' and also from the division heads' points of view. This will enable the L.R.C. to develop written annual goals and objectives that fit into, and relate to, major college and academic department goals. Accordingly, funding such library goals becomes easily justifiable at budget request time, not only because the library programs relate closely to the college program (and are therefore understandable), but also because the administration is not hearing of them for the first time.

Besides projecting the library services and materials to the college administration, the director must seek opportunities to showcase the professional caliber and contributions of the library faculty.

During annual college meetings to consider faculty reappointments, promotions, etc., presentation of library faculty should focus more on their achievements and contributions to the teaching/learning process. This is the language most clearly understood by the community college policy-makers. Appropriate examples of joint projects accomplished by library and classroom faculty should be used as illustrations of the candidate's professional involvement in the academic life of the college.

In addition, the director must endeavor to conclude the presentation of each candidate for promotion or reappointment with a concise statement of the unique quality of the individual which makes him/her a powerful asset to the institution. Again, the rationale here is to prove to the administration that librarians contribute at least as much as the classroom faculty in carrying out the mission of the institution, and therefore should be treated fairly with regard to distribution of the college budget.

Besides establishing a program for effective relationships with the college administration, the L.R.C. must also develop collegial relationships with other important groups on campus. These relationships become even more crucial when one considers that "competition for budget allocation will not diminish"[3] and in most instances, increasing funding for one area of the institution such as the L.R.C. means reduced allocation to another area.

The director must be quick to notice and make connections with other information-related centers, laboratories, and resources which abound on the community college campus under a variety of names such as: "Career and Transfer Resource Center," "The Archives," "Instructional Materials Production Center," "Microcomputer Labs," and a variety of departmental labs and mini collections. Attempts should be made to design mutually beneficial relationships with the directors or coordinators of such facilities, focusing on service to students as the common goal of both the L.R.C. and the facility in question. Quite often the L.R.C.'s offer of professional assistance in processing, organization and control of materials to these facilities is highly appreciated. However, the director must be sure to formalize, in writing, and clear this mutual arrangement and agreement with the appropriate dean or head of department in order to facilitate the provision of necessary funding for the project at the proper time.

As faculty throughout the college develop grant proposals involving media or instructional technology, the media services unit of the L.R.C. should work with the grants office to provide consultation with all grant developers regarding equipment and software needs to be incorporated into the proposal. This process not only increases the inventory of audiovisual equipment for instructional purposes but ensures the purchase of brand names for which parts and repair manuals are easily obtainable.

In this information age, the L.R.C., like other academic libraries, has a great potential for leadership in introducing the faculty and staff of the college to new technologies. Faculty workshops to introduce the online public access catalog, online database searching, periodicals indexes and other collections on CD-ROM, demonstrations of videodisc and various technologies are usually a very effective means of exhibiting the centrality of the L.R.C. to the life of the community college. As Clyde Hendrick aptly writes, "The library should develop a strong proprietary/ cooperative role toward new forms of information systems as these systems emerge. If it is a medium that has to do with knowledge or even 'mere information,' the library ought to be there ready and waiting to take over."[4]

Whether the L.R.C. is viewed favorably by the college administration and the other social/political entities on campus depends, to a large extent, on the political climate within the L.R.C. itself. The key ingredient to success is the L.R.C. faculty's attitude toward library programs and its adaptability and willingness to cooperate with the director in following the lead of the parent institution, even when such a move means going against the grain. The director's self image must be, by virtue of his/her position, first among equals, in need of the support and collaboration of the L.R.C. faculty and staff in carrying out L.R.C. programs. Consequently, the director must create a warm, caring, supportive and open atmosphere in which colleagues are willing to contribute ideas and carry out experiments without fear of failure.

Various types of activities should be undertaken at the L.R.C. level to prepare the library faculty to function effectively on the college-wide level. At regularly scheduled staff meetings, the director should brief the faculty on what the college is currently doing and the mood of the times as expressed by the college administration and academic departments. Brainstorming sessions may be held occasionally, to determine which L.R.C. programs will enable it to participate fully and actively in the targets set by the college. The L.R.C.'s involvement in intra- and inter-campus efforts must be carefully coordinated to ensure adequate representation of the library on the most important and appropriate committees, projects, task forces, etc. Library faculty assignments to these bodies should take into consideration each individual's skills and abilities and should aim at giving him/her a good opportunity to gain visibility by working with classroom faculty colleagues and/or college administrators. The L.R.C. can establish itself as a force to be reckoned with if its faculty members play leadership roles on campus.

Furthermore, the director must be available to lead, direct, motivate, support, review progress and encourage each library faculty member to excel in the tasks undertaken. It is also very useful to recognize promptly and commend achievements of the library faculty.

Finally, librarians must be encouraged and expected to act independently on creatively proselytizing the L.R.C. programs through their professional contacts and the services they offer. Each must form the habit of recognizing and seizing opportunities to project the L.R.C. as the nerve center of the institution.

An illustration of staff success along these lines took place quite recently at my L.R.C. The Humanities Department was cosponsoring a statewide annual conference of Teachers of English to Speakers of Other Languages (TESOL). The media librarian heard about it and offered not only to provide all the equipment needed by conference speakers, but volunteered to organize and chair a panel discussion on a topic very relevant to the theme of the conference, but which the conference planners had not considered. Her program was titled "Instructional Technology: What's New in AV Resources." The panelists included: herself, showing and discussing segments of films on the nature of language; another librarian, her immediate assistant, demonstrating videodisc technology; a television studio technician, also of the media services unit of the L.R.C., discussing production of instructional tapes; and an English as a Second Language ("ESL") instructor, showing the use of video in the ESL classroom.[5]

A reference librarian in the same institution learned about the conference and volunteered a selected bibliography of relevant resources to be included in the conference package for the conferees.

Needless to say, these efforts were highly appreciated and applauded by the colleagues in the Humanities Department and by over two hundred attendees from all over New York State, many of whom called back for more information on materials presented by the L.R.C. In a letter of appreciation to our media librarian, the conference organization co-chair stated: ". . .Not only did you and your staff see to it that presenters had exactly the items of equipment they had requested, on time and in place as needed, but you even managed to oblige an errant publisher who had left his computer behind! And managed to organize the second most popular presentation at the conference (right behind the plenary speaker!). . ."[6] Opportunities of this kind show up from time to time in many community colleges. The L.R.C. faculty must be alert, able, and willing to use them to best advantage.

End users—regular students, handicapped students, foreign students and adult students in extension programs—can be great allies to the L.R.C. Library services to these groups should be personalized by the acquisition of state-of-the-art equipment and materials and serious outreach efforts.

A strong, diversified bibliographic instruction program is one sure way of demonstrating the great value of the L.R.C. to its users. A credit-bearing bibliographic instruction course is especially useful in generating full-time equivalents ("FTE's") for the college, and obtaining additional funding for the L.R.C. The key to success lies, of course, in careful planning, securing an appropriate staff remuneration agreement from the academic dean, and program implementation on the part of the director and the faculty.

Cutting essential L.R.C. services in times of austerity is viewed by some, as an effective means of forcing fiscal officers to allocate more money to the library. Hendrick observes: "I have seen faculty scramble to protect the library during a budget crisis: there is an implicit attitude that the library is unable to scramble for itself. . . Like a fancy kept lady, the library must be protected and cared for. It seems not to occur to many faculty that the library could be aggressive in looking out for its needs and could administer real pain if its needs are not met."[7]

It is not clear what Dr. Hendrick means by "administering real pain." Whatever the situation, the last items to be tampered with should be essential and popular services. Cutting L.R.C. service hours, for instance, in time of austerity, should be done only as a last resort. This service, in particular, is essential in the urban commuter-type college where students attend at specified periods and must accomplish all their academic needs in fixed blocks of time.

Externally, the L.R.C., following at the heels of its parent institution, must develop cordial and fruitful connections in the surrounding environment.

Librarians must keep a watchful eye on new trends in higher education and be in a position not only to discuss them intelligently as appropriate, but more importantly, to discern ways of adapting these trends to the L.R.C. services. In 1979, an official from President Jimmy Carter's administration observed that the greatest challenge facing higher education was the profile of students being admitted to college campuses: "Reading skills of college students are not what they once were. Where yesterday's college student came to college predisposed to reading and libraries and took pleasure in them, today's college freshman is said to arrive on campus with an experience of 15,000 hours of television viewing. . ."[8] The public community college with its open-door policy, is not at all alien to this type of student body and has been in search of new ways to educate this population.

The same government official further challenged academic libraries "to use new technologies that make reading seem as much fun as television viewing. . .," "to be creative in finding ways to store and retrieve materials consistent with realistic space demands. . ." and to "persuade presidents, foundations, and legislators to increase their budgets."[9] A creative and ingenious use of the instructional technology unit of today's L.R.C. by librarians and classroom faculty, working cooperatively, should help achieve these results. Again, librarians must lead the way by finding out how "learning laboratories" are structured and utilized in other community colleges.

In addition, the L.R.C. must participate fully and actively in regional consortia, cooperatives and professional associations which facilitate sharing of resources and creation of national standards and guidelines pertaining to academic library services and operations. The more librarians participate in shaping national/regional policies, the better L.R.C. interests will be represented, and the more powerful our justification.

Where the community college is part of a district or university system, the librarians should be equally active in district/university-wide library and non-library related groups. Both the L.R.C. director and his or her faculty must seek positions and serve with distinction on the appropriate task forces, ad hoc committees, etc.

This has several benefits: it serves as professional development for the individual and makes him or her well known in the larger community. It gives the chancellor and the fiscal officers of the system an impetus to think of the library during the budget allocation process to the individual colleges that make up the system. It affords the L.R.C. representative an opportunity to push for funding for a system-wide establishment or project of tremendous value to individual libraries in the system. The City University of New York Office of Library Services is a good illustration. The CUNY Council of Chief Librarians, of which this writer is a member, lobbied for this office which was finally established and staffed with an Associate Dean in the Office of the Vice

Chancellor for Academic Affairs in the 1982–1983 academic year. Since then, this office has been successful in instituting valuable library investments—very much needed by CUNY libraries but unaffordable on an individual basis.

The major projects include the Union Catalog of all CUNY library holdings and more recently, CUNY + Plus, an integrated online system based on Northwestern University Online Total Integrated System (NOTIS). The seed money for these projects was provided partly by individual institutions. Obviously, many of the library directors in CUNY would have had difficulty in obtaining institutional funding for integrated library systems. Moreover, outside funding sources are not inclined to award grants for capital equipment purchases.

Other noteworthy elements in the L.R.C.'s external political environment are the businesses and organizations served by the parent institution. Depending on the local situation and arrangement, an "enterprising" L.R.C. director may want to follow the trend of offering academic library services to outside users. "Database searches, computerized interlibrary loans, translation service and literature searching service, can become revenue sources. This revenue may be important to the library's ability to continue to provide quality service to the outside users" and to upgrade the skills of personnel assigned to the task."[10] While paying for information is still widely debated, each L.R.C. should follow the norm in its own locality.

Finally, the L.R.C. has an ongoing relationship with outside funding sources such as the federal, state, city and private agencies, which have been, in recent years, tied very closely to the collective decisions and activities of the parent institution. The U.S. Title III grants, for example, which in the past provided funding for library equipment and personnel, can no longer do so directly. Each institution is required to submit one grant proposal. The L.R.C. has to compete then with other projects on campus. The college administration makes the final determination as to what projects should be represented in the proposal. Again, intracampus politics rears its head, and the L.R.C. has no choice but to continue marketing its services, programs and future aspirations in terms of their necessity for, and close relationship to, the teaching and learning process.

CONCLUSION

In sum, what has been outlined in this paper is not intended as specific solutions for fiscal problems in every community college library. It is meant rather, to suggest possible approaches for dealing with the various elements in today's L.R.C. political environment which exert influence on its funding. Joyce Edinger asserts that there exists a relationship between a library's contribution and the amount of funding it receives for its programs and services.[11] The L.R.C. should then not only endeavor to maintain its status as an indispensable source of information and services on campus but also, make those services known, appreciated and used by the college community.

The approaches suggested here for marketing the L.R.C. within the campus political environment are highly selective. They are based on the author's experience as a library administrator, rather than on a formal review of the literature. The reason for this approach is suggested by Lynden and Leonhardt. Their conclusion is that administrators have little time for writing papers about what one does to survive. They may consider these activities too mundane to be of any interest outside one campus. It may be impolitic in fact, to call too much attention to the very successes that one has had in competing for departmental funding.[12] But, as we evolve away from the traditional academic library model to today's more complex and institutionally-involved L.R.C., creative strategies must be devised to enable L.R.C. to deal successfully with the challenges of its political environments. Given the current fiscal crisis and the challenges of educating today's nontraditional college student, the L.R.C. must be willing to communicate to the market and to create within its institution the desire and the need for services which it can provide.

References

1. Marilyn Searson Lary, "Introduction," *Library Trends* 33 (Spring 1985): 439.
2. Edwin M. Ashley, "Reflections on the Image of the L.R.C.," *Community and Junior College Libraries* 1(Spring 1983): 1.
3. Gloria Terwilliger, "Forecasting the Future of Community College L.R.C.s," *Library Trends* 33 (Spring 1985): 536.
4. Clyde Hendrick, "The University Library in the Twenty-first Century," *College and Research Libraries* 44 (March 1986): 130.
5. The New York State Teachers of English to Speakers of Other Languages, *Eleventh Annual Applied Linguistics Winter Conference*, 28 January 1989, Long Island City, N.Y. Brochure.
6. Sally Mettler, Letter to Louise Spain. 12 February 1989.
7. Hendrick, *op. cit.*, pp. 129–30.
8. Mary F. Berry, "Higher Education in the United States: The Road Ahead," *College and Research Libraries* 40 (March 1979): 104–105.
9. *Ibid.*
10. Thomas C. Harris, "An Interlibrary Coordination Extension Program "

Austerity Management in Academic Libraries, John F. Harvey and Peter Spyers-Duran, eds. (Metuchen, N.J.: Scarecrow, 1984), p. 101.

11. Joyce A. Edinger, "Marketing Library Services: Strategy for Survival," *College and Research Libraries* 41 (July 1980): 328.

12. Frederick C. Lynden, and Thomas W. Leonhardt, "Intra-Campus Coordination and Austerity Management," *Austerity Management in Academic Libraries*, John F. Harvey and Peter Spyers-Duran, eds. (Metuchen, N.J.: Scarecrow, 1984), pp. 132–133.

The Private Academic Library and Its Political Environment

John Lubans, Jr.
Associate University Librarian
Duke University

Sheryl Anspaugh
Adjunct Professor
School of Library and Information Sciences
North Carolina Central University

I. INTRODUCTION

Politics, according to the nineteenth-century satirical writer Ambrose Bierce, is a noun representing a "strife of interests masquerading as a contest of principles."[1] While it would be curmudgeonly to accept this definition fully, it is true that as is the case with other organizations, opportunities for politics abound like ivy on the private campus. Here are some examples:

- Just prior to the library's annual budget review, your Provost sends you data from his budget officer showing that your staff's salaries are "significantly" superior to those paid at other private colleges. The source of the statistical data is not provided.
- A black student at your predominantly white university expresses dismay to the President about the inadequacies of the black history book collection. "It's third rate and all my friends say so, too!" he states. The university is under a self-imposed mandate to recruit black faculty.
- The faculty are at it again. You've opposed issuing keys to them for after-hours use of your branch located in the Arts building. It

houses the library, art faculty offices, studios, and classrooms. You've been successful for several years in staving off what is for you a serious security breech; however a new chairman of the art department has just arrived, and you're not sure where she stands on keys.

Our response to these situations rife with politics will have much to do with their resolution, which can be either favorable or detrimental to the library program and individual careers. This paper accepts the inevitability of the political process in the private setting, illustrates its existence through examples and the systems model, and advises that the process can be used or ignored with appropriate consequences. We provide an economic bent to our analysis through our implicit regard for the budget as a political tool.

II. THE SYSTEMS MODEL

This discussion of the open-systems model identifies the many reasons why politics is an unavoidable part of organizational life. Also it shows why there are differences, overt and implicit, among organizations, whether they are public or private. Such differences require varying political styles to advance the library's agenda on the campus.

Each organization, like each individual, has a unique personality. But when we talk about organizations, we often use the terms organizational culture or climate instead of personality. Both people and organizations, however, are a product of their environment, beliefs and values, experiences, and the influences of key people. Michael Beer depicts the elements of an organization's personality in his "social systems model of organization."[2] (See Figure 1.) He contends that while the organization is a distinct unit, it is not an island; rather it is encompassed by and interactive with its *environment* (including, for example, the economy, technology, geographic location, and socioeconomic variables). In *The Social Psychology of Organizations*, D. Katz and R.L. Kahn refer to such a model as an "open" system because of the impossibility of separating the components of the organization's culture from outside influences.[3]

In Figure 1, the *source of human input* is the hired staff (librarians, support staff, students) and to some extent the users of the library. They all have personalities, values, needs, educations, and skills that interact with the organization. Katz and Kahn conclude that because these people, too, are a product of *their* environment, they transmit these values to the organization as expressed through the *people* component. Of course, negotiating their different values is a political process.

The component, *structures*, includes the formal aspects of an organization that are designed to bring about desired behavior and results. *Behavior* of people and the *process* by which they interact is the means

FIGURE 1. A Social Systems Model of a Private Academic Library

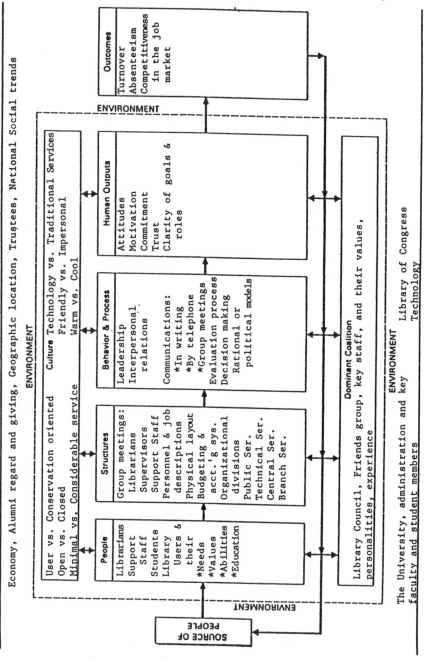

Adapted from: Michael Beer, *Organization Change and Development: A Systems View?* Santa Monica, California: Goodyear Publishing Co., 1980, p. 19.

by which work is coordinated and converted to results. The more congruent the behaviors and interactions with the organization's purpose, the more effective the organization will be in achieving its goals.

Human outputs will determine, in time, the health of the organization. There is a link between the condition of an organization's human assets and its performance. The organization does produce an *outcome* that, in the long run, is dependent on how well it has been interacting with its environment. For instance, the quality of work life will determine how well it will be able to attract and motivate employees and what kind of employees they will be. Each of these components makes up the organization and contributes to the perception of its organizational *culture* (e.g., warm and friendly or impersonal; formal or informal).

Finally, the key to the library's existence and success on campus is the congruency of its *dominant coalition* with the remainder of the campus, particularly the administration. Within the organization or social system, there are shared beliefs and feelings which form the *informal* (frequently unwritten and unstated) set of ground rules about what is expected and what will be rewarded. The closer the dominant coalition reflects the informal image of how these people see themselves, the more successful the library will be in its academic community, or within the social-political system of the university.

Obviously, and of direct relevance to campus politics, the more beliefs and values that members of the organization understand and share about how to do things, or what is right or acceptable, the stronger the culture will be. Culture performs a number of functions. It creates the organization's goals and values, by which success and worth are measured; it prescribes the relationship between individuals and the organization; it indicates how behavior should be controlled in the organization, and what kinds of controls are legitimate or illegitimate; it shows employees, trustees, university administrators how they should treat each other (e.g., honestly, competitively, or collaboratively); it establishes appropriate methods of dealing with the external environment (e.g., exploitative, negotiative, explorative); and it determines which qualities and characteristics of the organization are valued or vilified and what the rewards or punishments may be.

The systems model applies to any size unit, whether it is a department within the library, a library within the university, or a university within the community. One advantage that the private university has over its public counterpart is the smaller size of its community. Usually, it has fewer people with whom it must deal in terms of alumni, and in its funding process. A private university does not have to subscribe to state values nor compete with a multitude of state agencies for state monies. Thus its *dominant coalition*, those people who are responsible for key decisions, can be a fairly small circle. Trustees for a private university are often appointed to cultivate philanthropic sources. Thus, their agendas closely match those of the organization, and their efforts result in the continued strengthening of the organization's principle and capital. By their very nature, private universities can actually encourage what in a public institution would be labeled inbreeding, which is often regarded as politically unpalatable.

III. THE BUDGET AS A POLITICAL TOOL

Usually, the budget is an accumulation of past decisions, many of which are political. Although the cumulative nature of the budget may blur its political antecedents, their presence is worth noting. Because much of the library's budget is allocated to long-term staffing, the political decisions surrounding staff can inhibit the budgetary flexibility which most libraries seek. In addition, historical commitments to materials can restrict movement of dollars from waning academic departments to those on the rise. The entrepreneurial spirit found at many private institutions (remember that many were founded by businessmen who struck it rich) may introduce the permissive, even cavalier, attitude on the private campus that once money is raised for a program or an institute, library resources support will automatically follow. Partly, one suspects, the upper administration promotes this entrepreneurial spirit, because they too may share in the perceived benefits of expanding programs and initiatives: new students, grants, faculty, and prestige. This phenomenon can be found at public institutions as well, but the entrepreneurial spirit seems to flourish especially well in the capitalistic soil of the private setting.

Obviously, the library needs to be involved and aware of new ventures on campus. Involvement is not meant to derail healthy initiatives but rather to help assure their success. It is not uncommon for a new program to falter because existing resources could not meet great expectations. Occasionally, librarians are deliberately excluded or unheeded because of their tendency to exaggerate the cost of new ventures; presumably, they do so to guarantee adequate support. Such exaggeration can sabotage future projects. Proposal makers will avoid librarians, whose prognosis of excessive costs may sink their idea. Naturally, the adroit librarian will seek to keep information needs fairly high in the consciousness of the major players on any campus. The ways to achieve this visibility include: reporting structure; proposal review; membership on the upper councils where approval of any such venture is gained; and, most important, a communication link with the grapevines and the numerous other informal communication patterns found on any campus.

Some large private schools subscribe to the funding notion of "every tub on its own bottom." This refers to the Harvard model wherein each unit is responsible, more or less, for raising its own revenue and spending it. It is a decentralized model, usually including a separately administered library, that rewards the successful and flushes out the insolvent and may add to the penurious condition of some of the liberal arts. It should be noted that this model works best for professional schools.

A political conflict arises when a presumably shared resource such as the library restricts use by anyone other than the primary clientele. For example, it is galling for a professor in the liberal arts school to be denied borrowing privileges at one of the professional school libraries; this is also true for students who do not attend the professional school. The resulting campus perception of the restrictive library is that of a selfish child who refuses to share his or her toys while expecting others to share *theirs*. The central librarian usually finds trying to change such behavior politically explosive; few victories result for the common good. Compromises over service policies may be the best that can be achieved. After all, the "tub" model is supposed to let you keep what you raise; it's *yours*. A few libraries have come out with some gains from the tub model, primarily in "charging" (full cost recovery) the professional school for any central services provided. This could be applied to a shared online catalog and its costs.

To some extent, this political happenstance can also be found in centrally budgeted and administered branch libraries. Because of their location (i.e., in a teaching department among the *primary* clientele), most policies will first benefit the local users. Politically, the branch librarian is pulled in two directions: between the local teaching/research department and the central library. The most successful branch librarians generally choose, in practice, the departmental side on policy issues but also give the impression they are strongly supportive of the central library. As a result, *negotiation* best describes the relationship between the central library and its branches.

In technical and political terms, the private budget differs significantly from that of the public sector. Some of these differences follow:

1. *Line item vs. bottom line*: This item and salary savings, which follows, may make the greatest difference between the budgets of the private and public sectors. The private sector's bottom-line approach to budgeting permits latitude in moving monies from the various categories, ranging from binding to books, office supplies to student-worker budgets, travel to computer services, and so forth. In contrast, a strict interpretation of the line-item budget found on many public campuses restricts monies in one fund even if other funds zero-out in midyear and would benefit from receiving surpluses from other funds.

In the bottom-line approach, there is an implicit trust (until it is violated) that the manager knows best how to spend the overall budget and that the unexpected is best dealt with when it happens rather than delaying a response until the next budget process. Because the potential for abuse is greater, the bottom-line approach is politically more inflammable. A potential blunder such as moving book dollars into the staff lines can lead to a loss of political confidence in the library's leadership. Also, there is a trade-off for this flexibility. The library has no protection from local budget officers reducing certain parts of the budget. As line items in the public sector, these allocations would be politically inviolate.

2. *Salary savings*: Another feature that differentiates the budget of the private from that of the public sector is the former has greater access to salary savings or lapsed salary dollars that come from vacant staff positions. Many state schools simply do not permit the return of such monies to the individual unit; rather, they accrue to the general fund of the state. On the private campus some—if not all—of these dollars do return to the library. In good times, such dollars can fund new initiatives; in bad times, they provide a much needed buffer between having to do without and doing something.

These dollars are always at risk because others on campus perceive them as a windfall budgetary item not really needed by the library. Those with budget authority who are under relentless funding pressures for new university initiatives may look covetously at these funds. Therefore, it is not unusual to see some inroads made by the central budget office into salary savings through a tax in the form of a partial formulated return of lapsed salaries. The political aspects of defending this important resource should be obvious. Fortunately, other large employers on campus will resist giving up *their* salary savings so the library will not be alone in resisting centralization. Of course, it is mandatory to make budget policy officers aware of the university benefits achieved from salary savings in the library.

3. *Proximity of the budget office*: Unlike state legislatures and their budget-making activities, which sometimes occur in a distant capital city, the private budget decision makers reside on the campus, usually only a short walk away. In this setting, because all interested parties have ready access to the budget makers, the politically naïve may be trampled. The opportunities to influence the budget are considerable. All of the senior officials, with the possible exception of members of the trustees, are available to the librarian who seeks to cultivate a relationship.

We have seen several libraries adopt an adversarial role with the budget agencies and other university units. In our experience, this is suicidal. Such a tactic is seen as a defensiveness about the status quo when questions are raised about the budget, a refusal to keep important university officials informed and an unwillingness to accept a team member's share to help resolve university problems. An example would be to stonewall or otherwise ignore the dilemma faced by the university in recruiting special types of faculty. Often a position for the spouse may be part of the recruitment package. If the spouse is interested in working in the library, is it politically astute to show the unfairness, impracticality, and impossibility of doing this?

4. *Budget time line*: Generally, the budget time line for the private institution is much shorter than the one for the public institution, because there are fewer groups with approval authority in private institutions. Funding issues can be addressed rapidly, sometimes more than once a year, if dollars are available in the private sector. Politically, this applies to all units on campus. Thus, it behooves the library staff to stay in the fray of budgetary competition throughout the year.

5. *Iron triangle*: This now familiar term, thanks to Ronald Reagan, can be applied usefully to the private campus. It refers to the recognition that the agency, (the library) has a relationship with its client groups (students, faculty, friends) that extends to the university administration (the funding agency). If functioning well, the iron triangle protects the agency from punitive measures such as takeovers or budget cuts, usually undertaken by the funding agency. The concept is applied in the following case.

> One of the professional schools with a large commitment to computers, networks and "information management" regards the central university library as decidedly backward in its information services and facilities. If only the library staff (and budget) could be managed under a new vision, wondrous things would happen. The librarian, aware of the overtones and overtures being made, and, at the same time, genuinely appreciating the idea, broaches it to the Library Council, which is a group of a dozen faculty and students that meets monthly for a working lunch. Members are appointed by his boss, the Chancellor. Only one member is associated with the school seeking to take over administration of the library and its budget. They hear the pros and cons and recommend that this course not be pursued because too few gains are visible and, in fact, numerous liabilities may exist. With interest the Chancellor politely accepts the recommendation, including the dissenting minority view point of the one professional school representative and denies the takeover request.

This should show the impenetrability of the iron triangle by someone outside the triangle. Also, forces within the triangle, such as student and faculty groups and friends, can help keep the budget agency from eliminating services or cutting back in other areas. If well used, they can influence budget decisions to the benefit of the library. There is a risk, however, that a clientele group will rise in opposition to a sensible and objective library decision, such as closing the card catalog upon automation. Backing off and running a redundant service, at least temporarily, may be the library's only recourse to avoid too much damage elsewhere.

6. *Endowments*: Until relatively recently, endowments (i.e., cash gifts that are invested; the resulting income is *in addition to* the operating budget) were more often sources of income for private campuses than for public ones. Public universities, as recently as this decade, found fundraising especially difficult; according to would-be donors, the state was supposed to be subsidizing the educational mission. Thus, state university libraries were bereft of any endowment income. One could say that the private sector had the lion's share of this market. Although this is changing somewhat, many private libraries have endowment income that can provide dollars for both collection building and spending at the librarian's discretion. When it exceeds the operating budget, such money can provide needed equipment and serve as a carryover buffer at the year's end. From time to time, some attempts will be made to reduce the operating budget by some amount of the endowment income. Standing fast against such an incursion will often prove to be a challenge. Fortunately, other units on campus that benefit from endowment income will mount the barricades as well.

IV. CONSEQUENCES

Someone once remarked pejoratively, "When you lie down with dogs you get up with fleas." The political interpretation might be that you also get their allegiance. On the private campus we believe politics are a normal and healthy human aspect of the organization, which are practiced at all levels of the organization. (The stakes just get higher as you ascend the administrative ladder.) Politics exists everywhere, at all times; it is as natural and *necessary* a process as breathing. Participatory management efforts encourage it in our libraries, both public and private.

On some campuses, we have on occasion witnessed a seeming disregard for political influence. This studied and self-destructive indifference might be best illustrated in the way some librarians make decisions. The rational decision-making model can be compared against the darker political model. The idealized rational decision-making model is usually used to reduce risk, an objective not to be dismissed out-of-hand. This model, and the several other problem-solving versions of it, has as a basic tenet that there is one best answer, preferably untainted by politics. One such model recommends as a first step: "Ascertain the truth." Adherents of the rational approach usually do not mention that all that is needed to carry it out is ubiquity, omniscience, and omnipotence.

The political model (dare we call it irrational?) admits to shortages of time, energy, and brain power and depends on observation, intuition, readily available information, compromise, and a strong awareness of the politics surrounding most issues. A slavish adherence to the rational approach can result in a solution that, while admirable for its precision, simply won't work in the real world. Problem-solving models that recognize political influences usually include a final step (or two) that evaluates alternatives based on environmental conditions and studies what it will take to win acceptance of a solution.

While neither the rational nor the political model guarantees action-oriented results, we believe the political model will guarantee more successful solutions than will the rational model because of its implied coalition building and the seeking of acceptable solutions for all participants.

References

1. Ambrose Bierce, *The Devil's Dictionary* (Cleveland, Ohio: World Publishing, 1911), p. 258.
2. Michael Beer, *Organization Change and Development: A Systems View.* (Santa Monica, Calif.: Goodyear Publishing Co., 1980), p. 19.
3. D. Katz and R. L. Kahn, *The Social Psychology of Organizations*, 2nd ed. (New York: Wiley 1978), pp. 2–4.

IV

Supporting America's Libraries: Getting the Job Done

People in Washington Who Work for the Funding of Libraries

David R. Bender
Executive Director
Special Libraries Association

Although the United States has entered a new era in which President George Bush has declared himself an "education president," funding for libraries and library programs is at an all time low. In the eight years of the Reagan presidency, proposal funding for library programs has been consistently zeroed out of the executive budget, only to be replaced by the friends of libraries who serve in Congress.

Ironically, the only library initiative to be introduced during Ronald Reagan's eight years came in June 1988, when then Senator J. Danforth Quayle (R-IN) introduced the Library Improvement Act (LIA) at the request of the Reagan Administration. LIA was to be funded by $76 million. The Administration believed that LIA was a better approach than the existing funding mechanisms which supported library programs and services. In actuality, LIA was the first library program proposed by the Reagan Administration. The proposed bill did not meet with much enthusiasm or support from the library community. Yet, after seven years of struggle, many must have thought that their message was received: the federal government has both a role and obligation to fund library programs.

When one examines people in Washington who work for the funding of libraries, some of the most critical individuals, particularly in the years of the Reagan Administration, have been those senators and congressmen who have supported funding for library programs. One of the library community's fiercest advocates is Congressman Major Owens (D-NY). The only librarian in Congress, Owens made clear his support for libraries in a letter to his constituents in mid-1986. The letter expressed sentiments which reflect the attitudes of many library proponents who sit in Congress:

> The Congress is finally waking up to the unique and essential contributions that libraries are making to the well-being of the American people. The task ahead of us now is to maintain the momentum and work to translate this new awareness into the increased federal support that libraries need to improve and expand their services in the years to come.[1]

The effectiveness of members of Congress in securing funding for library programs cannot be underestimated in light of the Reagan Administration's desire to curtail funding. Among the library community's staunchest allies include Representatives Don Edwards (D-CA), William Ford (D-MI), William Natcher (D-KY), and Frank Annunzio (D-IL), who currently serves as the Vice Chairman, Joint Committee on the Library.

On the Senate side, library supporters are found in Senators Mark Hatfield (R-OR), ranking minority member of the Appropriations Committee, Claiborne Pell (D-RI), and Wendell Ford (D-KY), who is serving as the Chairman of the Joint Committee on Printing. Unfortunately, in the 1988 election, the community lost a valued friend in the person of Lowell Weicker, former Republican Senator from Connecticut.

The library community has endured years of little or no support from the Executive Branch. Under the leadership of the self-proclaimed education president, the future of support from the power brokers is still in question. Perhaps the emergence of First Lady Barbara Bush, who has made the eradication of illiteracy a goal of her own, will mark a change in the support of libraries from the Oval Office. At this writing, roles within the Bush Administration are only beginning to evolve and the key players to emerge. The library community can only hope that in addition to friends in the two Houses of Congress, that others will tilt the balance in favor of continued and increased funding for library programs in the next four years.

THE KEY PLAYER IN THE DEPARTMENT OF EDUCATION

The first federal library programs can be traced to 1956 when the Library Services Act (LSA) was created to serve the needs of citizens living in rural America. Since that time, LSA has evolved and in 1964 became the Library Services and Construction Act, better known as LSCA. This evolution marked the first time that funds were included in a federal budget for library construction. Over the last 25 years, the other titles of LSCA have been added to support resource sharing, networking, assistance for native Americans, foreign language materials and literacy.

Another funding source for libraries came in the form of the Higher Education Act (HEA) which supports the technological and training needs of the nation's research and academic libraries.

Together, these two acts are primary sources of federal funding for libraries; however, federal support accounts for only about four percent of library funding.[2] Excluded, of course, is funding for our national libraries: the Library of Congress, the National Library of Medicine, and the National Agricultural Library.

Support for school library programs is found in the Elementary and Secondary Education Act (ESEA) Title I program. This program was amended by the Hawkins-Stafford Amendment of 1988 which repealed the Education Consolidation and Improvement Act (ECIA) and reconstituted funding under ESEA Chapters I and II. Among the items funded are books, reference materials, computer hardware and software, and staff and curriculum development.

Leading the support of libraries in Washington is Anne J. Mathews, Director of Library Programs, Office of Education Research and Improvement (OERI) at the U.S. Department of Education. Dr. Mathews joined the Department of Education in 1985. Her work for libraries has touched nearly every aspect of the profession. She was a professor at the Graduate School of Librarianship and Information Management at the University of Denver and was program director of the Central Colorado Library System. She has served as a consultant to both the U.S. Intelligence Agency and the U.S. Agency for International Development.

Library funding obtained through LSCA and HEA support nearly every type of library. This funding has been "a major stimulus for the development of libraries and library services in this country."[3] According to Dr. Mathews, "For this reason, Library Programs must be intellectually, as well as financially responsible for the quality and usefulness of the projects funded."[4]

The work of Dr. Mathew's Library Programs staff cannot be overstated. For example, staff maintains close contact with state LSCA coordinators. Staff review and provide advice on both the annual and long-range plans prepared by state LSCA coordinators. Each state coordinator will annually prioritize the use of LSCA funds allocated in the categories mandated by Congress (i.e., programs for the aging, literacy, handicapped or institutionalized individuals). Library Programs' staff provide support and suggestions to state LSCA coordinators in a variety of specialized areas—community information referral centers, services to the elderly, the disadvantaged, the handicapped and literacy, to name a few.

Library Programs' staff administering HEA funds will maintain close contact with university grant project coordinators in order to advise on project plans and assure that funds are efficiently utilized.

A vital role handled by OERI's Library Programs is that of recommending improvements to library services to both the Secretary of Education and the library public. Dr. Mathews works closely with the Chiefs of State Library Agencies, the National Governor's Association, and the Education Commission of the States.

Among the crucial stated roles of the Library Programs are:

—Implement federal policies and programs to reform, revitalize, and revolutionize library and information services as we move into the next century;
—Provide creative guidance to programs based on the assessment of regional and national needs and on knowledge of current trends in research and practice;
—Collaborate with other Department of Education units and national library associations to extend and enhance the impact of program funds;
—Coordinate and gather statistics needed to plan for library development;
—Conduct research to establish a foundation for improved delivery of information services, and;
—Assume a leadership role on international issues, problems and cooperative programs related to library and information science.[5]

Obviously, OERI's Library Programs staff plays a key role in assuring the success of library programs funded by the federal government while recommending needed improvements to decision-makers at the federal and state levels. Additionally, Library Programs staff gathers and distributes information vital to the continued funding of library programs and serves as a vital bridge between the library community and the federal bureaucracy.

NATIONAL COMMISSION

Public Law 91–345 established the U.S. National Commission on Libraries and Information Science (NCLIS) in 1970. Included in the enabling legislation were eight functions, including advising the President and Congress on issues relating to libraries. NCLIS plays a vital role in advising Congress on reauthorization of LSCA and HEA, as well as on any legislation with implications for the library community.

Funding for libraries and related services was among the issues discussed at the first White House Conference on Libraries and Information Services in 1979. As the library and information community prepares for the second White House Conference, funding can be expected to emerge again as an issue. It is likely that a recommendation to the President and Congress will call for guaranteed funding for library programs and services from the federal government.

Susan K. Martin, NCLIS Executive Director, is an advisor to the Executive and Legislative Branches of the federal government and, therefore, is an important link between the library community and the decision-makers in government.

OTHER FEDERAL RESOURCES

While the bulk of funding for library programs at the federal level comes from LSCA and HEA, some 12 other agencies of the federal government provide limited funding in 65 programs for library-related projects, individual graduate study, or research. Among the agencies with monies for such projects are: the National Archives and Records Administration; the National Endowment for the Humanities; the National Science Foundation; the U.S. Departments of Agriculture, Commerce, Health and Human Services, Housing and Urban Development, and Labor; and the U.S. Information Agency.[6]

A publication of the American Library Association, "Federal Grants for Library and Information Services," is a handy guide to lesser known sources of funding for projects not covered by LSCA or HEA. Types of assistance available, eligibility requirements and deadlines will, of course, vary from program to program. A second, comprehensive source for federal grant programs is the *Catalog of Federal Domestic Assistance*, a looseleaf publication published by the Office of Management and Budget.

THE ROLE PLAYED BY LIBRARY ASSOCIATIONS

An important third core of individuals involved in the funding of libraries consists of library associations. The two associations most actively involved in library funding issues and legislation are: the American Library Association (ALA), which established its Washington, D.C. office in 1945; and the Special Libraries Association (SLA), which relocated to the nation's capitol in 1985 in order to step up its educational activities in the legislative arena.

Eileen D. Cooke, Director of the ALA Washington office, is well known in the halls of Congress. Priority areas of concern for ALA include access to information, legislation and funding, intellectual freedom, public awareness, personnel resources, and library services, development and technology.[7] Ms. Cooke and her staff of legislative experts track and support nearly all of the vital library legislation as it affects the funding and support of this nation's libraries. The *ALA Washington Newsletter* focuses specifically on legislation pertaining to the library community. Included in most issues, a chart on the "Status of Legislation of Interest to Librarians" will at a glance provide a capsule of current legislation and where each bill rests in the legislative process. The library and information community has come to rely on this chart and the invaluable information and insight provided in the newsletter.

Hearings on Capitol Hill will find Ms. Cooke, Carol C. Henderson or Anne Heanue, all from ALA's Washington Office, testifying or giving statements of support from the library point of view.

While ALA presents the public, school, and academic library's position, the Special Libraries Association (SLA) represents the special library perspective. Less visible in supporting general legislation for library programs such as LSCA or HEA, SLA is a vocal advocate for legislation supporting the library community, including implementing pilot projects which supply information to depository libraries in electronic formats, or decrying the cutback in data gathered from the 1990 census. While not supporting funding issues *per se*, SLA plays an important role in supporting library initiatives which further the goals and objectives of the library community at large.

David R. Bender, SLA's Executive Director, is actively involved in the Association's Legislative Agenda and for many years carried the banner of SLA to vital hearings in Washington. Sandy Morton, Director of Government Relations and Fund Development for SLA, has expanded SLA's legislative network to include representatives in each of the Association's 55 chapters and utilizes their specialized backgrounds in a witness pool for presenting and representing SLA's diverse membership on library issues.

Together, ALA and SLA are working partners in assuring that issues of importance to the library community are on the agenda for legislators and that discussion focuses on the unique needs of the library community as it serves the nation.

COUNCIL ON LIBRARY RESOURCES

The Council on Library Resources (CLR) is among the best known private providers of funding for libraries. Founded in 1956 with assistance from the Ford Foundation, CLR helps "libraries take advantage of emerging technologies in order to improve performance and expand services for an increasing number of users."[8]

CLR has been a recipient of funding through the National Endowment for the Humanities and combines that funding with grants from a prestigious assortment of private foundations that support programs which have concentrated in the academic and research libraries because of their key role in collegiate instruction.[9] In its 1986–1987 fiscal year, CLR awarded more than $512,000 in grants and contracts supporting an assortment of academic, public, and private projects. Five areas are of top concern to CLR for funding: research, access to information, bibliographic services, librarianship and librarians, and preservation.

OTHER FOUNDATION SUPPORT OF LIBRARIES

Depending upon the directory selected, more than 260 foundations provide financial assistance to support the needs of libraries and librarians. According to the Foundation Center, 927 grants of $5,000 or more with a total value of $85,861,762 were made in 1985 or early 1986,[10] an impressive show of support.

Not all foundations which support libraries are found in Washington; however, their support is critical to the improvement and expansion of library services. The money provided by corporate sponsors is tremendously significant in the development process.

CONCLUSION

Numerous players work to support the funding of libraries in Washington. They include elected officials in Congress, members of the federal bureaucracy, professional associations, and private institutions.

Regardless of their placement within or outside the political sphere, their interest and support helps to educate and persuade those who are not inclined to support the library community. Together, the library community and these library supporters are partners; their partnership ensures that America's libraries are supported in their educational and community goals.

What does the future hold for the library community? Now, during this "changing of the guard," we must all strengthen and revitalize in order to educate, influence and promote the needs of our libraries. Society faces a multitude of issues which can only be addressed and answered by a modern, well-prepared and well-funded library community.

References

1. Major R. Owens, Letter to Constituents. July 1986.
2. "The Nation's Libraries at Work for You," U.S. Department of Education Brochure, 1988.
3. Elaine Hill, "SLA Interviews Anne Mathews," *Special Libraries* 79 (Winter 1988): 1.
4. *Ibid.*
5. "The Nation's Libraries at Work for You."
6. Shari L. Weaver, *Federal Grants for Libraries and Information Services: A Selected Bibliography*, American Library Association (June 1988).
7. Margaret E. Chisholm, "American Library Association," *The Bowker Annual* (New York: Bowker, 1988), p. 162.
8. Mary Agnes Thompson, "Council on Library Resources," *The Bowker Annual*. (New York: Bowker, 1988), p. 222.
9. *Ibid.*
10. *Grants for Libraries and Information Services* (New York: The Foundation Center, 1987), Introduction.

People Who Work for the Funding of Libraries in the States

Howard F. McGinn
State Librarian of North Carolina

Successful consumer product companies have mastered the art of market segmentation. They know that the most cost effective and profitable way to earn revenue and to increase sales, is to tailor products and marketing campaigns to meet the needs of distinct, identifiable segments of a total market. Libraries, especially public libraries, are in many ways analogous to consumer product companies. Libraries can be viewed as companies that offer services and, as such, are subject to the same market demands and market environment influences as consumer product companies. Libraries face that age-old corporate mandate to earn the highest revenue for the lowest cost.

But how do libraries earn this revenue? What is the library's total market? What are the market segments served by libraries? This essay will use the business practice of market segmentation to discuss library revenue, markets, and market segments. It will explore the common sources of revenue, the total state library marketplace, and the segments of this market.

Viewing the total market of library support in a segmented manner can help library management more effectively invest valuable, finite personnel and financial resources to secure from the community the financial and moral support needed to prosper. The people who work for the funding of libraries in the states face a heterogeneous, massive, amorphous market similar to the one faced by the consumer product producers. Companies that thrive effectively segment this market; public libraries that thrive must have the same ability.

PUBLIC LIBRARY REVENUE

A public library director is constantly selling. Potential customers are found in every part of the community, and, like a profitable company, a good library will have a product or service for each. Moreover, the successful director is an inveterate door-to-door salesperson, a huckster who persistently sells library services to anyone willing to listen to the sales pitch. This director is successful because she or he is always aware of the basic fact of library selling—library sales are counted in tax dollars. One way or another, everyone pays taxes; consequently, everyone "buys" library services. Although the services may not be used by the purchaser, the purchase is nonetheless made.

Access to tax dollars by the library presupposes a willingness on the part of the community to invest in library services. This willingness by the community is similar to the business concept of goodwill. Goodwill is a collection of intangible factors relating to the reputation of a firm that enables that firm to sell its products and increase its earnings. In like manner, a library's goodwill is essential if the community is to decide to increase the library's earnings in the form of increased tax dollars. The library director, then, must work to increase the library's treasury of goodwill.

Goodwill also plays an important part in a library's other staple, revenues from gifts and grants. In this post-Vince Lombardi culture that idolizes winners, gifts and grants will come to the community agency that projects the winning image. A library without sufficient inventory of goodwill will not obtain the large gifts and grants that enable the library to obtain a few frills in its operations. If the library can project an image as the place where society's winners gather, the supplier of a public service that is essential to community survival, then gifts, grants, and, most likely, increased tax dollars will follow.

All of these major sources of revenue are intertwined: tax support, goodwill, gifts, and grants. All depend on the library's management, which must: understand the marketplace of the library; build an image of the library's economic importance to the community; create services to meet the needs of the marketplace; and aggressively sell these services to obtain various revenue. Through the use of market segmentation, a library director can effectively identify specific targets of opportunity to achieve library revenue goals.

LIBRARY MARKETS

The public library's marketplace is, at the same time, a burden and an opportunity. It is a burden because the market consists of everyone in the community. At some point, everyone needs information; thus, each citizen is a potential customer for library services. No library has sufficient financial and personnel resources to meet the universal information needs of its community. So, like Proctor and Gamble, General Foods, and General Motors, libraries have to become adept at dividing the community into manageable parts such as children's services, business services, adult services, and so forth.

The marketplace presents an opportunity for libraries in its sheer size and complexity. The market is almost infinitely divisible into smaller service segments. This traditional segmentation of library services is essentially the same as the market segmentation done by those consumer product companies to sell soap, toothpaste, and cars.

A market segment, according to Philip Kotler, is made up of customers who respond in a similar way to a given set of market stimuli.[1] Markets may be segmented in many ways. Diane Strauss notes that: "Traditionally, such variables as geographic location, age, race, sex, income, peer groups, life style, and political affiliation have been used to identify target markets, but any characteristic that identifies and defines actual or potential consumers can be used."[2]

Market segments are created based on these assumptions:

1. the people in a segment have similar needs to be filled;
2. the people in the segment will respond to marketing efforts in a similar manner;
3. the market segments created can be contacted or reached efficiently and economically;
4. the people in the segment have the resources to purchase the product or service; and
5. the product being marketed will fill the needs of the people in the segment.

The key idea in market segmentation is that by identifying distinct segments of a market, creating services to meet the needs of that segment, and devising special marketing campaigns to sell these services, an organization can produce a higher revenue return than if it attempted to sell to the market as a whole. Simply put, it is the classic notion of "divide and conquer."

Because of the many ways in which a market can be segmented, a company or library must choose "target markets" that will produce the highest return on the investment being made in "attacking" the market.

Target market segments for public libraries will be those that produce the highest amount of goodwill, tax dollars, gifts, and grants. These target markets may not necessarily be the market segments whose members are the most frequent users of libraries. Their importance rests in their potential as library revenue producers.

So, who are the people who work for the funding of libraries in our states? Can they be grouped into target market segments that will provide the highest revenue for the library? Do the segments have that distinctiveness necessary for effective selling? Let's move on, then, to those disparate market segments that provide the library's revenue.

LIBRARY MARKET SEGMENT I: FEDERAL, STATE, AND LOCAL GOVERNMENT

When asked why he robbed banks, the famous thief, Willie Sutton, replied "Because that's where the money is." There is no doubt where the library money is—it is in the banks named Congress, state legislatures, city halls and county governments. The political market segment is a peculiar combination of lifestyle (the politician), geography (state, county, city), and the most important factor of all, demography. Demography dominates because it includes the taxpayers, the people who pay the public library's bills.

In fact, the taxpayer is the real sales target for the public library director in the political market segment. Librarians spend much time courting elected and appointed public officials to assure a constant flow of tax funds, yet the key to influencing that official's decision should be taxpayer pressure in support of libraries. Librarians should always keep in mind that an elected official is constantly marketing a product— himself or herself. When a library devises a way to market the politician to the taxpayer through the politician's support of library services, the important tax dollars will follow. If the politician sees library support having little effect on political self-promotion, few tax dollars will follow.

Obviously, the goal of all of this courting and selling is to acquire state and local tax dollars. In 1986–1987, public libraries received $288,152,000 (7.9 percent) in revenue from state governments, $2,985,618,000 (82 percent) from city and county governments, and $425,000,000 (10.1 percent) from the federal government for all kinds of library service.[3]

But this is a market segment over which librarians exercise little or no control. In 1986–1987, the federal government spent $1,810,006,000,000, yet only $3,639,000,000 (.2 percent) was spent on library programs. In the 1986–1987 fiscal year, state and local governments spent a combined $775,318,000,000, yet only $3,274,000,000 (.4 percent) was spent on public libraries.[4] Why do libraries receive such a miniscule share of tax dollars? The following news item from *Library Hotline* provides a clear answer:

LIBRARY BOND ISSUE DEFEATED IN OKLAHOMA CITY:
Improved streets, bridges and intersections, and drainage bond issues, to the tune of $154,740,000, were approved while the $25,915,000 library bond issue was defeated on January 10 by 62 percent. The money was earmarked to construct a new, state-of-the-art combination library and art/history museum. The bond would not have raised taxes because other bonds were about to be retired. The current library is 34 years old and has 65,000 square feet on five floors—and no parking. Since the library has no money for capital projects, they have to wait for the city to select capital requests, from among all of those submitted by city departments, which will be put in the budget each year. The press was very supportive during the campaign, but a City Council member who was instrumental in getting the library on the ballot felt the economic climate was the cause of the defeat because "People just aren't used to spending money on what they consider 'frills'. We need to educate the public to think of libraries and museums as integral parts of the community, rather than as extras."[5]

What has to be done to effect this change, to alter the political perception that libraries are "extras"? Unfortunately, the first thing to do is break the public's perception of the library as a cultural institution. Linking the library and the museum harms the library. The future for libraries lies in its ability to link itself with "improved streets, bridges, and intersections," with water and sewer systems. The library needs to become part of the local public works infrastructure discussion, to position itself as the community's information public utility, its "information infrastructure," a service the community cannot afford to neglect. If the image of the library can be changed from that of the community's cultural haven, the provider of mysteries and romance novels, to an image of the library as the community's information center, the library can enter the battle for community infrastructure tax dollars on a more equitable basis.

After Reagan became President, tax support of vital community programs was transferred from Washington to state and local governments. This dollar migration has caused severe budget problems in many states and has made the competition for local tax dollars fierce. If libraries are to keep earning tax revenue from state and local governments, library marketing campaigns will need to emphasize the library's utilitarian nature and deemphasize its cultural nature. In times of tight money, taxpayers want tax dollars invested in essential services. Public officials, in turn, will certainly fulfill taxpayer wishes.

The people who work for the funding of libraries in our states are taxpayers. The library that builds strong taxpayer support gets the support of the public officials and the tax dollars. In this period of increased competition between state and local government agencies for decreased tax revenue, libraries must position themselves to compete more favorably with other essential government services. The following market segments are essential in the building of taxpayer and political support.

LIBRARY MARKET SEGMENT II: PROFESSIONAL LIBRARY ASSOCIATIONS.

Like the American Association of Retired Persons (AARP) or the National Education Association (NEA), state and local professional library associations are the lobbying agencies for library support in communities. The American Library Association (ALA) has little or no influence on local library matters. In fact, statewide and local library associations provide the philosophical, financial, and logistical support for ALA Washington efforts.

State and local library associations are a combination of demographic and geographic market segments. The membership list of associations in the typical state includes the following types of organizations.

State Library Associations

Major statewide library associations are multi-type umbrella organizations such as the California Library Association or the Georgia Library Association. These associations, in turn, are segmented by specific types of library services, functions, or markets to be served. Thus, there are special groups that lobby for the support of children's services, government documents programs, technical services, and so forth.

These special groups within the statewide association often have their own constituencies that help the association to pinpoint specific concerns and lobby the community and lawmakers more effectively and economically for the means to solve these problems or to begin new programs. For example, special groups promote access to government documents and information or defend intellectual freedom and oppose censorship. These groups can be very effective because segmenting the library lobbying market allows them to concentrate political pressure, philosophy, and dollars on very tightly defined objectives. Some statewide library umbrella associations have local or regional chapters. These chapters usually mirror the organization of the statewide association. There will be, then, special groups lobbying for their programs on a local basis, supplementing the local or regional chapter's hometown lobbying efforts.

Specialized State Library Associations

Most states have library associations that concentrate on the needs of specific segments of the library community. Examples of these types of associations include the North Carolina Public Library Directors Association or the Virginia Chapter of the Special Libraries Association. These associations function similarly to the special interest groups of the statewide library umbrella associations. They are effective because they have segmented their market and can concentrate political pressure to achieve their goals very effectively and efficiently.

Lay Groups That Support Libraries

Usually made up of non-librarians, retired librarians, or people who have legal responsibility for overseeing library administration, these groups concentrate their efforts on fundraising and political support for libraries. The most common of these groups are statewide and local friends of libraries organizations and statewide library trustee associations. These groups are very important in building support for libraries because they are a means of harnessing representatives from many segments of the community. But these groups are only effective if their leaders are also community leaders. Friends and trustees who are not community leaders will produce no support or tax revenue for their libraries. Thus, it is essential that local library administrators sell the library to their community leaders so that these leaders, in turn, can "buy into the library" and sell the library to the taxpayers and local public officials.

There are other statewide and community trade associations that can be enlisted in the fight for library support. Examples include AARP, associations working for the physically disabled, especially the blind, and school related organizations such as parent-teacher associations.

Local Umbrella Library Associations

Urban and rural areas spawn library associations that primarily serve the social needs of librarians in these areas. Often these local organizations will lobby taxpayers and local public officials for library support or for help in solving local library problems. The Metrolina Library Association is a multi-type library organization based in Charlotte, North Carolina. Because Charlotte's suburbs extend into

South Carolina, the Metrolina Library Association is a true interstate professional association with members in two states. But the Association also includes many rural communities in the Piedmont area of North and South Carolina. As a result, this local association must deal with multi-type library needs in urban and rural areas, small towns and big city bedroom communities, and the taxpayers and local public officials in two states as well as two state libraries. The Metrolina Library Association has been an effective library development and lobbying institution for over thirty years because it is, essentially, a geographically centered organization that concentrates its lobbying and development efforts on a specific geographic segment of the library market.

Many state associations employ professional lobbyists to promote library support in the state legislatures. While some state library agency employees are prohibited from lobbying by state law, other states will register the state librarian as a professional lobbyist. Perhaps it is time for the state associations to emulate the tactics of the most successful lobby of all, the National Rifle Association (NRA). Under the guise of the constitutionally guaranteed right to bear arms, the NRA has successfully—and notoriously—promoted its cause of unbridled ownership of any implement that fires a bullet whether it be an AK-47 assault rifle or a plastic gun that cannot be detected by airport surveillance. Its lobbying effort has been as successful in state legislatures as in Washington. In contrast to the efforts of the NRA, the efforts of national and local library associations appear anemic. Perhaps breaking the aforementioned linkage of the library and cultural institutions will help reorient the perception of taxpayers and politicians. Librarians, in turn, will need to engender the same ferocious zeal displayed defending first amendment rights when the time comes to promote basic—yet essential—issues that sustain daily library operations.

LIBRARY MARKET SEGMENT III: CORPORATIONS AND FOUNDATIONS

For some segments of the library community, especially the academic segment, corporate and foundation giving is the promised land of support. It is almost impossible to enter into planning discussions with academic librarians without the question of grant availability arising. In the world of "soft funny money," foundation or corporate giving is probably the most insecure source of financial support.

Libraries seeking these types of funds are fighting two trends. The first trend is the enormous increase in competition for these dollars. The same federal reduction in local revenue support that has affected state and local tax revenue has caused public and private agencies to deluge foundations and corporations for financial support. A real cause for concern by private academic institutions in many states is the sudden appearance of public academic institutions soliciting funds from those foundations and corporations that, in the past, had given exclusively to private institutions. The second trend faced is the growing amount of non-monetary support given by corporations. The Taft Group in Washington, D.C., publisher of fund-raising materials for nonprofit organizations, does note, however, that overall corporate giving in 1988 increased by 4 percent.[6] Corporate and foundation support has never been a major part of the normal public library revenue budget. But corporations and foundations do account for a substantial amount of financial support of local public library construction projects.

The corporate support market segment is geographic since corporations usually want to contribute dollars to projects in communities where the corporation maintains a headquarters, subsidiary or manufacturing plant. To benefit from this giving practice, the local library administrator should have county and municipal officials appoint local corporate managers to boards of trustees and should liberally salt the library friends leadership with corporate leaders.

The key to gaining corporate support is the answer to the old question being asked by the corporation: "What's in this for me?" The library must assure high local and regional visibility for the corporation if corporate contributions are to be forthcoming. Corporate giving is a kind of corporate advertising and, as with corporate media advertising, the more potential publicity and favorable exposure for the corporation, the greater the chance for the library's reception of a corporate check.

The foundation support market segment will usually be behavioristic or demographic. Foundations like to contribute to institutions or social causes favored by the corporation or person who established the foundation. Finding the right marriage between the local public library and foundation can be difficult. There are, however, a large number of local foundations whose existence are often unknown. These local foundations will concentrate awarding grants to local institutions or to institutions favored by persons affiliated with the establishment or management of the foundation.

MESSENGER TO THE SEGMENTS: THE MASS MEDIA

It is impossible for libraries, statewide or local, to market library programs to taxpayers as a whole or to taxpayer market segments without the mass media, especially the local newspaper. The simple facts are that taxpayers read newspapers, public officials read newspapers, and public officials respond rapidly to newspaper stories that help or harm the image they market to taxpayers. If the local library can maintain a steady drumbeat of local media coverage, especially controversial coverage that reflects positively on the library, political support will follow. The usual library newspaper fare of book reviews and acquisitions lists will not do the job. Libraries need to begin to place stories that emphasize the library's role in the infrastructure. The perception of the library as the community's information public utility will, in the long run, produce much more taxpayer and political support than the perception of the library as the town's cultural haven.

Who are the people who work for the funding of libraries in the states? Theoretically, everyone because a public library must be nonexclusive. But nonexclusivity creates an ill-defined marketplace that makes marketing libraries and library service difficult. This essay has argued that, by using the standard business marketing practice of market segmentation, the market segments that most directly affect the decision of investment of taxpayer dollars can be profitably targeted. This kind of approach may involve risks, but the risks are minimal. The true risk run by public libraries is the risk that they may become irrelevant. They won't disappear; they will just be ignored. By marketing the public library as the community's information public utility, the community's information infrastructure, the library will cause itself to be perceived positively by all. By altering marketing tactics and emphasis to fit the nature of each of the library's customer market segments, the support of the library market as a whole and, as a result, the support of the public officials who invest the public dollars can be achieved.

People invest large amounts of money in essentials. Librarians know the library is essential but establishing this same belief in the marketplace will require a change in thinking and some risk taking. Thomas J. Hennan, Jr., in the May 1988 issue of *American Libraries,* sums this well. ". . .if true leadership is risk taking, the nation's libraries may well be at risk. Many librarians, it appears, are unwilling to even identify, much less take the necessary calculated risks to make libraries truly necessary in 21st-century America. Public libraries may have a future only because they already exist, not because there is any compelling need for them."[7]

References

1. Philip Kotler, *Principles of Marketing,* 3rd ed. (Englewood Cliffs, N.J.: Prentice-Hall, 1986), p. 757.
2. Diane Strauss, "Marketing Fundamentals for Librarians," *North Carolina Libraries* 46:3 (Fall 1988): 133.

3. U.S. Department of Commerce. Bureau of the Census, *Government Finances in 1986–87.* Series GF-87-5 (Washington, DC.: U.S. Government Printing Office, 1988), pp. 2, 46.
4. *Ibid.,* p. 2.
5. "Library Bond Issue Defeated In Oklahoma City," *Library Hotline* XVIII: 4 (January 30, 1989): 4.
6. "Top 20 Corporations in Charitable Contributions," *Library Hotline* XVIII: 3 (January 23, 1989): 1.
7. Thomas J. Hennan, Jr., "Public Librarians Take A Cool View Of The Future," *American Libraries* 19:5 (May 1988): 392.

People Who Work for the Funding of Libraries at the Local Level

Virginia G. Young
Trustee, Public Library of Columbia

The local sources of funding for a public library can be as varied as are the imaginations of the people involved. Whatever the source, however, the funding itself falls into two specific categories. For purposes of separation, these categories can be referred to as "Type A" and "Type B."

"Type A" pertains to one-time funding for a particular project, i.e., funding for the construction or renovation of a library building, the purchase of a major piece of equipment, or for the support of a special programming activity. "Type B," on the other hand, pertains to the general funding of ongoing library operations.

In planning for additional funding, it is important to distinguish between these two funding types. Within a particular category, one individual may be more effective in raising funds than another. For example, a major fund drive requires a different kind of dedication and initiative than a drive for a particular project, which may need an individual who persistently dogs the footsteps of the local legislator until a point is made.

Again, the audience the local initiator addresses differs according to the kind of funding sought. Thus, to increase funding of the library's ongoing operation and service program, the audience will be the entire populace of the library's service area. The approach, the timing, and even the length of time required in order to reach a desired end will vary according to the nature of the endeavor.

Although most libraries need and receive support from the federal, state, and local levels, the major source of public library funding, by far, remains at the local level. For this reason, it is doubly important that all local resources be tapped on behalf of the library. In order to do this effectively, the cast of characters involved in fund-raising can never be too large.

LIBRARY TRUSTEES

One of the basic duties of library trustees is to secure adequate funds to carry out the library program. Consequently, trustees will be involved for the most part with "Type B" funding. Public monies for libraries may come as an earmarked library tax on property or from a single appropriation from the general revenue of the municipality. The former method is the more common source used to support the ongoing library service program.

State library laws usually have provisions regulating the tax rate a taxing body may levy for library purposes. Often a minimum or maximum tax rate is set. It is considered desirable to have no ceiling on the rate so that local citizens are not limited in what they wish to spend for library purposes.

With regard to funds raised through tax levies, the board of trustees should remember that they represent the general public of the areas in which the trustees reside. To effectively carry out their mandate, the trustees do not take upon themselves the exclusive right to determine when the climate is right for a tax levy increase. Their right, rather, is to present the library's situation and to seek the additional funding when needed. As in most democratic situations, the decision should be reserved to the electorate.

Consequently, it is incumbent upon the trustees to keep the governmental authorities and the public informed, in good times and bad, about the library program and its services. They can promote the library by explaining how it serves the individual and the community. It requires political intelligence and diplomacy to operate satisfactorily in this realm. In achieving their goal, trustees must be patient, pleasant, and, above all, persistent in their efforts.

If the board has been successful through the years in interpreting the library and explaining its position in a persuasive and enthusiastic manner to the corporate authorities, a generous appropriation or increased tax levy will be much easier to achieve.

Trustees' public relations with members of the community are equally important. They should never casually think of an individual as "just one vote." Many elections are won by just one vote.

Political action is, of course, based on knowledge. Thus, the librarian should judiciously brief and thoroughly discuss with the board why the library needs an appropriation or tax money for new services, equipment, or a new building. That way, everyone will be in a position to answer any questions that may arise.

LIBRARIAN

A librarian who is active in the community and who creates a positive image on behalf of the library and its services can have a constructive influence in securing funds for the library. The librarian can also recommend additional means of generating funds within the library. These sources include such options as: a fee service for database access through computer terminals in the library; rental of video cassettes; a rental collection of popular books to allow the library additional copies; income from copying machines; fines for overdue materials; establishment of a gift shop, which could be managed by Friends of the Library.

FRIENDS

Fund-raising for the library at the local level can be greatly enhanced through a well-organized Friends of the Library group. In fact, fund-raising is one of the fundamental activities of the Friends. Friends reach every segment of the community, and the methods these groups use are endless. From book sales to private solicitation, Friends have raised substantial sums for the benefit of the library.

Friends are often organized for the first time when there is a need for a new building or a major project. But once organized, their invaluable support continues.

A team of trustees, the librarian, and Friends working together can be a powerful force in creating an awareness in the community of the library and its services and in explaining its needs for funds.

ORGANIZATIONS

Organizations are already drawn together by a common purpose. When that purpose relates to the library, organizational members can work for improved financial development of the library. Service clubs, the American Association of University Women, the Chamber of Commerce, and the League of Women Voters are among the organizations that often take active roles in assuring adequate funding for the local library. The League of Women Voters is particularly helpful in getting "yes" votes when an increased tax or bond issue to fund libraries is on the ballot.

Some years ago the Louisville Chamber of Commerce took a full page ad in *Fortune* magazine featuring their public library as a means of attracting business and industry to their city. They recognized what a rich resource a library is for a business and for the families of its employees.

BUSINESS AND INDUSTRY

There seems to be an increased understanding on the part of business executives about the importance of the library as an information center. Contributions by business and industry to the library may take a number of forms such as cash grants, gifts of their products, or gifts of special equipment needed by the library. A loaned executive program is also sometimes set up so that one of the business's employees who is skilled in planning fund-raising or the political process donates these talents by working with the librarian, staff, and board. In addition, businesses may want to underwrite or help to promote special library programs. The banks in Atlanta, for example, helped with the library's reading program by using the slogan, "Bank on Books."

FOUNDATIONS

Local and regional foundations' trustees or administrative officers also help with library funding at the local level. Foundations often give grants for some specific project that ties in with their pattern of giving. It is usually hoped that such grants will result in measurable results. It may be library trustees, Friends, or the librarian who makes the initial contact with the foundation, but once a commitment has been made, those responsible for giving can encourage others to give. Sometimes foundations establish a challenge grant to encourage others to participate in private funding.

INDIVIDUALS

Individuals who have benefited from the library or who appreciate its service to the community are often those who work to secure library funding and who contribute their own funds.

The American Library Trustee Association gives awards to major benefactors of libraries. Although the individuals are honored nationally, the actual award celebration is held in the donor's home town. It is hoped that such exposure will inspire others to choose to make the library the beneficiary of their generosity.

Individual gifts have included entire library buildings and furnishings, valuable collections of books, modern electronic equipment, endowments for the library, and funding for special programs; the list goes on. Attorneys and estate planners can work for local library funding by recommending that the library be included in wills or as an appropriate memorial for an individual. An individual may also start an endowment fund for the library to which others may contribute. The income from such endowments can significantly augment the library's resources.

MEDIA

Newspapers, and radio and television stations have been major forces in promoting funding for local libraries. Editorials, news stories, and interviews with informed supporters have helped both public and private funding.

VOLUNTEERS

Volunteers who work in the library provide a service which makes it possible for funds normally designated for salaries to be used elsewhere. Also, since they are an informed group, volunteers can work for additional funding when needed. Of course, before a volunteer program is established in a library, the board needs to approve clearly-written policies and procedures that outline what they are expected to do and what their relationship to the staff is. It is also essential that volunteer programs have a coordinator, preferably a staff member who can inform and supervise the volunteers, and utilize their particular talents.

POWER STRUCTURE

Although it is clear that many people in the community can take a meaningful part in fund-raising for the library, if the decision-makers and leaders of the community are actively involved the chances of success will increase significantly. They are the individuals in groups and organizations already discussed; it is important to seek them out to ensure they are on the library team.

CONCLUSION

Public libraries are tax supported institutions. Thus, those working to raise funds for the library should be sure that the library is receiving the maximum possible support. Statistics show that private giving to publicly-supported institutions is increasing. If the library performs well, serves the community needs, selects a useful collection, uses modern technology, uses income wisely, and creates community awareness of its services, there is reason to believe that the library not only will attract private funds, but also will attract an increased number of people who will work to raise funds for the library at the local level.

Bibliography

Bonnell, Pamela G. *Fund Raising for the Small Public Library*. Chicago: American Library Association, 1983.
Fox, Beth Wheeler. *The Dynamic Community Library*. Chicago: American Library Association, 1988.
Howard, Edward N. *Local Power and the Community Library*. Chicago: American Library Association, 1978.
Young, Virginia G. *The Library Trustee: A Practical Guidebook*. 4th ed. Chicago: American Library Association, 1988.

Winning a Bond Issue

Richard B. Hall
Georgia Public Library Services

What do we have to do to convince the voters of our community that they want to tax themselves for a new library building? What kind of campaign techniques and strategies will we need to use to win a referendum in our community? What are the main reasons for the success or failure of this type of campaign in other communities? These are the questions that immediately come to the minds of library administrators and trustees who are trying to improve their library's physical facility through the use of the public initiative process most commonly called a referendum.

Most referenda for public library capital improvement projects result in the issuance of general obligation (G.O.) bonds. Other funding mechanisms used to raise capital through a referendum include sales taxes, property tax millage increases and even mortgages, but these methods vary tremendously from state to state. In this country, G.O. bonds may be issued by many funding agencies. For library buildings, the most frequent authorizing agency is the local municipality. In some localities, however, counties, school and library districts, New England towns, parishes and even states may issue G.O. bonds.

The decision to begin a referendum campaign is not one that should be taken lightly. The library board must be unanimous, if possible, in supporting the bond issue. From the outset, the board should plan to win. Strategic planning along with marshaling volunteer forces and raising the private funds necessary to run the campaign are critical. If these preliminary steps cannot be accomplished, the decision should be made not to begin the campaign at all, or at least not until those involved can make a strong commitment. In short, if support and commitment are now lacking, it is better to wait to build consensus.

CAMPAIGN ORGANIZATION

While half-hearted attempts occasionally do succeed, those who have an effective campaign strategy and a hard-working team significantly improve their chances of success. Library bond issues frequently fail not only because of voter apathy but because of neglect and lack of commitment on the part of campaign workers. There must be enough volunteers to do the work, and they must have a high degree of enthusiasm for the issues. The first step in any successful campaign is to organize a core of committed, influential individuals who will form the steering committee.

Be sure to allocate enough time for planning the campaign. Successful campaigns allow as much time for planning as they do for actual campaigning. The steering committee must study previous election results and carefully develop a strategy. Once the plan is established, there must be a strong commitment and almost fanatical attention to detail in carrying out the strategy. Take nothing for granted. The campaign coordinator should always follow up to ensure that things get done. It is particularly helpful to issue campaign calendars which clearly define individual tasks for all of the duties to be performed.

It is usually best to place the campaign primarily in the hands of one person. Preferably, this person should be a well-recognized community leader who has previously had this kind of campaign experience. This person may be a figurehead, but it is usually best if he or she also actively participates in running the campaign. There may be several co-chairmen and numerous subcommittee chairmen, as well as a campaign coordinator, to tie together the day-to-day details of running the campaign. The steering committee should be comprised of all of these individuals; presumably, many will be library board and Friends members. The steering committee must be representative of the community as a whole, especially if significant numbers of minorities form part of the community.

The subcommittee approach is particularly useful in organizing the campaign efforts, because it provides a link between the steering committee and various community groups. Subcommittees may be formed to establish a liaison with various groups such as lawyers, doctors, labor unions, realtors, religious groups, neighborhood associations, PTAs, and the Chamber of Commerce. Other subcommittees will perform specialized functions such as publicity, fundraising, speaker's bureaus, volunteer coordination, and planning of special events.

All of these subcommittees will distribute information, establish and detail duties of the membership, develop campaign calendars, and disseminate telephone numbers of campaign workers. They will help to keep the supporters informed of the campaign structure and strategy.

They will also provide an invaluable service by gathering information from the community. This will be vital if last minute changes in the campaign strategy are necessary because of an unforseen problem which arises during the campaign. Without this ability to adjust and fine-tune the campaign effectively and quickly, a minor issue can become life-threatening to a campaign.

Building credibility is essential. The library board and the campaign steering committee must be perceived as worthy of handling hard-earned tax dollars. Citizen involvement in all phases of the process is essential. These phases include not only the needs assessment process but also the budget development and campaign itself. Thus credibility is built for the project. In the taxpayers' eyes, it should not be a question of what campaigners are saying about spending tax money; instead, the taxpayers should view the campaign as a community effort to allocate the funds from a shared community chest. If this approach is effectively implemented, a successful outcome is usually a foregone conclusion when the issue finally comes before the voters.

Every campaign needs a rallying point. Most campaigns use one short, snappy, effective slogan as well as several themes. The slogan must be pertinent, catchy, and easy to remember. Although there may be several themes, all should be rooted in the need for the bond issue. It should be possible to develop several themes by analyzing the reasons behind the bond issue. These may include rapid population growth, being behind in national standards for library service, or simply the desire to have an attractive new building to foster community pride and demonstrate economic vitality. Campaigners can also promote the general economic improvement that results from most library bond issues. For example, good libraries help to strengthen minds. Strong minds foster increased economic growth: residents of the community are able to get better jobs, which in turn generally improve their chances for having a better quality of life.

It is important to humanize the issue as much as possible. The campaign cannot be won by talking about statistics and dollars. Campaign literature, press releases, and special events should focus on emotional issues such as children or young adults, and the value of education—not on finances. A personalized bond issue shows each individual voter how it will be of direct benefit. For example, the campaign can be localized by bringing it down to the neighborhood level. Show what the advantages in the bond package are for each area in the community. Will this area get a new branch or have its beloved branch expanded and renovated? This approach creates a grass-roots, vested interest in the bond issue which a discussion of money cannot buy and will likely translate into bond funds through votes at the polls.

It is important to define the issue so that it appears reasonable and is easy to understand. Simplicity is essential: the simpler the issue, the better the chance for success. Avoid the use of jargon and complex wording which confuse the electorate. Confusion over the issue will usually lead to negative voting. Bring the issue down to earth, especially when discussing money. Don't mention money at all if you don't have to. But if you must, keep it simple and describe the smallness of the tax increase in terms that are easy to grasp. For example, "the annual increase for the average home owner will equal the cost of a good book."

Obviously, there should be a demonstrable need for a new or improved library building. The quality of the library service provided in the past is also important. Success rarely comes overnight. The public approval of a referendum may well have been the culmination of many years of groundwork by the library board and staff. Years of frugal spending and confidence building creates credibility so that the public will trust and believe in the library's issue. No amount of slick public relations and campaign organization can make up for good, solid public representation and administration.

It is never too early to start working for support for a bond issue, and the best way to win support is at a grass-roots level. The library board should encourage local citizens to get involved in the needs assessment process. Citizens should oversee the development of the master plan for facilities and even the development of the building program. A grass-roots understanding of the beginning phase of the plan provides invaluable, broad-based support and potential volunteers for the campaign organization.

Pre-vote polls are useful tools in determining where the issue stands with the voters. The results help the steering committee gauge the chances of success and the degree of effort that must be expended in order to be successful. Another effective early campaign technique is the use of voter registration drives. Usually a very high percentage of voters registered by a campaign organization will subsequently vote favorably for the issue.

Timing is critical in a campaign. If the campaign starts too early, the opposition will have time to organize. If the campaign starts too late and is not well organized, the results may be disappointing. There may also be the perception that the library board is trying to "sneak the issue through" without proper public discussion. One of the most important factors that determines the success or failure of any campaign is the selection of the date of the referendum. This is one of the steering committee's more difficult decisions. The date of the referendum should be chosen to give the campaign planners their best shot at success. Unfortunately, setting the date is not always in the hands of the steering committee.

If the steering committee does have control over this decision, ideally it will be made by those who are well versed in the political and economic climate of the community. First it must be determined whether to hold the referendum during a regularly scheduled election or to call a special election. Since special election costs are considerable, this approach will not be looked upon favorably unless there is a very good reason to hold the library referendum separately. It is commonly believed that the smaller turnout of a special election enhances the chance for success of local bond issues, but as will be demonstrated later, this is not necessarily the case for library referenda.

Whatever the decision with respect to when the referendum will be held, the first phase in any campaign is to inform the voters of the need. To do this you will need to get their attention through some kind of publicity event such as a celebrity appearance at the kick-off rally. This first announcement of the campaign is critical because many voters make up their minds about a bond issue based upon their first impression. The kick-off celebration should be well-planned and well-publicized in order to introduce the bond issue to the voters in a positive light and to motivate campaign supporters and volunteers. This is a time that the campaign must avoid controversy at all costs.

COMMON CAMPAIGN TECHNIQUES

Many techniques can be utilized to communicate the library's position on the bond issue. The most frequently used "nuts and bolts" campaign method is to print fact sheets, brochures, bookmarks, postcards, and flyers that put the library's bond issue in a favorable light. This is a simple and relatively inexpensive method of communicating with voters. It is usually worthwhile to put a great deal of time and effort into planning the product and even to employ the services of a graphic artist. The promotional tools may show elevations and floor plans of the new building, highlight new services, picture children in the library, give the project budget, and demonstrate how little the resulting cost per household will be if the bond issue is approved by the voters.

Much of the information shown will be the basis for subsequent community group presentations, mass mailings, volunteer telephone pollings, door-to-door solicitation, and press releases to the media. The newspaper is the most commonly used media form since television and radio usually require significantly more technical sophistication and money. Providing frequent press releases to the newspaper and cultivating the editorial staff may result in important positive press coverage necessary to help win the campaign. This approach will also help to dispel inaccurate information, rebut false rumors, and even emphasize an important event such as an endorsement by a particularly influential community leader or group.

The process of obtaining endorsements can be a very effective method of bringing voters into the library's camp because endorsements create the perception of a successful bandwagon. This bandwagon image can be promoted by having effective speakers address as many potentially sympathetic community groups as possible. Endorsees and members of the steering committee, and members of the board or Friends group can constitute the speaker's bureau. Also, the Friends group can become an active supporter of the bond issue at various local functions by distributing promotional material.

Early in the campaign is the time to begin to communicate the library's need through longer, rational messages which attempt to describe the reasons for the bond issue. For example, "the funding is necessary because of the inadequacy of existing buildings." This phase may go on for weeks, or even months, in a preliminary, low-key manner. Later in the campaign, the messages must become shorter and move from factual to emotional in nature. These messages should affect the heart—not the head. Pictures of happy, well-educated children, as well as contented senior citizens, make strong images in promotional material.

The big push of the last week or two is the time when the majority of the funds for media advertisements will be spent. This media blitz should make the voter feel good about voting "yes" and supporting the library. It is essential to promote the issue vigorously during the last few days of the campaign, because this is when the majority of undecided voters make up their minds on an issue. In addition to voting for the issue, the voter must be encouraged to get out and vote.

Contrary to what one might think, a high percentage of the vote will not be determined by the campaign activities, but by the existing attitudes of the public toward the library and the funding agency. Thus, a successful campaign attempts to reach those people in the community who feel positive about the library to inform them of the importance of the bond issue, and subsequently to get them to the polls to vote. Because the campaign is not likely to change negative attitudes, it is important to concentrate limited campaign resources on those sectors of the community which are already favorably disposed toward the library in general.

Numerous studies have shown that the better educated, affluent, white-collar sector of a community is most likely to approve a library bond issue.[1] In addition, these people are the most likely to turn out to vote in the first place. In other words, the areas most likely to be favorable to the library are also more likely to have a higher turnout. This is one of the best things going for the chance of success of library bond issues!

It appears that the single most important factor is the education level of the voters. Adults with a college education and professional, technical, and managerial jobs are the most likely to vote in the highest numbers for library bond issues. It is essential to look at the educational level of the various precincts and target these individuals during the campaign. Turnout from these areas is critical. The campaign must concentrate its resources—time, energy and money—on the "yes" voter. It is much more productive to identify the "yes" voters and get them out to vote than it is to try to change the minds of voters who are already opposed to the issue.

Don't waste time on the "no" voters—ignore them and more importantly, don't antagonize them! If you get them fired up and give them an issue, those opposed to the issue may get organized. Areas of the community which have high percentages of middle-income industrial workers tend to have a low turnout rate and will generally not vote for library bond issues. It is wise not to spend much time in these areas unless they become pivotal to the election.

In a close campaign, reaching and convincing the undecided voter can frequently mean the difference between success and failure. The most appropriate tool for winning over the uncommitted voter, as well as enticing the committed voter to the polls, seems to be personal contact with highly committed individuals.[2] Personal communication through face-to-face contact is the best mechanism of reaching the undecided voter. This approach can be supplemented with printed material and media coverage, but there is nothing better than a friendly face and a handshake to tip the scales in the right direction.

Door-to-door canvassing by block worker volunteers under the direction of a precinct captain is a time-consuming method, but in a close election, it may make a significant difference. Voter turnout is higher in areas where door-to-door campaigning takes place. In this kind of one-on-one campaigning, volunteers should be well instructed on how to approach people, how to explain the bond issue, and how to answer questions or refer the voter to others in the campaign who have more in-depth knowledge of the issue.

The library's Friends group can form the basis of a volunteer organization that provides the muscle behind the steering committee for this activity. They should be effectively organized to get out mass mailings and make telephone contact with registered voters before the day of the referendum. The use of registered voter lists is an important tool, especially if they can be cross-checked with library patron files.

While all registered voters are important, library patrons who are also registered voters are the prime target group of sympathetic "yes" voters. They must be aware of the library's bond issue and encouraged to vote.

It is essential to have a good volunteer orientation program, not only for those who will be doing door-to-door canvassing, but for those who will staff the telephone bank as well. The telephone callers must have a good command of the basic information and issues of the campaign so that they do not create confusion in voters' minds.

Volunteers in telephone banks participate in three main stages of the campaign. The first establishes a baseline of support for the issue by early polling of registered voters. During this initial phase, the callers should make registered voters aware of the upcoming election while they determine the level of support. This kind of early information about how the community feels about the issue can help to establish an overall strategy as well as give the steering committee information about trends in specific precincts.

The next most important stage identifies potentially favorable voters. "Yes" voters should be identified along with undecided voters who seem to be leaning in a favorable direction on the issue. These undecided voters should receive special attention if the campaign is close. Basic information should be given, and a positive promotion of the issue should be made without an attempt to pressure the voter into a decision. "No" voters should be left alone and recorded so that they are not mistakenly called again.

The final stage of the telephone campaign comes in the week before the election, when the emphasis should be on getting out the vote. Volunteer callers should contact only "yes" voters and undecided voters who previously seemed to be leaning in a favorable direction. These voters should be encouraged to vote, asked to vote "yes" and offered transportation, if necessary, to get them to the polls.

In the week before the election, the majority of the paid advertising should also be released. Generally, electronic media ads will be a relatively small part of the campaign effort because of their great expense. However, they can be very effective if produced with sophistication and finesse. Television advertisements will reach a large number of people, as will radio ads, if they are placed in the prime time slots. It is wise to be careful about radio call-in shows because they tend to give the opposition an audience at your expense, even if friendly call-ins are carefully orchestrated.

Organized opposition can develop quickly in response to an issue which has emotional appeal, such as the waste of tax funds. Campaign planners must anticipate the strategies of these groups and must work to defuse or defeat the opposition. One commonly used technique for opposition groups is to attack an issue very late in the campaign and provide inaccurate and damaging information which gets headlines and the attention of voters just before going to the polls.

Last minute propaganda can be detrimental if the steering committee does not have time to respond appropriately. One approach to combat this problem is for the steering committee to plan a last minute push of its own. Since the last few days of the campaign are so crucial, the steering committee may want to plan a special feature article in the Sunday paper before election day or reserve funds for a last minute advertisement to rebut the opposition's false claims. Nothing should be taken for granted. The best offense must be prepared to defend the issue effectively. Furthermore, it should be recognized that the loyal opposition does not always play fair.

REASONS FOR SUCCESS OR FAILURE

The reasons for the success or failure of a referendum are a topic of much speculation and have eluded explanation over the years. Since every community is different, there is no sure-fire method or generic formula for success which will work everywhere. Thus, a campaign strategy that works well in one library district may fail miserably in another; therefore, each campaign must be tailored to the specific community. A strong, skillful grass-roots organization with forceful campaign arguments and high public interest is likely to produce a successful bond issue. Successful campaign strategy is the art, as well as the science, of political assessment. Knowing that emotional issues motivate voters is essential. A dry and logical campaign that does not touch the voter's soul in some way will often fall flat, while one that plays on the heart strings will frequently rally its constituency.

It is important not to make mistakes. The public relations aspect of building design, cost and location are good examples of this assertion. It is essential to minimize controversy over these factors. They should be addressed well in advance so that no last minute embarrassment arises during the campaign. It is difficult when the very building or site you are trying to fund is working against you.

Timing is one of the most important factors contributing to success or failure. Referenda for public library buildings which are held during a general election outnumber by a margin of approximately 2-to-1 those that are held during a special election. Contrary to popular belief, there appears to be little difference in the success rate of library referenda held during regular elections as opposed to special elections.[3] There also seems to be little data to support the assertion that a particular month of the year improves or lessens the chances of success. It is true that the spring and fall are the two most prevalent times for referenda to be held, but this is because of the regularly scheduled election days during these times.

The effect of competing items on the ballot has long been controversial. Although there is no conclusive proof, the presence of competing items does appear to be a significant factor for those referenda which fail. Frequently, competition from other items on the ballot, or a negative reaction to one or more issues which spills over and hurts the library issue, are cited as significant reasons for failure of a library bond question. This leads one to believe that, when selecting the time to place the library issue before the voters, very careful attention should be given to the popular sentiment toward other potential issues which will also be on the ballot.

Timing with respect to the economic climate is also an essential consideration. If the economy is in recession, or if there have been recent budget cuts or layoffs announced, the time may not be right to announce the library's new capital improvement plans. Quality of life is important to voters but not when an economic downturn threatens to curb basic services and individual pocketbooks. There will certainly be a recovery ahead. Thus, it may be wise to wait for better times than to plunge ahead and fail simply because the community feels economically insecure.

The same can be said for issues of taxation. If there has been a recent, unpopular tax increase or reassessment, it may not be time to act. Capital campaigns which are presented when the tax base is strained usually have a very difficult time passing. Opponents have traditionally used the concern over increased taxation to kill a bond issue. If the steering committee ignores this fact, or if it misjudges the political power of an organized tax increase opposition group, the results may be fatal to the campaign.

As an extra edge to insure success, the sophisticated steering committee may wish to retain a public relations firm or political consultant to help plan the campaign strategy. While this generates extra cost, the help may result in the rest of the campaign funds being spent more effectively. In the case history which follows, the library system employed the political and media consultant, James R. Turner, of Paxton & Turner in Virginia Beach, Virginia, with excellent results. He and Margaret P. Forehand, Director of Libraries and Research Services for the City of Chesapeake, Virginia, have collaborated to produce their perceptions of the important aspects of an actual campaign. This report is interesting not only because it embraces many of the campaign techniques discussed, but also because it was successful in overcoming almost insurmountable odds by utilizing only those techniques appropriate to the individual community.

THE CHESAPEAKE, VIRGINIA, CAMPAIGN

Following is a real scenario setting forth the specifics of a recent campaign. In the fall of 1988, our library system was well below state and national standards in terms of facilities and books. We knew of no additional municipal appropriations which were earmarked for our system beyond normal operating expenses. To stay viable, we had but one choice—a bond referendum. Accordingly, we convinced the city council to put a $10.6 million library bond referendum on the ballot, but there were problems.

The citizens of the community believed that uncontrolled growth had taken over the city, and they were being asked to pay for it. Bills reflecting a 17 cent real estate tax increase were scheduled to come out less than a week before the election. It was feared that an unpopular planning vote by city council was going to lead to a recall referendum on election day. On top of that, the city was entering the final stages of construction on an $18 million city hall which was controversial, both in cost and appearance. In short, despite very real library system needs, everything that mattered politically was going against us, and seasoned political observers had already proclaimed the library referendum dead on arrival. What to do?

First, we had to reorient our thinking. Increasing our circulation was not the objective here—winning was. As librarians, we naturally looked to our patrons, or user base, for support. But national voter statistics indicate that less than 50 percent of library patrons are also registered voters. Even worse, the statistics show that fewer than half of that number actually vote. Instead of concentrating all our efforts on a potentially unproductive audience, we attempted to communicate only with the group that mattered—the electorate.

Next, we recognized our shortcomings and got help from people who dealt with politics on a daily basis. It is natural for librarians to stay above the political fray, but we were now entering the political arena. Doing so without understanding what was going on could have had disastrous consequences. We knew that whether they are volunteers or paid professionals, political consultants understand the fundamental elements of political campaigns. There are three basic considerations which are critical.

The first consideration is to understand the electorate. A poll and previous election results can be significant barometers of voter attitudes, particularly when it comes to referenda. If funding and time allow, conduct a poll. It is only on the basis of a professionally designed and conducted poll that one can see into the electorate's mind. Be careful not to load the questions to get results that suit your perceptions. This only skews the results and seriously undermines your ability to position the campaign effectively.

Since funds did not permit a poll, our only guides were instinct, election results, and the experience of our political consultant. We knew it was important to try to keep the analysis of the election results separate from instincts. The "Committee of 100" theory holds that our attitudes and opinions are molded by those with whom we interact daily. Since we tend to associate with those with whom we agree, it is likely that their opinions are similar to ours or will color our views. Since the "Committee of 100" is not demographically balanced, it follows that the opinions of that group will likewise not be reflective of the population as a whole, much less the registered voters. A balanced view is needed, and often the only way to get that is to listen to what is said on the part of civic leaders and groups. Having said that, we urge you not to ignore what is said on the street. Sometimes rumors—which, as we all know, are the mother's milk of politics—can be significant warnings of future problems or shifts in the electorate. We paid particular attention to the public's perception of the negative aspects of the issue.

In our case, it was extremely important to listen to what people were saying. We were not running the traditional brand name campaign which utilizes the power broker, good-old-boy, political network. We were trying to appeal to the grass roots. We had to tailor our message to bring into the fold the common voter who was concerned about taxes and not happy with recent actions by the elected officials.

The second consideration is to position the campaign. At this stage, another theory of politics should be kept in mind. Voters act out of self-interest or the fulfillment of personal agendas. That being the case, voter trends and attitudes should emerge from the analysis of election results and polling data if it is available. Overlay the geographic distribution of the library bond referendum's offerings with voter trends by precinct. Look for common threads. Look for instances of bloc voting. Try to understand why the electorate did what it did. Try to understand what factors contributed to the failure of other campaigns. Most likely, the problems were not structural, but related to the message.

Out of this jumble of apparently unrelated facts will come an awareness of what the campaign message should be and to whom it should be directed. If it does not happen immediately, do not force the issue. The worst thing is to make faulty assumptions which may prove fatal on election day. Finally, remember that the voting is an emotional act. Do not be lulled into thinking that a recitation of facts—the need to meet library standards, the number of square feet involved and so forth—will be a sufficient impetus for the voter. The voter must be able to make an emotional connection with the issue. If none exists, you must create it. For instance, we stayed away from dollars and emphasized access to books and information.

The third consideration is to get the message out. The campaign message must be delivered in a consistent, repetitive manner if it is to penetrate existing advertising clutter and have an impact on the target audience. When that can begin and how that can be accomplished are often determined by fundraising capabilities. Since our campaign was short on funds, we concentrated our advertisements during the last ten days and ran four newspaper ads—the last of which was a two-page spread that came out on the Sunday before the election. We also targeted our door-to-door campaign efforts in precincts where this kind of labor-intensive effort pays off the best. Fortunately, the area where we distributed the lion's share of our 10,000 door hangers also had a high voter turn-out. We targeted this area because it had the largest number of new voters registered by our library branches. When canvassing door-to-door, we used a registered voter list so we would communicate only with the electorate.

If time is short, and people are not willing to commit to door-to-door campaigns, develop a grass-roots base. We built coalitions with civic leagues in areas that would benefit from the bond issue as well as other groups on the ballot. We talked the issue up with political leaders. They got the library in this mess, and they had an obligation to get it out. Pull out all the stops. In our case, we used the Girl and Boy Scouts. We had children passing out campaign literature on Halloween night. We did everything we could to generate interest and enthusiasm in both campaign supporters and the electorate.

Of the $15,000 we spent on the campaign, 25 percent went toward the newspaper ads. High quality campaign materials accounted for another 40 percent of the budget, while 20 percent was spent on the political consultant. The final 15 percent was spent on election day operations such as yard, poll and street signs, as well as guide ballots for the poll workers.

Remember, voters do not make up their minds until the final days of a campaign. Given that fact, the last two weeks of a campaign should be devoted to what is called the GOTV, or "get out the vote" effort. No matter what the merit of the issue is, at this stage it is worth nothing unless your campaign can get voters to the polls. This is where politics becomes less of a science and more of an art. Unless the campaign has the benefit of telephone banks and tracking polls which chart shifts in the electorate's mood, all that is left are feelings and experience with which to determine what last minute pitches can be made and how they can be constructed to do two things: draw undecided voters into campaign's camp and move everyone to the polls.

Since a voter's perception of events soon becomes reality, do not waiver from the charted course. Voters perceive unease and a lack of confidence very quickly, and the last thing a campaign should do is allow doubt to creep into the electorate's mind. In a sense, referenda are won or lost simply on the basis of that perception. If you can reorient your thinking, position the campaign and communicate effectively to get the vote out, you might overcome the odds. We did. On election day, the vote was 25,599 for (58%) and 18,656 against (42%). Against all odds, we are building libraries!

SUMMARY

As can be seen from the Chesapeake case, referenda can pass even in the face of long odds. The steering committee listened to the community, got a sense of its political beliefs and values, and responded effectively even in a political atmosphere which was unfriendly. The case illustrates clearly that no one campaign strategy or combination of campaign techniques can work in every case. Each community is different. Thus, the library steering committee must develop its own approach to a referendum based on the local situation.

There are many techniques which can be used. It is important for the steering committee to plan the strategy carefully, humanize the message, and gain credibility with the voters in order to succeed. The committee must concentrate limited resources on the educated, affluent, white-collar sector of the community. These people will usually be sympathetic to the library's issue and will have a high voter turn-out rate. Finally, success is frequently influenced by the timing of when the vote is held, economic realities, ballot competition, taxation issues, and the prospect of organized opposition.

References

1. Guy Garrison, "Voting on a Library Bond Issue: Two Elections in Akron, Ohio, 1961 and 1962," *Library Quarterly* XXXIII (July 1963): 239.
2. Ruth G. Lindahl and William S. Berner, *Financing Public Library Expansion Case Studies of Three Defeated Bond Issue Referendums* (Research Series No. 13) (Springfield: Illinois State Library, 1968), p. 51.
3. Richard B. Hall, "Referenda for Public Library Buildings 1987," *Library Journal* 113 (June 15, 1988): 31.

Building a Sound Case for Support: Statistical Evidence and its Attractive Presentation

Keith Curry Lance
Research Director
State Library and Adult Education Office
Colorado Department of Education

Statistics. The mere word sends cold chills up backs, wipes smiles from faces, and silences a room faster than the mention of E. F. Hutton in their commercials. It recalls the purgatory of math classes and the sweaty-palmed dread of standardized tests. And, for all too many of us, it still makes our eyes glaze over as we ponder seemingly endless pages of numbers that are supposed to mean something to us, but do not.

This chapter is about the *art* of using statistics to build a sound case for support of libraries. Five strategies for using statistics are recommended, and success stories exemplifying them are shared. Also, library and non-library sources of useful, available data are discussed.

STRATEGIES THAT WORK

Five statistical strategies proven to win support for libraries are:

1. presenting figures from the user's point of view,

2. presenting trends for a library,
3. comparing one library with another (or group of others),
4. relating the library to its community, institution, or the economy, and
5. using graphics to present statistics.

These strategies succeed, because they package figures in ways that make them meaningful to decision-makers.

The User's Point of View

Presenting library statistics from the user's point of view is an easy way to make them meaningful to decision-makers. Knowing that a library's annual circulation was 200,000 might not mean a lot to the typical board member; however, knowing that the library loaned an average of six items to each of its clients would probably mean much more. Per capital measures of circulation, in-library use, and reference questions, to name a few instances, have become popular in recent years among public libraries.[1]

In addition to reporting that the library circulates six items per capita, suggest what those six items might have been. The six items might be selected from the paperback and hardcover best sellers lists published in each issue of *Publishers Weekly*. This "market basket" strategy was used as part of a successful fundraising campaign by the Montgomery County (Maryland) Public Library in 1985, and was presented by Julie Pringle Smith in a session entitled "The Numbers Game" at the 1986 American Library Association Conference in New York. The following example from the Colorado State Library's 1987 public library bookmark, illustrates how this strategy has been implemented recently.[2]

A DOLLAR'S WORTH OF VALUE FOR EVERY PENNY

In 1987, Coloradans paid $13.39 each for public library service. In exchange for that small contribution, the average Coloradan:

- borrowed six circulating books such as:

Bill Cosby's *Time Flies*	$15.95
Donald Trump's *Trump: The Art of the Deal*	$19.95
Mikhail Gorbachev's *Perestroika*	$19.95
Garrison Keillor's *Leaving Home*	$18.95
Stephen King's *Misery*	$18.95
Arthur Clarke's *2061: Odyssey 3*	$17.95

- used two items in the library such as:

Wall Street Journal	$119/year
Encyclopedia of Associations	$240

- received assistance in finding information
  using reference material such as:

Thomas Register of American Manufacturers	$225
Standard & Poor's Daily Stock Price Record	$228/year
Standard & Poor's Earnings Forecaster	$350/year

If an individual had purchased only these materials, the cost would have been about $1,339.

VISIT YOUR LOCAL PUBLIC LIBRARY AND CHECK OUT THE VALUES AVAILABLE THERE!

To give the figures substance, go beyond mere per capita use statistics to suggest actual materials which individuals can remember using.

Presenting Trends for a Library

Presenting statistical trends for a library is another easy statistical strategy for garnering library support. In 1989, the library media coordinator for the Canon City (Colorado) school district won an increase in the per student allocation for library media materials by comparing the allocations made over a four-year period. Having made modest increases between 1985 and 1989, officials proposed a reduction in 1990. The damage that would have done to the library media program was shown by presenting figures in both actual and constant dollars. The School Library Acquisitions Price Index[3] was used to calculate constant 1985 dollars, thus controlling for inflation:

PER STUDENT EXPENDITURES ON
LIBRARY MEDIA MATERIALS, 1985–88

Year	Actual Dollars	1985 Dollars
1985	$ 8.80	$ 8.80
1986	$ 9.00	$ 8.57
1987	$ 9.00	$ 8.04
1988	$11.00	$ 8.80

Taken separately, the comparison of 1985 and 1988 allocations in constant dollars suggested that the district had maintained the status quo. When the intervening years were considered, however, the return to 1985 levels in 1988 was less impressive. Thus, such funding, albeit an improvement, was insufficient to begin correcting the damage done by two years of reduced buying power. A 1989 price index was not yet available; however, its effect on the continuation of $11.00 per student funding in 1989 was clear. While the district regained its 1985 buying power in 1988, $11.00 per student for 1989 meant the beginning of a new downturn in library media spending. Understanding this, district officials were persuaded to make a substantial increase in the allocation, rather than reduce it.[4]

Comparing One Library with Another (or Group of Others)

Certainly, comparing one library with another or group of others is the prevailing strategy in using statistics to build the case for library support. Groups of comparable libraries are usually selected on the basis of population served or operating expenditures.

The University of Southern Colorado Library provides an excellent example of this strategy. Since the library had few in-state peers, they compared their library to its peers nationwide:

SELECTED STATISTICS FOR THE
UNIVERSITY OF SOUTHERN COLORADO LIBRARY
AND ITS PEER INSTITUTIONS NATIONWIDE, 1985

Measure	University of Southern Colorado	Peer Average
Materials expenditures	$206,432	$453,415
Materials expenditures per student	$45	$77
Materials expenditures as a percent of operating expenditures	27%	29%
Operating expenditures	$757,526	$1,525,551
Operating expenditures per student	$166	$263

University administrators were very unpleasantly surprised by the USC Library's standing in relation to its peers, and were thus persuaded to increase the library's materials budget by $100,000 over a three-year period.[5]

The library administration was very fortunate that USC had a set of national peer institutions that had been selected by the very decision-makers to whom they would be appealing for support. Before selecting a comparison group, study the audience to identify an existing comparison group which was selected by them or which has instant credibility with them. One of the easiest ways for decision-makers to dismiss comparisons is by questioning the use of the comparison group. Conversely, playing to the predispositions of decision-makers can pave the way for a successful presentation. For example, the director of a school library media center (LMC) might win a budget increase by comparing her LMC to those at schools which are her school's sports rivals.

Relating the Library to its Community, Institution, or the Economy

Relating the library to its community, institution, or the economy is another strategy for building library support. This strategy is useful when dealing with those who do not understand the library's scope or importance and whose priorities lie elsewhere.

In 1988, Colorado's governor questioned the need for state-level library programs in light of the state's need to promote a new airport and increased tourism. The state library provided a good example of this statistical strategy by responding with comparisons which suggested the scope and importance of those programs in relation to these hot issues:[6]

- Circulation of books and other materials by libraries outnumbers passenger traffic out of [the Denver] Airport—in fact, all Colorado airports—two-to-one.
- Visits to libraries outnumber ski lift ticket sales six-to-one annually
- As many Coloradans are registered to use public libraries as are registered to vote.

Because these comparisons related libraries to issues on the state's political agenda, they contributed to a successful effort to not only maintain, but increase, the state's support of library programs.

This strategy—combined with the user's point of view strategy—was employed by the Boulder (Colorado) Public Library in 1987 as part of its successful bid for a .38 cent sales tax increase:[7]

ARE YOU GETTING YOUR MONEY'S WORTH?

The .38 cent sales tax increase will cost the average Boulder citizen
approximately $17.00 per year.

For $17.00, you can buy:

1/3 of a filled pothole OR
3/4 of a new hardback book OR . . .
1 tankful of gasoline OR
1 extra large pizza with the works OR . . .
3 movie tickets with popcorn and soft drink OR . . .

Unlimited use of an improved and expanded
Public Library, open full time, including free
attendance at Library concerts and films.

This item helped voters to consider the annual cost of increased library services—$17.00—by comparing those benefits to alternatives which might be purchased elsewhere in the community for the same cost.[8]

Using Graphics

It is a cliche, but it is true: "A picture *is* worth a thousand words." Presenting statistics graphically is probably the best way to head off the reactions to statistics described at the beginning of this chapter. Consider the following example. If you were a decision-maker being presented with library statistics, which of the following would speak to you more clearly and immediately—the table or the bar graph?[9]

COMPARATIVE STATISTICS FOR OREGON LIBRARIES
SERVING POPULATION OVER 100,000: FY 1988

Library	Circulation per capita	Volumes per capita	Expenditures per capita	FTE Staff per 10,000
Eugene	10.52	2.57	$17.77	4.65
Jackson Co.	6.31	2.16	11.24	3.34
Salem	9.16	2.14	11.28	3.70
Multnomah	7.55	2.15	17.58	5.15

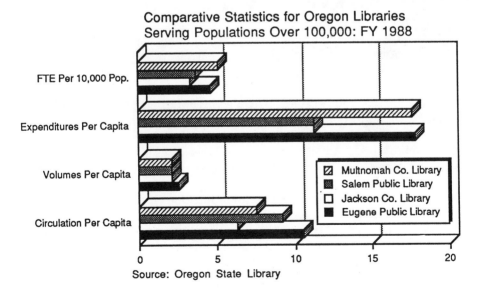

Comparative Statistics for Oregon Libraries
Serving Populations Over 100,000: FY 1988

Source: Oregon State Library

The graph is a superior means of communicating this information. One need only look at it to ascertain the relative standing of the four libraries on the four statistics. The table is a block of letters and numbers which the reader must picture mentally in order to understand it. The problem is that most readers will not get that far. The table raises the spectre of statistics, obscuring the data rather than turning it into information.

Use of computer graphics is increasing in both popularity and sophistication, due to the availability of inexpensive, high-quality graphics software. A little graphics goes a long way. In fact, most graphics software provides more options (e.g., color, multiple bars, three dimensions) than are often justified by the data or the audience. In the bibliography, sources are listed for this chapter for anyone interested in graphics. The references were suggested by Joel Fingerman during a session entitled "The Big Picture" at the 1988 American Library Association conference in New Orleans.

SOURCES OF PUBLIC LIBRARY DATA

During the last half of the 1980s, the availability of comparative public library data increased dramatically. Four sources of such data are: state library agencies (SLAs); the Federal/State Cooperative System (FSCS) for Public Library Data; the Public Library Data Service (PLDS); and the American Library Association's Office for Research (ALA/OFR).

All SLAs collect annual statistics from public libraries. Most states have data on: populations served and borrowers registered; staffing, income, and expenditures; and circulation and interlibrary loans. Many states are also responding to the Public Library Association's Public Library Development Project by collecting other output data, such as library visits, in-library use, reference transactions, and a variety of "fill rates."[10] Only since 1985, however, have SLAs begun to use common definitions of statistical terms and procedures for collecting data.[11] Annual reports of public library statistics are available from most, if not all, SLAs.

In 1988, the National Center for Education Statistics (NCES) received substantial legislative and administrative mandates to begin collecting data on all types of libraries more systematically and rigorously. Specifically, the School Improvement Act of 1988 (PL 100-297) charges NCES to "acquire and diffuse among the people of the U.S. useful statistical information on subjects connected with education (in the most general and comprehensive sense of the word)." Libraries are among the specified subjects. The law also mandates that NCES "shall develop and support a cooperative system of annual data collection for public libraries" via the state library agencies. At that time, a 14-state ALA pilot project begun in 1984 was succeeded by FSCS. By December 1988, 41 states had expressed interest in participating in FSCS.

FSCS is still in a pilot project mode, because the number of participating states tripled in one year and because NCES data must meet rigorous statistical standards for publication. At this writing, FSCS reports are expected to begin print publication with FY 1988 data in 1990. These data will also be available on magnetic tape and diskette. Statistics being collected as part of FSCS include the types listed above.

In 1988, PLA established its Public Library Data Service and published *PLDS Statistical Report '88*. In addition to items gathered by state library agencies, it provides percentages of the population in selected age and education groups; fill rates for titles, subjects, and browsers; and major roles.[12] Besides these data, strengths of PLDS include the availability of library-by-library data, especially for libraries serving over 100,000, and the timely publication of its report. Its weaknesses include the omission or under-representation of libraries serving smaller populations and the fact that its data are published unedited.

One of the most popular types of public library data—salary statistics—is sometimes available from state library agencies, often, as part of the annual statistical report. For national comparisons, the best source is the annual *ALA Survey of Librarian Salaries* published by the ALA Office for Research. Public library salary statistics can also be found in *The Municipal Year Book* and its state-level counterparts.[13]

SOURCES OF ACADEMIC LIBRARY DATA

Academic library statistics are available from state departments of higher education, NCES, and two associations, the Association of Research Libraries (ARL) and the Association of College and Research Libraries (ACRL). NCES now collects academic library data every two years via the Integrated Post-secondary Education Data System (IPEDS). This survey is administered by state departments of higher education. For data on other states, contact either NCES for magnetic tape or one of the private companies which will provide data on either magnetic tape or diskette (e.g., the National Data Center for Higher Education in Boulder, Colorado). The IPEDS academic library survey includes the general categories listed for libraries as well as data on student workers, circulation from reserve collections, and online database searching. Comparable statistics published by the academic library associations cover their members only.[14] In addition to the machine-readable IPEDS files available from NCES, ACRL is publishing a four-diskette data set entitled *ACRL Academic Library Statistics, 1978/79–1987/88* in 1989.

Academic library salary statistics are included in the annual *ALA Survey of Librarian Salaries* and the *ARL Annual Salary Survey*. The College and University Personnel Association (CUPA) is another association which collects salary data on academic librarians annually. Salary figures for academic librarians may also be available from the state department of higher education or detailed institutional budget reports.

SOURCES OF SCHOOL LIBRARY MEDIA CENTER DATA

Few state library agencies—even those located in state departments of education—collect LMC data on a regular basis or, for that matter, at all. When they do, some of the data (e.g., materials budgets, staffing, and salaries) may be available from the state department of education.

In 1985 and 1986, NCES surveyed a nationally representative sample of school library media programs. Those data have been used widely, owing to the timely publication of the original NCES report, *Statistics of Public and Private School Library Media Centers, 1985–86* (1987), and its incorporation into *Information Power: Guidelines for School Library Media Programs* (1988). In addition to these statistics on LMC programs, *Information Power* also contains formulas for generating budget requests and estimating space needs.

In April 1989, the National Commission on Libraries and Information Science established a Task Force on School Library Media Centers to advise NCES on incorporating LMC items into the School and Staffing Survey (SASS). If that is not possible, a separate mechanism for surveying LMCs on an ongoing basis will be sought.

SOURCES OF DEMOGRAPHIC AND ECONOMIC DATA

The U.S. Census Bureau is a rich source of statistics on population characteristics (e.g., age, sex, ethnicity, family status, income, education, and employment). The Bureau of Labor Statistics (BLS) is a rich source of figures relating to employment, unemployment, and general economic trends. BLS is the source of monthly and annual updates on the consumer price index, a figure useful for calculating the effects of inflation on a library's income and operating expenditures (excluding materials). Price indices for academic and school library materials are developed by Research Associates of Washington (1988) and reported in the *Bowker Annual*. In addition, BLS calculates general price indices for books and periodicals.

Every state has a state data center. Most often, it is located in the state department that works closest with local governments (e.g., the department of state or local affairs). It can provide invaluable assistance in organizing data by the sometimes quirky boundaries of public library branches. In addition, it can usually provide annual estimates of local and county populations as well as periodic updates of other figures. Likewise, the state department of labor or employment is a useful complement to BLS, and the state department of revenue or taxation is a source of statistics, such as assessed property valuation—a figure useful in demonstrating a jurisdiction's ability to spend more on its library.

Beyond these national and state agencies, there is a growing private data industry which makes available demographic, economic, and lifestyle data. Annual updates for counties and metropolitan areas of selected data items are available in publications of Standard Rate and Data Service, Arbitron Ratings Company, and *Sales and Marketing Management* magazine (see References). The most noteworthy example of a private data company is the Claritas Corporation, whose packaging of such data by zip codes led to the nationwide community analysis reported in *The Clustering of America*.[15]

This chapter merely scratches the surface in describing successful strategies for using statistics to garner library support and recommending sources of such data. Many of the examples used are based on Colorado experiences; however, success stories can be found nationwide. In fact, most of the strategies implemented successfully in that state were borrowed from successful campaigns elsewhere. Library managers who need to use statistics to garner support are encouraged to make contacts with people who have data or successful support-seeking experience which they need to tap.

References

1. See Nancy Van House et al., *Output Measures for Public Libraries: A Manual of Standardized Procedures,* 2d ed. (Chicago and London: American Library Association, 1987), pp. 37–71 for details about calculating per capita measures.
2. For permission to use this example, the author thanks the Colorado State Library.
3. *Bowker Annual,* New York: R.R. Bowker Co., 1989.
4. For permission to use this example, the author thanks Martha Bass, Library Media Coordinator for the Canon City, Colorado, School District.

5. For permission to use this example and a report of the impact of this statistical strategy at the University of Southern Colorado Library, the author thanks Beverly Moore, Library Director, and Tony Moffatt, Planning and Budgeting Officer.

6. Keith Curry Lance, *The State Library Regional Library Systems and Interlibrary Cooperation: Investments in the Information Infrastructure of a More Competitive and Productive Colorado* (Denver: Colorado State Library, 1988), pp. 3, 5.

7. Boulder (Colorado) Public Library, *The Public Bridge*, Fall (v.4, n.5) 1987.

8. For permission to use this example, the author thanks Marcelee Gralapp, Director of the Boulder, Colorado Public Library.

9. For permission to use this example, the author thanks the Oregon State Library.

10. See Van House, *op. cit.*

11. See Task Force on a Federal-State Cooperative System for Public Library Data, *Action Plan for a Federal-State Cooperative System for Public Library Data* (Washington, D.C.: U.S. Government Printing Office, 1988) for a list of common statistices, definitions of statistical terms, and suggested methodologies for collecting data.

12. Charles McClure et al., *Planning and Role-Setting for Public Libraries: A Manual of Options and Procedures* (Chicago and London: American Library Association, 1987).

13. See, for example, Colorado Municipal League, *CML Benchmark Employee Compensation Report* (Denver: The Colorado Municipal League, 1989).

14. See Association of Research Libraries, *ARL Statistics* (Washington, D.C.: The American Library Association, 1989) and Association of College and Research Libraries, *ACRL University Library Statistics, 1987–1988* (Chicago: The American Library Association, 1989).

15. Michael J. Weiss, *The Clustering of America* (New York: Harper and Row, 1988).

Bibliography

American Association of School Librarians and Association for Educational Communications and Technology. *Information Power: Guidelines for School Library Media Programs.* Chicago and London: American Library Association, and Washington, D.C.: Association for Educational Communications and Technology, 1988.

American Library Association/Office for Research & Office for Personnel Resources. *ALA Survey of Librarian Salaries.* Chicago and London: American Library Association, 1989.

Arbitron Ratings Company. *Arbitron Ratings, Radio, Market Survey Area Guide.* New York: Arbitron Ratings Company, 1989.

Association of College and Research Libraries. *ACRL University Library Statistics, 1987–1988.* Chicago: Association of College and Research Libraries, 1989.

Association of Research Libraries. *ARL Annual Salary Survey*. Washington, D.C.: Association of Research Libraries, 1989.

Association of Research Libraries. *ARL Statistics*. Washington, D.C.: Association of Research Libraries, 1989.

Boulder (Colorado) Public Library. *The Public Bridge*. Fall (v.4, n. 5) 1987.

Bowker Annual. New York: R.R. Bowker Co., 1989.

College and University Personnel Association. *Administrative Compensation Survey*. Washington, D.C.: College and University Personnel Association, 1989.

Colorado Municipal League. *CML Benchmark Employee Compensation Report*. Denver: Colorado Municipal League, 1989.

International City Management Association. *The Municipal Year Book*. Washington, D.C.: International City Management Association, 1988.

Lance, Keith Curry. *The State Library, Regional Library Systems, and Interlibrary Cooperation: Investments in the Information Infrastructure of a More Competitive and Productive Colorado*. Denver: Colorado State Library, 1988.

Lynch, Mary Jo. "Salaries of Library Directors, July 17, 1989: Data from *The Municipal Year Book 1988*." *Public Libraries* 28 (1) (January/February): 40–43.

McClure, Charles, Amy Owen, Douglas Zweizig, Mary Jo Lynch, and Nancy Van House. *Planning and Role-Setting for Public Libraries: A Manual of Options and Procedures*. Chicago and London: American Library Association, 1987.

[National] Center for Education Statistics. *Statistics of Public and Private School Library Media Centers, 1985–86*. Washington, D.C.: U.S. Government Printing Office, 1987.

Research Associates of Washington. *Higher Education Prices and Price Indexes: 1988 Update*. Washington, D.C.: Research Associates of Washington, 1988.

Research Associates of Washington. *School Price Index: 1988 Update*. Washington, D.C.: Research Associates of Washington, 1988.

Sales and Marketing Management. "Survey of Buying Power," New York: Market Statistics, Inc., 1989.

School Improvement Act of 1988, The. (PL 100–297).

Standard Rate and Data Service. *Spot Radio Rates and Data*. Evanston, Ill.: Standard Rate and Data Service, 1989.

Task Force on a Federal-State Cooperative System for Public Library Data. *An Action Plan for a Federal-State Cooperative System for Public Library Data*. Washington, D.C.: U.S. Government Printing Office, 1988.

Van House, Nancy; Mary Jo Lynch, Charles McClure, Douglas Zweizig, and Eleanor Jo Rodger. *Output Measures for Public Libraries: A Manual of Standardized Procedures*, 2d ed. Chicago and London: American Library Association, 1987.

Weiss, Michael J. *The Clustering of America*. New York: Harper and Row, 1988.

Successful Lobbying in Support of Libraries

Eileen D. Cooke
Director, Washington Office
American Library Association

There is an old saying that success has many fathers but failure is an orphan. Success in the legislative arena calls for eternal vigilance and perseverance. There are no shortcuts or easy victories. If you are faint of heart, the legislative process is not for you. In addition, flexibility is essential. You must be willing and able to negotiate or compromise. *Compromise* is not a dirty word. Rather, democracy is all about compromise. In fact, the vast majority of our public laws are passed after having differences ironed out or reconciled by the House and Senate conference teams appointed to work out points of conflict between the House- and Senate-passed versions of legislation.

Often, legislative proposals may be ahead of their time. As a result, they have not yet gathered sufficient grass-roots support to convince Congress or legislators at any level of their merit or justification for expending taxpayers' dollars. That appeared to be the case when the Washington Office of the American Library Association (ALA) was first opened by Paul Howard in October of 1945. The "Public Library Demonstration Bill" (the forerunner of the Library Services and Construction Act) was introduced March 12, 1946, in both the House and Senate of the 79th Congress. However, it failed to be brought up for a vote in the Senate, did not even make it out of the education committee in the House, and died when the 79th Congress adjourned. In 1948 the legislation was again introduced. It was sent to the respective House and Senate education committees and was actually passed by the Senate but failed to make it out of the House Education and Labor Committee; it subsequently died when the 80th Congress adjourned.

The next time around, the bill got sidetracked in the Senate but made it to the House floor for a debate and lost by a vote of 161 to 164. Throughout the 82nd and 83rd Congresses, the legislation gained additional support but not enough to get it passed. Finally, in the 84th Congress, after ten years of persistent effort, it passed in both the House and Senate and was signed into law by President Eisenhower in June of 1956. At last success had been achieved; perseverance had paid off.

The Library Services Act, as it was called at that time, authorized a five-year program at $7.5 million annually for the development of public library service in rural towns with populations under 10,000. Then, with victory and the law in hand, the annual campaign began for an appropriation of funds to carry out the provisions of the law. Even though the law authorized $7.5 million, all that was appropriated the first year for allocation to the states and territories was $2,050,000. It was not until 1964, after a 1960 extension of the law, that the full $7.5 million was appropriated. And it was also in 1964 that another five-year extension was approved. Additional amendments removed the 10,000 population limitation, thus opening up the program to all public libraries regardless of size, and authorized the Title II Public Library Construction Program. At that stage, the Library Services Act became the Library Services and Construction Act or LSCA as it is referred to today.

In 1966, 20 years after the first bills had been introduced and ten years after the first law passed, at the height of President Johnson's "Great Society," LSCA was again amended and expanded. Title III, Interlibrary Cooperation, and Title IV-A, State Institutional Library Services and IV-B, Library Services to the Physically Handicapped, were added to the list of charges the Act was to carry out under the administration of the state library agencies. Between fiscal years 1964 and 1966, funding increased dramatically for Title I, Public Library Services: it jumped from $7.5 million first to $25 million and then to $35 million where it stayed through fiscal year 1969, when President Nixon came into office and began trying to cut back on the Great Society spending programs. However, after an impressive start with $90 million appropriated over three fiscal years, the LSCA Title II, Public Library Construction Program ran into the "guns versus butter" issue of the Vietnam War and was cut back to $18 million in fiscal year 1968 and $9 million the following year.

From then on, despite the great grass-roots need expressed, funding for LSCA Title II continued to languish between $7 million and $9.5 million, with President Nixon recommending zero and Congress beginning to withdraw general support for all construction programs because of its inflationary multiplier effect. By 1973, the law authorized $84 million for LSCA II, but Congress provided nothing. And when Nixon's fiscal year 1974 budget went to Capitol Hill on January 26—at the beginning of the ALA Midwinter Meeting in Washington, D.C.—it not only proposed zero funding for LSCA II but it recommended eliminating all the federal library grant programs under LSCA, the Elementary and Secondary Education Act Title II school library program, and the Higher Education Act Title II college library resources and training programs, as well as several other education activities.

Long before, when the Nixon Administration began in early 1969 to cut back on existing federal aid, the education community fortunately had seen the handwriting on the wall and established a coalition to fight for education funds. The Emergency Committee for Full Funding of Education Programs was formed in the spring of 1969 to lobby for adequate appropriations for all of our respective programs. Altogether, about 100 education-related organizations or associations, including ALA, were represented. Each had the responsibility to provide current information and justification for its own programs and to provide a united front in support of education in general. The first successful test of the group's considerable collective lobbying skills came on July 31, 1969, when the U.S. House of Representatives voted 393 to 16 to approve a $1 billion increase over the Nixon budget for education funding.

The highly successful ALA trustees' "March on Washington" on July 9, organized at the 1969 ALA conference under the auspices of the American Library Trustee Association (ALTA), had been an impressive forerunner and inspiration paving the way for the Emergency Committee's victory. Over 100 community leaders representing 33 states and the District of Columbia responded to ALTA's call for action. The day started with a pep talk by Representative Daniel Flood, then chair of the House appropriation subcommittee with jurisdiction over education and library programs. Then, the ALTA marchers visited more than 100 Representatives and received commitments of support or inclinations to do so from 95 members. The Emergency Committee representatives were clearly impressed with ALTA's demonstration of lay leadership and commitment to libraries. Twenty years later, some chapter Emergency Committee members still remember the time "those library people" charged up to Capitol Hill and won some early commitments in the battle for education funding which continues to this day.

In 1972, after Nixon was reelected, the education coalition dropped "Emergency" from their name and became The Committee for Full Funding of Education Programs. We decided emergency no longer accurately described our situation. We had signed up for a way of life. A couple of years later, Senator Warren Magnuson, Chair of the Senate Appropriations Committee, opened that year's hearing for the education community by saying that he didn't want to hear anyone talk about full funding. Inflation was out of hand and they had to hold the line on increased funding. Subsequently, we opted to become the Committee for Education Funding or CEF as we are currently called.

Although the committee has had countless successes, the process has become more complicated due to some extent to the Budget and Impoundment Control Act of 1974, whereby Congress established its own Congressional Budget Office and House and Senate Budget Committees to assert their independence from the Administration's Office of Management and Budget (OMB). The impetus for this action stems from the massive impoundment of education appropriations by President Nixon in 1972, which led to a series of class action suits against him and Casper Weinberger, the Director of OMB. After consultation with several state attorneys general, we succeeded in persuading some of the state librarians to join in a similar class action suit, which eventually succeeded in winning release of nearly $52 million in impounded LSCA funds. But it took until the spring of 1974 to actually get the money in hand for expenditure.

A book entitled *The Dance of Legislation,* by Eric Redman, gives a blow-by-blow account of how, among other things, a major health bill was enacted. Based on that book, my experience with the vagaries of the legislative process, and tales of Pyrrhic victories on other fronts, I would say that the dance of legislation is the minuet. For each step you progress, be prepared to take two to the side and possibly three back. Patience and persistence are essential in the legislative process. Think of the ten years it took to get LSA, the first federal library law, on the books.

Other laws that moved along with great dispatch in comparison with LSA were the Elementary and Secondary Education Act (ESEA) and the Higher Education Act (HEA). In both cases, the timing was right. The long-standing bias against federal aid to education was fading and President Johnson, who was deeply committed to increasing support for education, was pushing through proposals which had their roots in the Kennedy Administration as memorials to the assassinated President. The combination of working with eager education groups in Washington plus grass-roots support from the states helped to win passage of both with relative ease.

Generally, it is easier to rally the troops periodically for the support required to pass the authorizing legislation for such programs as LSCA, ESEA, and HEA than it is to generate and maintain perpetually the grass-roots personal contacts and correspondence from constituents essential to winning the annual appropriations to implement the various provisions of the laws on the books. Of course, it is even more challenging to compete with the constantly increasing number of other worthwhile activities promoted by colleagues in education, especially when tax dollars for discretionary domestic programs lose ground to inflation, military spending, social security, medicare entitlements, and interest on the federal debt. In fiscal year 1989, 26 percent of federal spending went to defense; 34 percent to social security, military and civil service pensions; 15 percent to debt service; and an additional amount to medicaid, housing subsidies, and nutritional aid for senior citizens. Some time ago, it was reported that only about 17 cents of every tax dollar was controllable. Ten cents of that went to run the government and what was left was earmarked for federal grant programs.

The fiscal year 1990 budget (October 1, 1989–September 30, 1990) submitted by President Reagan, estimated that 26 percent will go to defense, 43 percent to direct benefit payments to individuals, 11 percent to grants to states and localities, and 5 percent to other federal operations. Sizeable appropriations victories are rare because the available dollars are few. Just maintaining current services in the face of inflationary increases is an extraordinary achievement. By the time the House and Senate Budget Committees finish slicing up the fiscal pie for the appropriations subcommittees to consider funding their respective priorities, there is slim chance in these deficit-driven days of anyone winning a major increase. A gain in one area usually means a proportionate loss in another area.

One of the best examples of long-standing commitment to a cause where patience and persistence finally paid off was achieved by the ALA library trustees, ALTA. Understanding the difficulty of continually maintaining support for public libraries in the face of shifting local priorities and financial circumstances, they decided to push for a White House Conference on Libraries to focus nationwide attention on the plight of libraries as well as their great potential. They began their campaign in 1957, but it fell on deaf ears within ALA, where many members were just getting used to the idea of having the new Library Services Act, and others were still resisting the concept of federal aid to education, not to mention aid to libraries. Various ALTA members over the years attempted to win ALA's support for a White House Conference, but it was not until the 1972 Midwinter Meeting that the ALA Council approved a resolution supporting a White House Conference on Libraries.

On October 13, 1972, as the 92nd Congress was getting ready to adjourn, Senator Claiborne Pell, Chair of the Senate Education Subcommittee, announced that he was preparing legislation that would authorize the President to call a White House Conference on Library and Information Services. He believed that the conference should be based upon conferences in every state and territory and should involve the lay leadership of the states' communities and the library leadership from their libraries of all types. He said he was confident that the process would promote greater appreciation and support for libraries.

It will forcefully acquaint legislators, public officials, the news media, and the public with the abiding concerns of librarians, educators, library trustees, and the governing boards of school systems and institutions of higher education. A White House Conference can review the accomplishments, the unmet needs, and, above all, the magnificent potentialities of our libraries, and I am sure that, once they are made aware of the facts, the American people will see the wisdom of enlarging their support for their libraries.

On January 26, 1973, Senator Pell introduced Senate Joint Resolution 40 (S.J.Res. 40), authorizing a White House Conference on Library and Information Services to be called by the President in 1976. When President Nixon's budget was transmitted to Congress three days later proposing to eliminate the major federal grant programs for libraries in fiscal year 1974, many ALA members urged that the conference be held then and not wait until 1976. However, a number of steps had to be taken before that was possible.

The Senate Education Subcommittee held a hearing on S.J.Res. 40 on July 24 and passed the bill on a voice vote November 20. Meanwhile, on the House side, House Minority Leader Gerald Ford introduced a companion bill, H.J.Res. 734, on September 19, and the House Select Education Subcommittee Chair, Representative John Brademas, introduced a similar bill, H.J.Res. 766, October 11 and conducted a hearing on November 29. But the House legislation wasn't brought up for a vote until the following year. Then, to expedite passage, Brademas brought up an amended S.J.Res. 40 under "suspension of the rules," a shortcut procedure which requires a two-thirds majority vote instead of a simple majority under the regular procedure. The vote on the bill was only 223 to 147 and therefore failed to pass. The next step was taken October 2, 1974, when the House Rules Committee cleared the way for another vote on the bill, this time under the normal procedure calling for a simple majority for passage. The House debate was set for December 12 and this time it passed 259 to 81. Subsequently, differences between the House and Senate versions were resolved and both bodies approved the conference report December 19, ending a cliff-hanger situation. The legislation would have died if still pending when the second session of the 93rd Congress adjourned the next day.

On December 31, President Gerald R. Ford signed the legislation authorizing $3.5 million to implement the new law. Public Law 93-568 provided an unprecedented opportunity. For the first time, a law calling for state conferences and a White House Conference on Library and Information Services focused nationwide attention on libraries. Needless to say, ALTA members were jubilant over achieving this long-time goal. At last, there would be fresh troops recruited to help them in their never-ending, countless campaigns to increase public awareness and support for libraries.

Action moved on to the appropriations front in 1975, but it took more than two years, until May 1977, to finally get the $3.5 million to begin the conference process. The first state conference was held in September in President Carter's home state, Georgia, and after all the state and territorial conferences, the national conference was held in Washington, D.C., November 15–19, 1979. This historic first White House Conference on Library and Information Services (WHCLIS) brought together over 900 delegates representing more than 100,000 people who participated at the state and local level in 58 pre-conferences in the states, territories, and the District of Columbia. By law, two-thirds of the delegates were interested citizens, while one-third were librarians and library trustees.

Some 3,000 resolutions developed during the pre-conference stage were subsequently distilled into 64 resolutions approving recommended changes and improvements in various aspects of library and information services.

Libraries were seen as community, cultural, educational, and information resources which needed greater support. The delegates wanted all citizens to have equal and free access to information. This was reflected in resolutions to strengthen services to Indians, the handicapped, children and youth, the elderly, the homebound, the institutionalized, minorities, illiterate, and other inadequately served groups.

The resolutions asked for a national information policy to guarantee equal access to all publicly held information and to encourage networks of shared resources. The federal government was urged to fund fully library-related legislation including LSCA, HEA, and ESEA. Several resolutions dealt with improving library and information services through technology. Goals included the increased use of satellite communication, video techniques, and cable television in the expansion of library and information services. Reduction of telecommunication and postal rates were called for. Other resolutions dealt with improved technology to preserve deteriorating collections and education and training of librarians for the changing information needs of society.

One of the most significant but intangible results of the first White House Conference was an increase in public awareness of libraries and their impact on individuals, the economy, and the nation. Friends of Libraries, U.S.A., a fledgling affiliate of ALA established in June of 1979, experienced impressive growth following the conference. Now in their tenth year, they represent over 1,700 Friends groups nationwide and about 300,000 citizens. In addition to raising money, the Friends now use their projects and clout to promote reading, library use, and increased state and local funding. Although Friends groups have most often formed to support public libraries, in recent years school and academic libraries have been increasingly interested in forming Friends groups.

As a direct result of the White House Conference recommendations on library networking and resource sharing, LSCA Title III (Interlibrary Cooperation) was increased 140 percent in one year. President Carter recommended an increase from $5 million to $12 million in his fiscal year 1981 budget and Congress appropriated that amount. In the first ten years of Title III's existence, the annual appropriations never budged beyond $2.6 million. Through the period concluding the White House Conference process, a total of $39.2 million had been appropriated for Interlibrary Cooperation. From fiscal year 1981 through fiscal year 1989, a total of $141 million has been appropriated. Thus the first conference succeeded in educating and informing the nation, from the grass-roots level up, of the critical importance and great potential of resource sharing as a basic approach to opening up access to library and information services to people wherever they reside.

However, as always, there is need for continuing education. Moreover, the world changes, other opportunities arise, unexpected crises shift priorities, and new challenges compete for scarce tax dollars. Now, we have a new opportunity after a three-and-a-half-year struggle to get the legislation enacted. On August 8, 1988, President Reagan approved what is now Public Law 100-382, which calls for a second White House Conference on Library and Information Services, or WHCLIS II.

The new law authorizes $6 million to carry out the process this time, and takes into consideration the inflationary impact over the past 12 years. The immediate challenge is to get the appropriation as soon as possible. Time is of the essence since WHCLIS II is to be held July 9–13, 1991. That means governors' conferences and other state or regional activities must precede the national conference to be part of the process.

As stated in the law the purpose of the conference is to develop recommendations for the further improvement of the library and information services of the nation and their use by the public in accordance with the findings set forth in the preamble of the law. Among the 11 findings listed are the following:

> ...the economic vitality of the United States in a global economy and the productivity of the work force of the Nation rest on access to information in the postindustrial information age;
>
> ...the White House Conference on Library and Information Services of 1979 began a process in which a broadly representative group of citizens made recommendations that have improved the library and information services

of the Nation, and sparked the Nation's interest in the crucial role of library and information services at home and abroad; and. . .

. . .emerging satellite communication networks and other technologies offer unparalleled opportunity for access to education opportunities to all parts of the world, and to individuals who are home-bound, handicapped, or incarcerated. . . .[1]

Participants in the second White House Conference will, undoubtedly, identify some of the same issues which were highlighted in 1979 that still demand attention. There is always need for ongoing support for basic activities. Other topics discussed at some length such as literacy and preservation have evolved to higher levels of importance having previously been brought to nationwide attention.

Other issues will reflect problems which stem from the Reagan Administration's push for privatization of government activities, e.g., the contracting out of federal libraries and the sharp reduction in government publications in the name of paperwork reduction.

Once again, access to information and public awareness of the role of library and information services are bound to be key issues as plans are drawn to keep libraries and the public good on track in this decade and for the twenty-first century. Meanwhile, on with the dance and be not faint of heart.

References

1. PL 100-382.

Public Relations and the Financial Support of Public Libraries

Robert B. Ford, Jr.
Medgar Evers College
City University of New York

In this era of diminishing resources and uncertain financial support, libraries need all the ammunition they can marshal. In addition to lobbying efforts, a library's story can be an effective fundraising device. The story must be told in terms that most laymen and the community the library serves will understand. In telling that story, fundraisers can use public relations techniques. In fact, the success of the lobbying effort may well depend upon the effectiveness of the public relations program and how it functions. As initially distasteful as this writer finds the idea of using Madison Avenue techniques in the library setting, these techniques are needed in order to generate additional financial support in the fiercely competitive environment in which libraries find themselves.

This chapter examines public relations both as a concept and a process and then analyzes how it can help to generate additional financial support for libraries. Furthermore, it focuses on the application of marketing and communication techniques in libraries and concludes by examining how to manage the human climate of an organization.

Our society is composed of many, diverse organizations that are interconnected in a variety of ways. This interconnectedness results in individuals and organizations being highly interdependent. It also requires an elaborate communications/media network in order for all of these groups/organizations to be continuously informed about what each is doing. In fact, an organization must be able to explain or communicate its actions to the various publics that it serves or else it will face scathing criticism. Since libraries are always vulnerable, an effective public relations program is no longer a luxury but a necessity.

Public relations has been defined by several authorities. In their book, Cutlip and Center stated that public relations is "the planned effort to influence opinion and action through socially responsible performance based on mutually satisfactory two-way communication."[1] The British Institute of Public Relations defines public relations as "the deliberate, planned and sustained effort to establish and maintain mutual understanding between an organization and its publics."[2] Finally, Nolte, another expert in the field, defines the phenomenon as "all the things done (or not done) that affect public opinion (whether favorably or unfavorably)."[3] Of the three definitions cited here, it is the first that seems most explicit and inclusive. What is most important about the definition is its focus on the socially responsible performance of the organization combined with the essential process of two-way communication.

There is a formula often expressed in public relations literature that states:

x (the deed) plus y (the way the deed is interpreted) = public attitudes[4]

Another configuration that leads to the formation of public attitudes starts with:

Basic Objectives (Organization) *leads to:* Implementation of Objectives through Specific Actions and Planned Programs *leads to:* Communication with External Publics *leads to:* Public Attitudes[5]

Part of the general confusion about public relations lies in the fact that it is a combination of both management and communication concepts, as well as a staff function that has evolved over the years. In other words, public relations is both policy and practice. As policy, it reflects the management function; as practice, it embodies both the communication concept and the work of the practitioners who, as media/communications experts, arrange the activities that continuously inform the various publics about an organization's policies, decisions, and other actions.

While public relations is both policy and practice, it is also process. As process, the manager and public relations practitioner go through four successive steps:

1. *fact-finding and feedback* (includes listening): determining and identifying the specific problem to be dealt with;
2. *planning and programming* (includes decision making): bringing attitudes and opinions to bear on an organization's policies and programs—in other words, "here's what we can do";
3. *action and communication:* conveying information to all who will be affected and whose support is essential—in other words, "here's what we did and why";
4. *evaluation:* assessing the results as well as the techniques utilized—in other words, "how did we do?"[6]

One writer has devised a "Public Relations Interaction/Flow Chart".[7] By analyzing this flow chart, an observer can further understand the dynamics of how public relations functions. The analysis begins with *media,* i.e., everything that the public is exposed to through books and journals, radio and television, etc. Then it moves on to the various *publics* whose attitudes and opinions are likely to affect the actions of the organization. From these different levels of the public, either a favorable or unfavorable *opinion* is generated. Then the analysis moves on to that sphere where the organization is *"integrated" with its environment,* which means that either success or failure is experienced in achieving organizational objectives. In this sphere, inbound communications are analyzed, and public relations policy and program recommendations are formulated. At this stage, all of this data goes forward to the organization's management. What ultimately happens depends on *organizational characteristics* (history, values, objectives, etc.) and *intervening variables* (status of public relations and quality of public relations performance). From this process emanate the *decisions* and then *action* (includes outbound communication) followed by a *feedback loop* that takes us back to the starting point: *media.* It is apparent that the success of a public relations program depends on many variables (as reflected in the flow chart)—some of which are controllable internally and others that are seriously influenced by the external environment.

Because public libraries provide services to the general public and thereby are accountable to them, they must be concerned about their public relations image. At a time when libraries must compete with other essential services for financial support, public libraries need to publicize effectively all of the positive things that they do for their communities. In fact, opinions vary on whether library services are as essential as fire, sanitation and schools. The fact of the matter is that library service is essential only if a majority of the community perceives it as essential. The only way to develop that perception is with an effective public relations program.

According to a 1978 Gallup study, most adults in the United States do not use libraries and are unfamiliar with the services they provide.[8] The study suggests that public relations has *not* been a top priority for public libraries. Of course, this does not mean that public libraries have not provided good service for their communities or do not offer a good bargain in terms of costs versus benefits. What it does mean is that the library message must be effectively and systematically communicated so that the positive feelings that most people have about libraries can be transformed into active and informed support. This support can then be further translated into more money for operating expenses and other needs.

For the library message to be as effectively communicated as possible, there is a definite need to utilize certain marketing techniques and concepts, as described below. First, one must acknowledge that most nonprofit enterprises, including libraries, do not have a marketing orientation. One author has defined marketing as a "continuing process of identifying unmet needs and the development of products and services to meet these needs."[9] The library manager must continually question whether certain decisions, policies, activities, or programs will affect the behavior of a selected target audience (or market), and if so, how they will affect the market's behavior. After first determining its mission and objectives, the individual library should turn to the phenomenon known as market research (also known as community analysis or community needs assessment). The information and data gathered during this process can be utilized by dividing the community into various segments or user groups and then looking at the characteristics of each. Then, of course, the market research information must then be related to the overall objectives of the individual library.

Unfortunately, libraries have been more product-oriented than user-oriented, i.e., they often have produced new products and services without truly determining the basic need for such products and services. The capacity to produce has often taken precedence over an actual need or demand that should have been met. In such a situation, what often happens is that the marketing resources and strategies must attempt to influence market behavior rather than determining the needs and characteristics of the market in advance of new product development. This can often lead to a high degree of product failure.

Basically, there is a five-step process to dealing with new product development:

1. the relevance of the product must be determined and applied to the library's purpose and objectives;

2. the fit between the needs of the target audience and the attributes of the product must be established;
3. the product concept (but not the product itself) needs to be tested by asking for reactions from the target audience;
4. criteria must be established in order to judge the success or failure of the product;
5. the product should be introduced for a trial period and, subsequently, success or failure can be determined or, more importantly, measured.[10]

Under this approach, a market-oriented library gathers data about market needs, and brings professional judgment and a sense of public responsibility to the process of selecting and designing products and services. Furthermore, it investigates each product offering to establish whether it really satisfies the needs of the market segment for which it was intended.

Another team of writers in the marketing/information services field has identified the responsive organization in marketing terms. It is clear that, for their ultimate survival, libraries must shift their focus from the traditional bureaucratic modus operandi to the client-centered and responsive approach to doing business from a marketing vantage point. There are basically five major steps or key concepts in the marketing process or cycle:

1. *market segmentation* (mentioned earlier in this chapter): includes information gathering and quantification;
2. *market positioning:* prioritizing clients, groups, and services, and includes policy making;
3. *consumer analysis:* determining needs and preferences, and includes information gathering and quantification;
4. *marketing program:* the optimum mix of product, price, delivery mode (place) and promotion, and includes planning, customization and coordination;
5. *marketing audit:* evaluation of plan and implementation, and includes information gathering, quantification, making judgments, and reporting.[11]

It is important to note that three of these steps or phases indeed demand measures for quantification (steps 1, 3, and 5).

The application of marketing to the library/information field is still in its formative stages. However, increasingly, it will be a tool that will help libraries shift from a reactive to a proactive position and from a service that is based on products to one that is increasingly client-centered.

Often, users have a variety of perceptions about the library based on individual positive or negative experiences. The public relations process will keep library users informed about the positive benefits to be gained from utilizing certain services. Furthermore, certain communication strategies should be activated in order to reach out to unserved segments of the potential user population and persuade and educate them about the positive force that libraries can make in their individual lives. The important point is to strongly influence the attitudes and perceptions of actual and potential users about the services offered by the library. This can only be achieved by systematically communicating relevant information to the public about those special events and occasions that can likely lead to increased usage of the library and its facilities.

In the final analysis, communication forms the link between the services offered by the library and the awareness of the public about these available services. There are at least six components to developing a viable library communications/public relations program:

1. outline a public relations/communications program that will focus on a specific time period;
2. identify those media channels that are likely to reach the targeted population segment;
3. provide a budget that will support the development of a goal-oriented media program;
4. assign a staff person who will be responsible and accountable for communication activities;
5. develop a timetable for news releases and program announcements;
6. formulate standards for evaluating the degree of success of the communications/public relations effort.[12]

An important component that all managers must learn to deal with is the human climate of an organization.[13] There is a broad range of attitudes of the various publics that interface with a given organization. The atmosphere that surrounds these attitudes is likely to determine the success or failure of many other factors with which managers must deal. Especially in the decision-making process, managers must learn to reckon with the human climate or people factors. Without a doubt, these factors are likely to be a decisive element in the future survival of any organization.

Of course, many processes can help to maintain this human climate such as an analysis of the organization's position regarding the direction of various trends, planning the program's structure and commanding the course of change in attitudes (i.e., helping to create the human climate or being overwhelmed by the inevitable changes that will occur and then being forced to react to them), and careful implementation of the proposed communications/public relations program. The visibility of the organization is extremely important in this context while the cloak of anonymity is potentially dangerous in such a volatile situation. What is also crucial is how the messages to the various publics are selected and then how these messages reach their intended audiences. This is done by utilizing elements that are capable of persuading people and affecting their opinions. The key element appears to be the adoption of a pro-active rather than a reactive stance by the management.

It is clear that effective public relations must "build public confidence as well as increase public understanding and awareness."[14] This requires careful planning once agreement has been reached on organization goals and objectives. During the past decade, there has been an increase in library public relations programs. Unfortunately, a survey in 1983 revealed that, for many libraries, public relations still remains an unplanned effort that does not generate the level of support that is required in such a contemporary environment.[15]

Some positive activities are taking place on all three levels (local, state and national). Certain projects have been sponsored by the American Library Association, the Library of Congress and the National Library Week. In addition there have been various statewide efforts (Florida, Pennsylvania and North Carolina). Furthermore, several state libraries and large public library systems have added public relations specialists to their staffs. As mentioned earlier, several libraries have taken the initiative to utilize marketing practices once considered important only for the private sector and the profit-making enterprise. Increasingly, some libraries are turning to the expertise offered by external firms and consultants especially with regard to the mechanics involved in bond issue campaigns and fund-raising efforts for capital improvements.

In conclusion, the original question posed in this chapter was how and in what way can public relations help to generate additional funds for public libraries? The answer is that effective public relations tells the library story in such a powerful manner that it will positively influence public opinion to the extent that city and county commissions and state legislatures are forced to deal with the financial ramifications of an effective library public relations campaign. The importance of such efforts depend on how well-planned and well-executed such a program can be. If the library adds the skills of an experienced lobbyist who will work closely with the public relations specialists, the public library can then deal from a position of strength rather than weakness and vulnerability.

However, in addition to public relations, libraries must become more sophisticated about the political process that always surrounds any effort to generate additional financial support. Herbert S. White, former dean of the Indiana University School of Library and Information Science, has, in a recent publication, discussed seven observations about libraries and the political process.[16] While these observations seem like the application of common sense to the library setting, so many practitioners obviously have not heeded their import. Here are the seven observations:

1. *Self-Evidently Good.* The library profession has generally subscribed to the premise that library support should be based on the fact that libraries are self-evidently good. That can no longer be an assumption in these conservative and reactionary times. What is really necessary is to gain *a basic understanding of how politicians make their decisions.*

2. *Lack of Powerful Friends:* It is a great irony that libraries have not done so well in the political arena since they obviously have no enemies. Indeed, what is so sad is the fact that libraries simply *do not have enough powerful friends who will fight and risk for them.*

3. *All We Can Afford:* It is sheer nonsense to believe the old story that whatever is being provided is all that the particular locality can afford. The fact is *we afford what we want to afford* and we can certainly afford libraries; crying poverty has no basis in reality, but we have made an obvious strategic error in requesting too little.

4. *No Neutrality:* In a political setting, there are *no neutrals;* people are either for you or against you, and if they are against you, then they must be for someone or something that wants the same money that you do.

5. *Making Libraries Indispensable:* We must find a way to *make libraries indispensable* to the work and life habits of a wider constituency that is the core of a given community. Furthermore, some degree of growth and expansion is necessary for the survival of libraries.

6. *Dealing With Friends and Enemies:* One basic reason for librarians' ineffectiveness in the political environment is that they have not figured out ways to *reward their friends and punish their enemies.*

7. *The Sacrificial Lamb:* Library costs in the overall budgetary context are truly trivial. It is *the appearance of economy rather than actual economy* that dominates political thinking. Politicians perceive that more votes are likely to be gained from cutting expenses, library budgets not withstanding; *libraries make good sacrificial lambs* because they don't wiggle as much when their heads are on the chopping block.

It is time to stop being a sacrificial lamb and also make politicians aware of the fact that there is a price to be paid when they cut library budgets. When politicians reach that awarenes and act accordingly, then libraries can drop the image of always being "the sacrificial lamb." With the assistance of effective public relations programs that point will be reached and the image will be dropped sooner than one might expect.

References

1. Scott M. Cutlip and Allen H. Center, *Effective Public Relations* (Englewood Cliffs, N.J.: Prentice-Hall, Inc., 1971), pp. 4–5.
2. British Institute of Public Relations cited in Cutlip and Center, *op. cit.*, p. 6.
3. Lawrence W. Nolte, *Fundamentals of Public Relations* (New York: Pergamon Press, Inc., 1974), p. 5.
4. Cutlip and Center, *op. cit.*, p. 6.
5. *Ibid.*, p. 7.
6. *Ibid.*, p. 186.
7. Nolte, *op. cit.*, p. 16.
8. Mona Garvey, *Library Public Relations: a Practical Handbook* (New York: H.W. Wilson Company, 1980), p. 7.
9. Andrea Dragon, "Marketing and the Public Library," *Public Library Quarterly* 4 (Winter 1983): 37-46.
10. *Ibid.*, pp. 41–42.
11. Martha Jane Zachert and Robert V. Williams, "Marketing Measures for Information Services," *Special Libraries* (Spring 1986): 61–70
12. Dub Ashton, "Marketing and Communications: Activities That Support Library Growth," *Arkansas Libraries* 42 (December 1985): 13–16.
13. Philip Lesly, *The People Factor: Managing the Human Climate* (Homewood, Ill.: Dow Jones-Irwin, Inc., 1974), p. ix.
14. Alice Norton, "Library Public Relations: New Opportunities in a Growing Field," *Library Trends* 32 (Winter 1984): 291–302.
15. *Ibid.*, pp. 292–293.
16. Herbert S. White, *Librarians and the Awakening From Innocence: a Collection of Papers* (Boston: G.K. Hall & Co., 1989), pp. 171–177.

Skills in Fund Raising: Give, Get, or Get Out

Pamela G. Bonnell
Manager, Plano (Texas) Public Library

The need for private funding to enhance a library's operating budget has become the focal point of many library administrators; whether a library is public or academic, administrators are seeking new found private dollars from individuals, corporations, and foundations. Private funds have become an integral part of the budget process to supplement a stagnant materials budget, to build a new facility, to provide a level of excellence, to establish an endowment, or to fund a myriad of other institutional needs.

Fundraising is both a science and an art. Although not an exact science, certain techniques and methods apply to all fundraising programs. The art of fundraising is only limited by the imagination; thus, a fundraising program should include creativity in public relations when approaching individuals for donations.

PURPOSE

Before venturing into any fundraising campaign, determine the purpose of the campaign and the amount needed to accomplish the goal. Any fundraising campaign falls into one or a combination of the following categories: 1. annual appeal; 2. capital campaign; 3. deferred giving; 4. memorial gift program; or 5. a special event.

This chapter addresses a major capital campaign in which the money may be designated for renovation, a new facility, or an endowment.

PROFESSIONAL COUNSEL

Once ready to consider a capital campaign, employ a professional funding counsel to minimize guesswork and to maximize the chances of a program's success.

A professional counsel almost always recommends a pre-campaign or feasibility study. This is an examination of the fundraising capital potential of the institution through confidential interviews with previous and potential donors. The function of a professional counsel is not to raise the money, but to help you achieve your goal.

In *Quality Education,* Richard Meeth did a study that found that every $1.00 spent on development brought in $4.40 (or a yield of 23 percent). The average cost of every dollar raised is approximately 29 cents.

A professional counsel brings both an outside point of view and the benefit of experience. Some of the things that a professional counsel will do for you are:

1. Assist in appraising your potential and in sharpening your priorities.
2. Determine the amount to be raised.
3. Identify strengths and weaknesses of an institution.
4. Establish a time frame.
5. Establish campaign budget and maintain budget controls.
6. Assist the leadership to organize key volunteers.

When selecting a professional counsel, follow these guidelines:

1. What is the firm's reputation as a development consultant? What successes has it had and with whom?
2. How many of the firm's experiences have been in your area and specifically with your kind of institution?
3. What do the firm's present and past clients say about their work?
4. What is the professional competence and background of the principals of the counseling firm?
5. Who in the firm will be assigned to your institution? Does he or she personally have the background and successful experience to help your organization's particular development program?
6. If possible, visit their office.

PRE-CAMPAIGN (ENTER THE CONSULTANT)

Feasibility and Planning Study

The feasibility and planning study will tell whether the giving community can support the plans as outlined in the "case." A "case for support" is carefully planned and thought out and rises from the particular needs of the institution. It is not contrived for the purpose of a campaign. The case should illustrate strategic planning. The board and staff must be totally behind the need. The preparation of the case is performed by staff and approved by the board. It should include the reason for the institution's existence and its philosophical purpose and goals.

The consultant will need a one-page summary of the case, and a chart of standards of giving needed for success. The community leaders to be visited should be identified and the board chairman or chief executive officer should send letters to each, telling of the plans for the study. Then, each should be called for an appointment. The consultant should also be provided with other materials from the institution such as a copy of the budget, a list of board members, a case statement, and levels of giving.

During the interview process, the consultant conducts confidential interviews with 60–100 (variable) of the institution's major and leading supporters to determine how they feel about the project described in the "case." Examples of questions the consultant might ask are:

- Is the project urgent?
- Will the supporters give in a range described?
- Will they work?
- Does the institution have a favorable reputation in the community?
- What other local campaigns do they contribute to?
- Do they have any suggestions for leadership or top gifts?

The interviewer may leave the one-page case summary with the interviewee. When interviews are completed, the consulting firm summarizes everything: data, conversations, information learned, ideas, opinions of interviewees, and others. An analysis is prepared, and recommendations are made to the institution as to the next steps to take, how to proceed, and when.

Based on the results of the feasibility study, the consultant will recommend one of the following:

1. The institution is ready to begin a campaign immediately;
2. A public relations or information program is needed to inform the institution's constituency of who and what it is before venturing on a capital campaign;
3. A prospect (or constituency) cultivation program is required first; or
4. No campaign is recommended at this time.

In addition, the consultant will state how much can be raised (goal), how long it will take (timing), what it will cost (budget), and who will help (leadership gifts).

THE CAMPAIGN

The consultant will assist in setting up office systems in close cooperation with the institution's present system. A campaign plan will be developed within the scheduled time frame. A giving chart will be developed identifying individuals and corporations for each level. Eighty percent of the money is given by 20 percent of the donors.

STANDARD FUND RAISING GIFT TABLE
$100,000 Goal

Gifts	Amount	Totals
1	$15,000	$15,000
2	7,500	15,000
3	5,000	15,000
4	2,500	10,000
		(10 gifts equal $55,000)
20	1,000	20,000
50	below 1,000	25,000
		(80 gifts equal $100,000)

In any fundraising campaign, the board must make the first commitment to demonstrate its belief in the project. Harshly stated, each board member must give, get, or get out. In other words, each member must give a substantial donation, solicit major contributions, or gracefully submit a resignation.

Using the above gift table, the gifts are solicited for the three groupings outlined below.

To identify prospects for the gift table, the consultant will assist in researching the ability of each individual and corporation. The prospects will be gathered by collecting names from the board, staff, past donors, community leaders, and volunteers.

A chairperson must be enlisted along with other key leadership. Only the most respected leaders should be recruited. The consultant will assist in training all volunteers in the art of approaching prospective donors and the importance of the case. The volunteers will be given deadlines and report at scheduled meetings. It is important that a tremendous amount of enthusiasm be generated to keep the volunteers excited and motivated to solicit. When the end of the campaign finally arrives, announce the victory, publicize the amount raised, reward

Board of Trustee Segment

1	$15,000	$15,000
1	7,500	7,500
1	5,000	5,000
2	2,500	5,000
5	1,000	5,000
		(10 gifts equal $37,500)

Gifts from Individuals

1	$ 5,000	$5,000
1	2,500	2,500
10	1,000	10,000
25	below 1,000	12,500
		(37 gifts equal $30,000)

Gifts from Corporations

1	$ 7,500	$7,500
1	5,000	5,000
1	2,500	2,500
5	1,000	5,000
25	below 1,000	15,000
		(33 gifts equal $32,500)

volunteers with recognition and a wrap-up party, and recognize major donors.

The two goals of every fundraising campaign are, of course, to attain or surpass the goal and to establish a new army of volunteers who are enthusiastic about their accomplishments and your institution.

Building Coalitions to Support Library and Information Services

E. J. Josey
Professor, School of Library and
Information Science, University of Pittsburgh

About twenty-four years ago, in 1966, I accepted a position with the New York State Library, which is a part of the New York State Education Department. I was attracted to the New York State Library at the time, because it was about to embark upon the development of the first multitype library system, the development of the reference and research library resources systems, which is now affectionately known as the "3 R's." In this network, the configuration structure included all types of libraries working towards a common goal. While this was a fascinating experience, I don't think that I really became converted to coalition building in terms of support for libraries until many years later.

As I think about coalition building in 1990 and beyond, my message is that this is a development in which librarians must become involved. We have been fairly successful in developing an army of librarians, library advocates, library trustees, citizens groups, and library friends to battle for legislative support for libraries. What is still needed in the 1990 s and beyond is to develop a cadre of people at the grass-roots level or the neighborhood-action level in our communities. This kind of group is not only needed at the local level; I see the need at the state level, and of course, at the national level.

Librarians, library trustees, and library supporters must now turn to community organizations and press them into action for more state support for libraries. We have been told that "the relationship between community organizations and elections has long been fraught with controversy. Community organizations, in the main, have traditionally shied away from election campaigning for a number of reasons. On the one hand, the nature of the election process—putting a premium on politicians' personalities and public relations packaging—seems a far cry from the concerns with organizations and coalition building, which provides for political empowerment at the heart of the community effort. Moreover, community organizations focus on building the inner resources and unity of specific communities, and they have been fearful that involvement in politics would split their membership and engage them in issues not immediately relevant to their goals. This kind of fearfulness of being involved in politics seems to have died out in the 1970s.

Citizen activism exploded at the grass-roots level in the 1970s and spilled over into the 1980s. During the 1970s, working people in America awakened to defend their neighborhoods from corporate and governmental bulldozers. Ecologists fought against the destruction of the natural environment and human life. Workers exposed the problems of health and safety on the job. Consumer groups investigated carcinogens in food and water. During this same time, minorities and women in America fought valiantly for their rights in various arenas, and older people, veterans, and the handicapped formed coalitions to gain political power and recognition.

The protests of the 1960s did not die completely; if anything, they became more and more rooted in the lives of ordinary men and women. Nevertheless, it was not until 1981 in Albany, New York, when we found out that the South African Springboks Rugby team was coming to Albany to play, that I became convinced that the road to salvation in terms of community action for libraries and library services was a highway of coalition building. A small interracial committee of about ten persons was formed to talk about the impact of this apartheid team coming to Albany. Before we realized it, over a period of two or three weeks, we had involved about 40 organizations in Albany in a dynamic coalition. This was easily done in the Albany area, primarily because every neighborhood had some kind of neighborhood association. In addition to the neighborhood associations, we involved the unions, all of the churches, synagogues, and mosques and religious leaders, including the Roman Catholic Bishop, the Episcopal Bishop, the Methodist Bishop, in the area, the Board of Rabbis of the Albany area, and the Moslem leadership.

This was a diverse group, and many of the people had never worked together; but there was one common goal that we were striving towards: to uphold the United Nations cultural boycott against the racist South African government. Our goal was to keep the South African Springbok

Rugby team out of Albany. Although we had a court battle all the way up to the United States Supreme Court, we did not necessarily reach our goal of keeping them out of Albany; nevertheless, on the rainy night of September 22, 1981, more than 3,000 people in Albany were galvanized into a powerful demonstration around the baseball park, Bleeker Stadium, and as one group we made a powerful protest statement proclaiming our disgust for what South Africa stood for before the world. I can guarantee you that no South African team will ever set foot in Albany again until apartheid is crushed. This came about, primarily, because of community organizations getting together to build a coalition to achieve one common goal.

As a result of this experience, I became convinced that this same kind of coalition building could be developed to support libraries. One organization alone in Albany never could have achieved what we accomplished as a coalition. Our voices were heard around the world. Every major newspaper in the world, including the *London Times*— even the USSR's Tass wire service—carried word about our protest from Albany; and this was because more than 60 organizations came to work against a common foe. I became convinced at that time that any library advocacy group, whether the Friends of the Library, the library trustees, or citizen groups for library programs could garner support from other community organizations, to be successful in lobbying for library funding, and to strengthen library programs in their local area, in their state and, of course, in our nation.

The combined voices of many organizations are far more effective in exerting political influence than the single voice of one organization. We have been reminded that:

> A politician can discount the complaints of a health group, for example, about the health hazard posed by a air pollution. However, when labor organizations, neighborhood councils, senior citizens groups, and medical associations add their voices to those of the health group, the politician can no longer afford to ignore them.[1]

Let us now examine the proposition that librarians should form coalitions. When I became president of the American Library Association six years ago, I chose as my theme, "Forging Coalitions for the Public Good." I developed that theme because libraries and their capacity to serve the public good was being seriously threatened by forces in American society that believed the federal funds should not be used to support certain domestic programs, including libraries. My goals were to explore and reaffirm the concept of the public good and to develop coalitions to foster public support for libraries and other services which contribute to the general welfare of our country.

We brought together representatives of more than 60 of the nation's leading organizations and more than 1,500 librarians, who spent a full day in a president's program grappling with this particular subject. I felt that this was necessary, because librarians had not done a good job in explaining the library's vital role, and we were constantly assumed to be engaged in empire building as well as feeding from the federal trough. It was important to bring together organizations across the spectrum to look at the importance of libraries as educational and information institutions and this coalition would be helpful not only to ourselves but also to other organizations that were having the same problem with federal government as well. As you know, "a coalition is a temporary alliance of persons, institutions, or groups for joint action. We already have library networks, Friends of the Library groups, cooperatives, and other means of increasing influence or power by the force of numbers. Coalitions are viewed not as an alliance of discrete entities, but as a joining together of large, usually national groups. The sheer size of the Federal government, its intricacies and complexities, the bureaucratic sand in its gears—all require more power to effect even a small change. Libraries certainly can no longer 'go it alone.'"[2]

Librarians should also join coalitions because they are competent planners and decision-makers who should be personally involved in the planning efforts within their communities, organizations, and institutions. They should be members of groups making policy decisions, especially in assuring access to information, information equity, or developing and maintaining information and communication networking structures and channels. Librarians must take an active role in identifying social, cultural, educational, and economic issues at whatever level they occur. Librarians should urge their national or state professional organizations to join coalitions or themselves join existing coalitions. At times, librarians must step out themselves and form working relationships with organizations having common goals and objectives. Librarians need to build timely coalitions that anticipate rather than react to challenges and opportunities, some of which may not yet be recognized even at the national level.

Library trustees play a very important role in the formation of coalitions. In general, they represent the power brokers of the community. Trustees are usually involved in the politics of the community. They are often leaders in education and business and thus have their fingers on the pulse of the community. Because of their leadership roles in the community, library trustees are very important to the success of library coalition building.

We know that coalitions work. One example of a national coalition formed in the early 1980s to bring about recognition for the fine work that libraries do is Betty Stone's partnership program to bring about awareness about public library service in the community. In spite of a few success stories, there are problems and opportunities. While we have a great number of active issues groups—probably more than any other advanced industrial country—forming coalitions of these groups has repeatedly proven extremely difficult. One major reason behind these difficulties has been single-group sectarianism—a position that many single issue group organizations take. Unless their issue is the basis of the coalition, the group will not participate. My point is that the various groups that are invited to join the coalition might have their single issue or their concern, but we must be able to sell the library package as a broader issue that affects more people in the community. We must keep in mind that we live in an information society and that libraries are the base of the information society. Moreover, we should try to impress upon our coalition colleagues that the library cuts across all socio-economic lines, all political parties and philosophies, and that it is the institution for all the people. Thus, supporting the library will in the long run support the total community.

S. M. Miller, Professor of Sociology and Economics at Boston University, tells us that, "building and maintaining a coalition is no easy business; each organizational member of the coalition has its own ideology, agenda, and strictures—none of which is likely to coincide exactly with those of other members."[3] Many organizational leaders are known to have egos that feed on publicity and are quieted only by time-consuming stroking. Suspicion, perhaps a healthy paranoia, is a necessary ingredient of success, because of the likely dangers of agent provocateurs, crazies and infiltrators pursuing their own special goals. Thus, decisions are made under rushed arguments, difficult conditions that contribute neither to wisdom nor to trust. Complicating the situation further is that each of the constituent members and units of the coalition is very likely to have differences if not splits within it. As a result, these factions within a movement or organization continually jeopardize the formation—and longevity— of a coalition.

Commenting on this same subject, Joan C. Durrance tells us that, "most successful coalitions bring together groups which may not be in general agreement but which agree on a single issue. The most effective coalitions do not require common positions on a number of issues; differences need not weaken them. An environmentalist recently pointed out that when a coalition is formed to preserve a wild river from development, some people may support it because they are avid fishermen, others because they like to canoe or kayak, still others because they don't like to see money put into a poorly conceived water project. . . . In fact, coalitions often make strange bedfellows."[3]

While some of these things are problems, there are opportunities in coalition building. We can avoid the mistrust and the problems enumerated above by building trust and effective working relations within the coalition. This can be done by having an understanding on the part of all members of the coalition, and by prescribing certain norms, and procedures that will be followed to effectuate change or to achieve the goal that the coalition is seeking. In my experience many tensions and difficulties between member units of the coalition frequently arise because they do not understand what the other units stand for politically or philosophically, or how the other organizations make decisions and what some of their problems are. Nevertheless, I am convinced, that once understanding is achieved that things can move pretty easily.

Let me give you an example from my NAACP experience. When I was the President of the Albany, New York NAACP Branch for four years, from 1982 to 1986, we were involved in a coalition against police abuse. The coalition was formed as result of a needless police killing of a young black deranged homeless man, Jessie Davis. The man was shot down in cold blood. It was discovered that he was unarmed except for having a fork and a table knife. It took five policemen to pump six bullets in the man; in spite of all their police training, they could not restrain the man, who was armed with only a fork and a table knife, except to kill him. Since this had happened in Albany three times before, the community—as you can imagine—became outraged and alarmed.

Several organizations joined the Albany NAACP Branch. These included both white and black churches, with black and white ministers, and many other groups. As the president of the Albany NAACP, I asked the Legal Redress Committee to provide legal assistance to the family of Jessie Davis. When the chair of my Legal Redress Committee, a woman by the name of Dr. Alice Green, tried to explain to the coalition the procedures that the NAACP usually takes in such a case, some black young people from a radical group were a little chagrined. They felt that the legal approach was too slow a process. They were anxious to do something immediately. We spent about two hours arguing and wrangling. However, those two hours were not lost, because once the members understood the legal implications and effect of immediate action, not only on the community, but on Mr. Davis' family, members of the coalition began to accept the sound advice and admonition of Dr. Alice Green. In short, in coalition building, if you try to achieve your goal, you will spend many, many hours trying to build consensus on various subjects that sometimes might seem to be extraneous, but the dialogue is necessary to try to clarify what the likely connections as well as the divisions among the coalition members might be. Once that clarification has been made, success is inevitable.

Opportunities and achievements can be had if certain norms are followed. You must accept the differences and the divisions of labor. For example, you cannot accept sameness in action or belief from your constituent members of the coalition, and you must respect their differences. If your local AFL-CIO tells the library coalition that it cannot support a certain political position because it appears to be contrary to labor policy, I don't think that we should spend all night arguing and wrangling on that particular point. Nevertheless, I suggest that you take the opportunity to use the AFL-CIO or any other union in the areas when they can work with you in achieving whatever goal you are trying to achieve at that particular moment. Of course, the condition that the union might object to may be a local problem that the union has with the politician in your state senate or in your state assembly who may be handling the library bill, and who may be perceived as anti-union by the union. And so, while the politician may be prolibrary, to the union people he is anti-union. As a result, they don't feel too happy with the person. To get around this awkward problem, work with the unions in some other agreed-upon way. For example, in printing out flyers, unions can make a contribution, in spite of this one minor difference. We must remember that coalitions are marriages of convenience.

One norm that we must understand is to separate what is done as a movement or organization from what is done as a member of a coalition. Joining a coalition does not mean giving up the particular qualities of each of the members of the coalition. The members can continue to speak in their own names or as an organization in the community; however, they have to make clear that they speak for themselves and not for the coalition as a whole. In the experience that I have had in coalition building, the NAACP, the churches and the Urban League, the Catholic Charity Organizations, and the Jewish Federation are the most widely known organizations in the community in terms of longevity of operation, and, most importantly, of having not only a local base but also a national base. Therefore, whenever you speak as a representative of your library association or library, you have to be sure that you are speaking for your individual organization, and when you are speaking for the coalition, you must also make that crystal clear.

Translating this into library parlance, one of my colleagues told me the story about a Friends of the Library Group having functioned in a certain way by approaching local legislators for assistance in obtaining funding for a library building. This idea for a campaign for a new library building was completely rejected by the members of the coalition, and of course, the Friends of the Library Group was rather angry. We cannot wear our feelings on our sleeves and become angry when our suggestions are ignored or if we proceed unilaterally without authorization or support. We must do our homework to find ways of bringing the members of the coalition around to our point of view. So the coalition members must police themselves carefully and anticipate reactions to what they do so as to avoid confusing their particular library issues with coalition policies. This is also true in community coalitions from my experience.

Another norm that we must follow is to share the credit for our successes. The library trustee board should not get all the credit nor should the Friends of the Library, the Jewish Federation, the Labor Union, the League of Women Voters, the NAACP. All constituent members of the coalition that worked hard to achieve the legislative goal should be given credit. It is better to give too much credit than too little for those who may not deserve credit may work harder the next time.

There are many success stories about coalition building. Let me share a few with you:

Bill Eshelman reminds us that:

> . . . the friends of the Detroit Public Library, in a desperate drive to "keep the doors open," scoured the city to identify groups that would join with them in a coalition to help keep DPL afloat—at least one more year. In one of the cities hardest hit by unemployment, the DPL had been struggling to preserve even the basic services. Some years ago the library was designated as a statewide, not just a city, resource, and qualified for state funding. But it became clear that the only lasting solution was an increase in the local tax rate. Thanks to the good work of the coalition, the hard-pressed citizens of Detroit voted to tax themselves an additional one million dollars to support their public library. It will mean about five million dollars more each year for the library. Some of the credit for this successful campaign must be attributed to the goodwill resulting from the Information and Referral Service, an everlasting tribute to the vision of Clara Jones. The linkages will bind the Detroit community to its libraries for years to come.[4]

Libraries and librarians have already experienced some success with building coalitions at national and local levels through library associations. State organizations often form successful legislative coalitions. The American Library Association has been an active partner in—and often an initiator of—coalitions on education funding, telecommunications legislation, access to government and information, literacy, and similar issues. During my presidency of ALA, I initiated the Coalition for the Public Good, which had more than 60 members. I also established, at the request of the ALA Council, the Coalition on Government Information to fight the restriction of access to government information.[5]

Now we should take a few moments to look at what libraries and library associations are doing for coalition building across our borders. In upstate New York, the North Country Reference and Research Library Resources Council has fostered an affiliation between the medical libraries in the north country section of New York and the medical libraries of Ontario, Canada. In addition there is the New York and Ontario Chapter of the Medical Library Association. The St. Regis Mohawk Reservation Library, which is funded from New York State funds, works with the Ontario Library Association of Canada in providing library service to Indian libraries in Ontario through the Akwesane Library. Margaret Jacobs, the librarian, takes credit for this creative work. Helen Maul of the Nogales/Santa Cruz County Public Library of Arizona reports that in Nogales there is an official policy that Mexican citizens who never crossed the border may have a card for use in the library. There is also an exchange of materials between that library and the Mexican library. Helen Maul also serves on the Arizona/Mexico Governors' Commission, which finds ways to work on common concerns including libraries. A woman of strong faith she says, "librarians sharing their resources and profession can and should be active players in the game of peace and understanding."

Colleagues in the great state of Washington should be congratulated for the fine work that they have been doing in developing coalitions. The famous Western Library Network stretches across national borders all the way to Australia. The Washington Library Association's continuing education workshops with the British Columbia Library Association and the activities of the Pacific Northwest Library Association are truly international in scope. The work of the Washington State library's planning and development divisions in its work with the South Alberta Institute of Technology is something that other state libraries can envy.

Finally, there are other excellent coalitions around the country. Campaigns around jobs and peace have taken place in a number of cities across America. There have been attempts to combine job safety with ecological concerns, and to put an end to the struggle for better schools and housing. The library community must learn from these efforts. We must take a single library issue, although it is single issue, and make it a broader issue by showing the American people that libraries support the economy, that libraries support education, and, more importantly, that libraries support the infrastructure of America, so that our so-called single library issue effort can be translated into structures and coalitions that work for political power to support libraries and information services. As we plan for the twenty-first century, we must find more creative strategies to support library and information services by a renewal of our efforts through coalition building.

References

1. Dina Cowan, and Judith Kunofsky, "Building Coalitions: The More Diverse the Members, the More Likely the Success," *Sierra Club Bulletin* 67 (September/October 1982): 94.
2. William Eshelman, "Serving the Public Good: Coalition for Free Library Services," E. J. Josey, ed., *Libraries, Coalitions and the Public Good* (New York: Neal-Schuman Publishers, 1987), p. 104.
3. S. M. Miller, "Coalition Etiquette: Ground Rules for Building Coalitions," *Social Policy* 14 (Fall 1983) p. 47.
4. Joan C. Durrance, "The Effective Coalition," E. J. Josey ed., *Libraries, Coalitions and The Public Good* (New York: Neal-Schuman Publishers, 1987) pp. 118–119.
5. William Eshelman, *op. cit.,* p. 105.
6. Patricia Glass Schuman, "Libraries and Coalition Building," E. J. Josey, ed., *Libraries, Coalition and The Public Good* (New York: Neal-Schuman Publishers, 1987) p. 129.

Notes on Contributors

Ngozi Agbim, Chief Librarian, LaGuardia Community College. City University of New York.

Sheryl Anspaugh, Adjunct Professor, School of Library and Information Sciences, North Carolina Central University.

David R. Bender, Executive Director, Special Libraries Association.

Pamela G. Bonnell, Library Manager, Plano (Texas) Public Library System.

Dennis P. Carrigan, Assistant Dean, College of Library and Information Science, University of Kentucky.

Eileen D. Cooke, Director, Washington Office of the American Library Association.

Arthur Curley, Director, Boston Public Library.

Paul J. Fasana, Andrew W. Mellon Director of the Research Libraries, New York Public Library.

Robert B. Ford, Jr., Associate Librarian for Reader / Information Services and Professor, Medgar Evers College, City University of New York.

Richard B. Hall, Division of Public Library Services, Georgia Department of Education.

Michael H. Harris, Professor, College of Library and Information Science, University of Kentucky.

Cynthia Jenkins, Member, (Democrat), The Assembly, State of New York.

E. J. Josey, Professor, School of Library and Information Science, University of Pittsburgh.

Keith Curry Lance, Research Director, State Library and Adult Education Office, Colorado Department of Education.

John Lubans, Jr., Associate University Librarian, Duke University.

Howard F. McGinn, State Librarian, North Carolina Department of Cultural Resources.

Marilyn Gell Mason, Director, Cleveland Public Library.

Major R. Owens, Congressman (Democrat, New York), United States Congress.

David Shavit, Associate Professor, Department of Library and Information Studies, Northern Illinois University.

Kenneth D. Shearer, Professor, School of Library and Information Sciences, North Carolina Central University.

Joseph F. Shubert, State Librarian and Assistant Commissioner, New York.

Benjamin F. Speller, Jr., Dean, School of Library and Information Sciences, North Carolina Central University.

Gary E. Strong, State Librarian of California.

Thomas B. Wall, Public Services Librarian, School of Library and Information Science, University of Pittsburgh.

Janet M. Welch, Executive Director, Rochester Regional Research Library Council.

Barratt Wilkins, Director, State Library of Florida.

Virginia G. Young, Trustee, Public Library of Columbia (Missouri).

Index